AT THE PRECIPICE OF POVERTY

At The Precipice of Poverty

A Croydon Chronicle

D. T. Blakeley

JANUS PUBLISHING COMPANY LTD
Cambridge, England

First published in Great Britain 2001
by Janus Publishing Company Ltd
The Studio
High Green
Great Shelford
Cambridge CB22 5EG

www.januspublishing.co.uk

Copyright © D. T. Blakeley 2001
British Library Cataloguing-in-Publication Data
A catalogue record for this book is available from the British Library

ISBN 978-1-85756-484-6

All rights reserved. No part of this publication may be reproduced,
stored in a retrieval system or transmitted in any form or by any
means, electric, mechanical, photocopying, recording or otherwise,
without the prior permission of the publisher.

The right of D. T. Blakeley to be identified as the author
of this work has been asserted by him in accordance with the
Copyright, Designs and Patents Act 1988.

Cover Design: Mick Dickinson

Printed and bound in Great Britain

Dedication

I would like to dedicate this book to my beautiful granddaughter Ellie Lloyd. A child who has brought so much love and happiness to my life. Also thank you to my wife for all her understanding and support while I was writing this book.

CONTENTS

Introduction		ix
Chapter 1:	The Move to Wilford Road	1
Chapter 2:	Trouble in Forster Road	26
Chapter 3:	The Killing of a Best Friend	48
Chapter 4:	The Vicar's Daughter	70
Chapter 5:	Death from Lockjaw	88
Chapter 6:	Tales from the workhouse	107
Chapter 7:	In the infirmary	131
Chapter 8:	The final fight	153
Chapter 9:	Corrosive poisoning	182
Chapter 10:	The final journey	208

INTRODUCTION

This is a story about a young man's life in one of the roughest areas of South London in the year 1907. This young man had a dream, it was just a simple one: to try to give his parents a better life and a better place to live, away from all the drunkards and trouble that made life so unbearable in and around the area where they lived. He adored his parents, especially his mother. She had been the only woman in his life, until the day they moved into Wilford Road. Before he had finished unloading the cart, a young lady who lived down the road had already introduced herself to him, and by the end of the day he would fall deeply in love with her. But it wasn't to last. He found out the hard way what it was like to fall in love and then have your heart broken in the space of a short time, but he never gave up on his dream and one day, this young man's dream was about to become a reality. He had the chance to take his parents away from their depressing way of life and also to give up the reputation he had of being one of the best bare-knuckle fighters around, but one thing stood in his way: the young lady, who was his first love and who had then left him to go off to marry another man. When she came back she told him some news that would ruin the lives not only of his parents, but also of his new girlfriend, his best friend and eventually his own.

    This book tells the story of a young man who had to fight every inch of the way in order to protect his parents, and I also hope that it will give the reader some idea of the day-to-day life of working-class people – from the infirmary to the workhouse and from the public houses to the drab little rooms where they lived. Everyone had it hard and everyone, even the women, had to be tough to survive. It was nothing for a fight to break out in a public house between two women and in the end a kitchen knife would be pulled from a woman's apron and be used. This was the normal way of life.

Most of the events in this book are based on true stories that actually happened at the time so, if you can put your imagination to work, try to picture the places where the events took place and fit faces to the people in the story – you might be lucky enough to take a trip back in time and get the feel of what life was really like in the year 1907.

Chapter 1

The Move to Wilford Road

At twenty past three on 22 February 1907, Violet Blake gave birth to a baby boy. Violet was only 18 years of age at the time and had been forced from her parents' home to find refuge in a friend's room to give birth to her first child.

Violet had spent the last few years living in Wilford Road, said to be one of the roughest roads in the south of England. It was so bad that even the police would only go down there in twos or threes, they would never take a chance of walking down Wilford Road alone; even if they were in pursuit of someone, they would stop at the top of Wilford Road and blow their whistles until assistance arrived.

Wilford Road was given a nickname – 'Banghole', which is still used today. This wasn't the original nickname. Over one hundred years ago, the people of Croydon nicknamed the road 'Bangall', because the men who lived there would 'bangall' the strangers who walked down it, in other words, if your face wasn't known, then you would get a good beating just for coming down the road.

Another road that was just as bad and ran parallel with Wilford Road was named Forster Road – it had the same reputation as Wilford Road. Most of the buildings in Wilford Road consisted of blocks of two houses, each with an alley at the side, big enough to get a horse and cart down to the back yard, and most had stables built at the rear. The majority of the houses were lodging houses where you would have two to three families living in one house. Some lived in one room and some two rooms, but if you were quite well off, compared to other families down the road, then you would have one whole floor to yourself; but each family shared the outside toilet and the only washing facilities were a jug and bowl. Violet's family was one of the lucky ones – they occupied the whole ground floor of their house.

Violet Blake was an only child and her mother and father were typical parents of that time. There were two types of parents; they were either very strict and laid the law down on every little thing or they never cared about their children until they were old enough to earn or steal enough money to provide them with ale. Violet's came in the category of very strict. They were not the usual type of people to live down Wilford Road: her father had spent most of his life in the army, but was discharged through ill health and now worked as a clerk, not bringing home very much money. Wilford Road was all he could afford, but he was working, which was more than most of the men from the road.

Coming from an old regiment, he still had the army blood inside him, which made him very strict towards his daughter. Some say he was too strict, for Violet enjoyed the good life. She would do everything her father had forbidden her to do but, of course, not in front of him. She was too afraid of the beating she would receive. It was not uncommon in those days for husbands or fathers to beat their women, in fact it was seen as quite normal, especially after the public houses turned out and the men were full of ale. This never applied to Violet's father for he wasn't a drinking man. That would have brought him down to the level of the people he hated the most – the drunken men and women of Wilford Road.

Violet was always out and about behind her father's back and she was always seen in most of the local public houses. Because there were no televisions or radio and no entertainment at all in their rooms, the public houses were a place of refuge. As soon as they had earned, stolen or borrowed a few pennies, they would be off up to the public houses.

No one cared if they were spending the rent or food money, it never mattered and there were no shortages of places to go for a drink. In less than five minutes' walk from Wilford Road and Forster Road there were no less then eight public houses and these were where most of the people congregated, perhaps just to get away from their dark, depressing rooms and their uninteresting, monotonous lives. There they would stay until the drink had taken over their thoughts. This was the life Violet enjoyed. Maybe she thought she was just that bit better than other people in the road, her parents were certainly snobs and she was better spoken then most, or perhaps it was because you could always find the young men in and around the public houses. She would always be seen with one on her arm. The good people wondered if this was her way of forgetting the dull life she had at home or was it to rebel against her strict parents who, of course, never knew of her goings on outside the home.

Violet was also very crafty; she would never ever come home smelling of drink and if one night by some misfortune she had one too many, then she would make sure there was always a friend's room she could stay at. She was certainly one for the good times and one for the young men who were the rough and ready type, who never cared about anything, except having a good time, even if it meant spending their mothers' rent money. If Violet's parents had found out how she had spent her spare time, her father would have beaten her senseless for bringing disrespect to their good name and then would have thrown her out and disowned her. They never found out because the only people they spoke to in that area were well-to-do and respectable. If they did know what Violet got up to, they were certainly too embarrassed to mention it to her parents. Violet's way of life was not the thing to talk about around the dinner table, and she knew it. Violet was not out of the ordinary, many girls of her age, and some a lot older, led the same sort of life, they needed to get out and to mix with other people; sometimes it was their only release from the depressing lives they had at home.

Nine months before the birth of Violet's child, on a bright summer morning, Violet was sitting quietly in her room with nothing to do. Both her parents were out so she was passing her time looking out through the front window and watching the poor people of Wilford Road going about their business. The women were on their way to the wash house with all their washing piled up on an old pram or pushchair. They never had many clothes to wash, in fact, some only had the clothes they stood up in, and of course, their Sunday best. But any rags would do, an old tablecloth or blanket; they wouldn't always wash what they took up there, it was just a trip out, something to look forward too, for anything was better then sitting in those rooms all day.

Also it was a good excuse to meet the other women and have a good chin wag and catch up on all the gossip from the road. The men, well most, were still getting over the drink that they consumed the night before. Some were still drunk trying to find the house where they lived, after spending most of the night asleep on the footpath, and the ones whose bodies were immune to the ale were struggling along on their way to town with large baskets of flowers. The men who had their own horses and carts were slowly trying to guide them out on to the road to go about their daily business, some with their heads bowed down and letting the horse decide which way to go.

Violet thought to herself that there had got to be more to life than this. She turned and leaned forward, to see what was going on at the top of the road. She noticed a young man driving a horse and cart towards her; he was coming straight down the middle of the road and causing some confusion with the other horses and carts, which were made to pull over to one side of the road, for he certainly wasn't going to move. She strained her neck to get a better look and then thought, I have never seen this man before. She lifted the curtains right up and nearly fell off the windowsill. As he drove closer towards her, she noticed that there was a woman sitting next to him and a man walking by the side of the horse, holding the reins. As the cart went past her house at a slow walk, her eyes were locked on to the young man. I haven't seen him in any of the public houses, she thought, I wonder what he is doing down here? She knew no one would use Wilford Road as a short cut as it was too dangerous. So she came to the conclusion that they must have business there.

Violet quickly pulled the curtains back and rushed to the door stumbling over the foot stool as she went. She removed her shawl from the back of the door, put it around her shoulders and rushed out of the front door and on to the road. She then stopped to make sure no one was looking at her, then crossed over the road. She walked slowly along the footpath, just keeping behind the driver's seat of the cart, making sure she was not noticed. She was trying to look out of the corner of her eye, trying to see what was on the back of the cart under the canvas. It's a load of furniture and mats, she thought. Perhaps the young man was moving into a room close by or was he just the driver of the cart and the old man and woman were moving in? Well, I should soon find out, she thought.

The Move to Wilford Road

The cart carried on and then stopped, two houses from the end of Wilford Road. Violet was stuck – she couldn't just stand there or she would look a fool and she couldn't keep walking as she would end up in Princess Road. She wasn't sure what to do. The young man was about to turn round and get off the cart; he would have seen her if she had stayed where she was. She looked across the road and saw two women whom she knew standing outside their house talking. This is my chance, she thought. She slowly turned round and walked to the back of the cart and then made her way over to the two women. At first she made out she was joining in with their conversation, but really she was keeping a close eye on the young man.

She watched carefully as the old man tied the horse to the gas lamp, put the nose bag on the horse and made his way up to the front door of number 54, looking down at a bit of paper he had in his hand. He banged on the door and when it opened, Violet could see the landlady standing there talking to the man. She then exchanged a key for some money. Violet's heart started to beat faster. Only one more thing to find out – was the young man just the driver of the cart or was he moving in with his mother and father? She was still making out she was talking to the two women, without having a clue what the conversation was about. Her eyes kept focused on the young man as he climbed down from the cart. He was tall, broad, and had thick, jet-black curly hair and a handsome face with dark, clear skin. While all of this was going on, the two women were beginning to realise why Violet had joined them. They started to make suggestive and rude remarks, in a loud manner just so the young man could hear. But this never embarrassed Violet, who was used to all the dirty remarks, she just looked over the road and hoped that the good-looking young man would look back and perhaps take some notice of her.

The young man made his way around the cart, removed his coat and threw it over the back of the horse. He then walked up to the old woman, who was still sitting on the cart, placed both hands around her waist and lifted her down, then held her hand as he walked her into the house. What a gentleman, Violet thought, you don't get many of them around this way. Most would have left the old woman to climb down on her own. After a while he returned to the cart and started to untie the sheet to remove the furniture. As Violet looked on she couldn't believe her eyes; he was built like a horse with muscles bulging out from everywhere. The beads of sweat were now hanging from his brow and reflecting off his dark skin by the sun. Violet stared and watched his every move, but the young man still never looked over.

One of the women whom Violet was standing with pulled at her arm. 'Perhaps he is one of them shy boys, you know, one of them who don't go with every woman he sees,' she said to Violet.

'It looks like you might have to make the first move, girl,' the other woman said.

'I can't do that,' replied Violet, 'how can I go walking up to him for no reason, he would think I'm a right old tart.'

'Well, you will have to make your mind up and do something soon,' the first woman said. 'We are off indoors now to get the old man's dinner ready and unless you want to stay out here on your own looking like a prat, you had better think of something and quick.' The two ladies looked at each other and laughed. 'Go on Violet, run over there,' one of them said. 'You won't get anywhere standing here on your own.'

The two women left Violet standing on the footpath and both walked to their front doors. They looked back at Violet, laughing. 'Go on, you're not normally this backward with the young lads. Go over there and get stuck in, my girl,' one of them shouted.

Violet was now getting embarrassed; she was sure the young man could hear the two women shouting. She looked around, not knowing which way to turn. 'Hold on, Bet,' she shouted, 'I know what I can do, would you do me a big favour and lend me a jug of ale? I'll bring it back tonight, I promise.'

'Well, make sure you do,' the woman replied, 'my Bert won't be too happy if he's got no ale to go with his dinner tonight.'

Violet waited for Bet to bring the jug of ale out, still looking over her shoulder to make sure the young man had not disappeared. When Bet came out with the jug of ale, she was still laughing in between taking sips from the jug. 'That's good stuff,' she said. 'Now you will remember to replace this before the night's out. I can't afford to go and buy another one.'

Violet took the jug and held it close to her chest, trying not to spill it. The two women were still watching from their doorways. Violet looked across the road – the young man had just taken some furniture in, so she waited until he came back out and then made her way over to the back of the cart. She walked up to him as he was lifting off an old chair and tapped him on the shoulder. 'Good morning,' she said, 'you look really hot and in need of a rest. Would you like some cold ale to cool you down?'

The young man turned round, the sweat rolling off his face and cascading down his broad bare chest. 'No, thank you, I don't drink,' he replied.

Violet wasn't expecting him to say that. She never knew of any young man who didn't drink ale. 'Well, would you like some help getting the lining down from the cart?' she asked. She knew she couldn't walk away from him, not now she was this close.

'Yea, if you don't mind,' he replied with a voice strong and deep. 'Do you live around here?'

'Yes', she replied, 'just over the road. Are you just the driver or are you moving in here?'

'No, I'm moving in with my parents. Are you sure you can manage those boxes. My mother was coming out to help with the liner, but she is not as strong as she used to be and can't manage too much these days.'

Violet put the jug down by the side of the cart and made her way to the back. She nearly tripped on the reins from the horse that were tied around the gas lamp and hanging down on the footpath. She took a box from the cart that contained some sheets and pillow cases.

'You go on and I will follow you in,' she said, 'and you can show me where to go.' The box was too heavy for Violet and she rested it down on the wheel of the cart. She again tried to lift it and walked away from the cart, but tripped over on the reins again. The box hit the ground and broke open and the bedding went everywhere. The young man heard the noise and came back to see if Violet was all right. When he saw what she had done and the frightened look on her face, he started to laugh.

She looked up at him. 'It's not funny, I've hurt my bloody ankle. You shouldn't leave those reins hanging all over the footpath, it's bloody dangerous.'

'No, I know, I'm sorry, it was just the look on your face. That was my mother's best bedding; she had only just returned from the wash house before we left and it was all cleaned, pressed and ready to go on the bed, before you took hold of it.'

Violet forgot about her ankle and quickly picked up the lining, folding it back into shape so only the clean parts were showing.

The young man remarked, still laughing, 'You have already dirtied my bed sheets young lady and I don't even know your name.'

'It's Violet Blake,' she said, as she bent down trying to sort the pillowcases out from the bed sheets.

'My name's Barny, Barny Sturt, and don't worry too much about the lining, I will tell my mother that I dropped the box and got them dirty, she'd blame me, anyway.'

'So she should, it was your fault.'

Barny turned to the cart and removed a big chair, picked it up and threw it straight up and on to his shoulder. Violet looked on in amazement, it was no effort to him at all; it was as if he had just picked a scarf up and was putting it around his neck. Violet couldn't believe just how strong he was.

'Follow me in, Violet,' he said 'and mind you don't trip over, I will introduce you to my parents.' Barny walked into the house first, forgetting that Violet was still outside picking up the lining. She was just putting the last sheet in the box when she heard someone shout out her name from across the road.

She looked over the top of the cart and saw two young men waving at her. She knew both of them and had walked out with them in the past, but she had no interest in them now. One of them shouted across the road, 'Got yourself a job in removals, Violet, my old love, or have you found a nice place for me and you to settle down in together?'

Violet grinned and tried to lift the box again, but this time the bottom fell out and the lining ended back on the footpath. She threw the box down and shouted back to the two young lads. 'If this was my place, you two wouldn't stand a chance and you would be the last two I would move in with, now be on your way, you toe rags.'

The two boys crossed the road. 'Come on, Violet, let's go for a drink,' one of them said.

'No, I'm too busy, now go away both of you and leave me alone.'

The two boys were used to having a good laugh with Violet and weren't going to leave it at that. They bent down and picked up some of the bed sheets. 'Well, Violet, we might as well make use of these since you got them out, you must have known I was coming,' one of them said.

Just then Barny came out of the house and asked Violet what was going on and if the two lads were bothering her.

The Move to Wilford Road

'No,' she replied, 'don't worry, it's only a couple of my friends playing about and having a game.'

Barny walked up to the two lads. 'Come on, put the bed sheets down and be on your way.' He helped them along with a gentle nudge.

The two boys looked up with a shocked look on their faces. This was where they had been born and brought up, it was their ground and they weren't going to let a stranger to the road tell them what to do, a friend of Violet's or not.

One of them pushed Barny and then took a step back. He removed his coat and tightened his belt and then put his fists up in a fighting attitude.

Violet shouted across to Barny, 'Go back into the house, I will get this sorted out. I will get rid of them.' She knew how rough the boys were and she knew that if they started, they wouldn't stop beating Barny until he was near to death.

The two boys had now challenged Barny to fight and he couldn't back down now, even if he wanted to. If he did, his reputation would be gone. Barny told Violet to stand behind the cart.

'You can't take these two on, Barny,' she said, 'you don't know what they are capable of; they will kill you.'

'Yea that's right, Barny boy,' one of the lads shouted to him. 'We are going to teach you the biggest lesson of your life – you don't mess about with one of the Bangall boys.' The lad started to move around with his fists up in a fighting attitude.

Barny stared at the boy as he moved around him. Barny then took two steps back and one forward and then put an almighty blow on the boy's chin. It sent him falling backwards out of control until he hit the side of the cart, he then bounced back off the cart and on to the pavement. As he came back, Barny put another blow to the boy's face. This one landed on the boy's lips, which immediately split open and allowed two teeth to leave the boy's mouth. He stumbled for a while and then fell to the ground, knocked out completely cold. Barny turned to take on the other boy, but he was already half way up Wilford Road, running like a screaming pig. He had seen the force of Barny's punches and wasn't staying around to find out how they felt. Violet had never seen such a blow. The boy on the ground was not the hardest in the road, but he was no push over; but two blows from Barny had stopped him in his tracks.

Violet stood there for a moment with her mouth open, looking down at the boy. 'How did you do that, Barny?'

'Do what?' he replied.

'Well, you just knocked him down and made it look so easy.'

'I'm sorry you had to see that, Violet,' he said, 'but they left me no choice. I couldn't turn and walk away.'

Violet turned and looked up at Barny with her big brown eyes that were filled with envy at all that power. 'You know you have done it now, Barny. Everyone around here will want to fight you, just to see how good you really are.'

'I don't mind that,' he replied, 'as long as they are willing to put their hands in their pockets and pay for it.'

'I don't understand, what do you mean?'

'It doesn't matter now, help me pick up the lining and then you can come inside and meet my parents.' Barny walked in with the box of lining and Violet followed. He took her through to the scullery at the back of the house. Violet looked in and saw Barny's father on his hands and knees trying to light the fire with no success, and his mother standing by the table, sorting through some boxes that Barny had brought in.

'This is Violet,' Barny said, as he pulled a pair of long john's off the table and threw them under a chair.

'Pleased to meet you,' Violet said in a soft, shy voice.

His father looked up from lighting the fire.

'What was all that trouble about outside, boy?'

Barny looked back at his father on the floor. 'Nothing for you to worry about, Dad.'

His father got up with the help of the fireplace and looked his son in the eyes.

'You haven't been in this road for five minutes and you're out there fighting. Why can't you just leave it alone for once and walk away?'

'It wasn't his fault, he wasn't to blame,' Violet said, her voice getting a bit louder and stronger now.

The old man turned his back on Violet and returned to the fire. 'You don't know us, you don't know what Barny's capable of, so you should keep your opinions to yourself, young lady.'

Barny turned to the door. 'Come on, Violet, let's go. We will come back when he is in a better mood, whenever that will be.'

Violet followed him back out to the road. 'Where are you off to now, Barny?'

'I have to take this cart back to the coal yard before six o'clock. How would you like to come with me for a ride?' He didn't have to ask her twice, she was out, up on the cart and ready to go. She didn't even notice the young man still sitting against the cart wheel whom she had to step over to get on to the cart.

Barny looked down at the young man and then took his arm. 'Come on, friend, get up.' He tried to pull him off the ground. It was no good, the boy was still out cold and looked as though he would be there for the rest of the day. Barny put him back down and then noticed the jug of ale, which Violet had offered him earlier. He picked it up and poured it over the young man's head. The boy soon came around when he felt the cold ale run down his neck. Barny helped him to his feet. 'Come on, friend, be on your way. You're all right now.' The boy was still stunned and was stumbling around. He never had a clue where he was, but Barny walked him over to the house and he slowly moved off with the walls to help him along. Barny watched him for a short while and then jumped up on the cart. He turned the horse around and they slowly made their way out of Wilford Road.

On the way Violet turned to Barny and asked him why his father had been so grumpy.

'He never used to be like that. He has been a carpenter ever since leaving school. He was one of the best around here but, a few months ago, he was leaning out of a first-floor window, trying to fix a frame that he had made and, while he was trying to put it in, his foot slipped and he fell out. He hit the ground and couldn't move. They found out later that he had badly injured his back.'

'The poor soul,' Violet said, 'how bad was he hurt?'

'Well, he was in the infirmary for about four weeks. He couldn't move for the first two weeks and when he came home we knew he wouldn't be able to return to work and that's when the trouble started. I was bringing some money into the home, but without my father's money we couldn't live. It wasn't long before we were behind with the rent and then we had to leave our old house. We were on the street with all of our furniture on the back of a cart that we borrowed from a neighbour and it was only a good friend of the family's that saved my parents going to the workhouse. I tried to get in more work, but we never had the time to get the money together for other lodgings. Anyway, this friend of ours, he looks after the coal yard down by the station. That's where we are going now, he let us use this horse and cart so that we could move to Wilford Road. Well, when he knew we had nowhere to stay, he offered us one of the old railway carriages that stands in the coal yard and we have been there until today when I finally got enough money together to pay for the rent on the house in Wilford Road. He said that we could have the carriage until my father was back on his feet, but his back injury won't get any better now and he has had to stop work altogether.'

'So, how do you live without your father's money coming in?' asked Violet.

'Well, my friend Fred, who let us have the carriage to live in, he gives me a bit of work every now and then, early mornings and weekends unloading the coal from the trains and loading it on to the carts ready for the drivers to take out, so that helps, and I also do a bit of bare-knuckle fighting,' he said.

Violet now knew why it only took him two hits to knock her friend out cold. 'Is that why your father was worried about the fight outside your home?' she asked.

'Yea, he feels guilty about not bringing any money into the home and he knows most of the money we live off, we get from the fights I win. My parents both think it's bad enough me having to fight to earn money to live, without having a brawl in the street for no reason.'

'It's a shame that your father has such a great knowledge of carpentry but can't put it to any good use.'

'No, I know, but he is trying his hardest to teach me the trade, but it takes so long and we need the money now.'

When they finally reached the coal yard, Barny drove the cart through the gates and over to the stables. He looked across the yard and saw three man arguing. 'There's Fred, over there with the black overcoat on, he's the one who took pity on us when we had nothing. He's been really good to us, a really nice bloke.'

'Well, he doesn't look that nice,' she said, 'not the way he is having a good go at those two men.'

Barny shouted out to his mate: 'Are you OK, Fred, or do you need a hand?' When the two men heard Barny shouting across the yard, they walked away and Fred came up and took hold of the horse's bridle.

'Did you have a bit of trouble there, Fred?' Barny asked.

'No, it was nothing I couldn't handle,' he replied. He then noticed the pretty dark-haired girl sitting next to Barny. 'Who is that, Darky? Your new girlfriend?'

Barny looked at Violet and smiled. He then turned back to Fred. 'Thanks for the loan of the cart, Fred, it really helped us out.'

'That's quite all right, mate, you're welcome. How are your parents settling in?'

'Yea, they seem all right, but I had to leave them to it; my old man had the hump again.'

'Well, he has got a lot to have the hump about. Do you fancy a mug of tea before you go back?'

'Yea, that would be nice.' Barny helped Violet down from the cart and they made their way across the yard to an old railway carriage that Fred called his office. Fred followed them in and filled the kettle, while Violet and Barny sat down on an old wooden bench, which Fred had pinched from the station and covered with horse blankets.

Violet whispered in Barny's ear. 'Why does he keep calling you Darky?'

Barny smiled, 'It's when I have finished unloading all of the coal, I'm covered in coal dust from head to foot, and Darky's my nickname; everyone calls me it around here.'

Before Violet could say another word, Fred walked over to them. 'So, how is your old man getting on, Darky?'

'Well, not too bad, Fred, he's still not happy about being off work, he gets fed up so quickly.'

'He ought to think himself lucky to be alive,' Fred replied, 'that was a bad fall he had. Anyway, here's your tea. I have to be going now, a bit of business in town. Will you let the fire burn itself out and lock up before you go?'

'Yea, don't worry, Fred, I'll take care of that.'

Fred walked out of the door, but he came back quickly. 'I forgot to ask you, Barny, will you be able make it tomorrow morning, for the four o'clock coal train?'

'Yea, I'll be here, Fred, I'm only too glad of the work.'

'It was nice to meet you, Violet,' Fred said as he walked out of the door again, 'keep your eye on that Darky, he can be a bit of a terror sometimes.'

Barny and Violet sat there and watched the fire burn itself out.

'It's getting a bit cold now Barny, would you give me a cuddle?' she said as she snuggled up to him.

'What do you mean?' he replied, looking shocked.

'I mean, I want you to put your arms around me.'

Barny sat there all awkwardly. 'I bet you have never been with many girls have you?' Violet asked.

'Well, to tell you the truth, I have never had the time, but it feels really nice being close to you, Violet,' he said.

During the next few hours Barny went through a totally new experience without knowing he was falling deeply in love with this girl he had only known for a few short hours. Violet, well, although this was the first time she'd gone all the way, she couldn't remember being with such a nice, kind, caring and considerate man as Barny. He was as strong as a horse but, at the same time, as gentle as a baby and out of all the men she had walked out with, Barny was the only one who had made her feel this way. After a while they both woke up with their arms around each other.

Violet looked up at Barny. 'It's late, I must go home. I'm not supposed to be working tonight and my father will be wondering where I have been.'

'Where do you work?' Barny asked, as she was trying to sort her hair out.

'I'm a nanny's auxiliary in one of the big households near the woods, up on the hill. It's handy because, being an assistant, I don't have to work many hours, so if I want to stay out all night I can tell my parents that I'm sleeping over at work and then stay out with my friends.'

'Are you not frightened that your parents will find out one day?' he asked.

'No, there is no reason for them to ever meet my master or mistress, so there's not much chance of them finding out. The only way they will is if I stay out all night and forget to tell them that I am working, like tonight, so I will have to hurry.'

Barny helped her on with her shawl. 'Do you have many men friends, Violet?' he asked in a soft voice.

'Well, yes I have to, living down Wilford Road with parents like mine. If you're not friendly with everyone they would make it really hard for my parents and myself, just because we had a better life before we lost everything and moved to Wilford Road.'

The Move to Wilford Road

'Well, you don't have to worry now, I will take care of you.'

Violet turned and put her hand on his face. 'Talking about the people of Wilford Road, you will have to be careful now. That young man you hit has three older brothers and they are really evil; he also has a lot of nasty friends. They are always having a dig at the poor people of Wilford Road, most are too frightened to even look at them. They would think nothing of taking an axe to you if you cross them and that's what you have done, Barny, in a big way. They won't forget what you did to him. I would imagine that they are out there now looking for you, so make sure you are on your guard walking home tonight.'

'Don't worry about me,' he replied, 'this has been one of the happiest days of my life and I won't let them spoil that.'

Barny made sure the fire was out and locked the door behind them. Violet asked him if he had the money for the tram fare. 'No, I'm sorry we will have to walk.' So off they went, arm in arm until they reached the top of Wilford Road.

Violet stopped at the corner. 'I will have to leave you now, Barny, just in case my father sees us together. He will go mad if he sees me walking out with anyone who lives around here, so I can't risk walking with you. But please be careful and remember those boys – they will try and get you down here rather than anyway else; they feel safe in this road. They know there is only a slim chance of any police being around, so watch your back. They won't fight you face to face, not now they know how good you are, and remember there will be more than one of them. They will wait until you're not expecting them and then pounce on you.'

Barny put his arms around her and held her tight. 'Don't worry, I will be all right. Will I be able to see you tomorrow?'

'Yes, but I will come to your house. I can tell my parents that I am going to help your mother sort her rooms out, they won't mind that.' She left him standing there looking like a lost child. He watched her run down the road and laughed as she tripped again on a loose cobble in the middle of the road.

When he could see that she had arrived safely in her house, he started to make his way down the road, keeping a close eye out for trouble, but only because Violet had told him to – he wasn't afraid of anyone – but he didn't want to let her down. When he reached his house he found that the front door was ajar; he slowly pushed it open in case someone was inside waiting for him. As he looked in he could see a figure standing by the bottom of the stairs in the darkened hall way.

'Is that you Barny?' he heard someone say.

'Mum, what are you doing out here? What's wrong?'

'Come here, son, we have had trouble here tonight.'

He walked up to her and put his arm around her. He could tell by her voice that she had been crying. 'Tell me what's happened, Mum. Where is Father, is he all right?'

She looked up at him. 'Yes, he's in the scullery, he wants to be on his own, but he's been hurt.'

Barny left his mother and rushed through to the scullery. Where he found his father lying on the floor by the fire; he looked as if he was doubled up in pain. 'What's happened, Dad? Who's done this to you?' Barny screamed.

His poor old dad looked up at him and groaned, 'It's all right, son, I just stumbled and hurt the old injury in my back. I'll be all right in a little while. Go and make sure your mother's OK.'

Barny stood towering over him feeling helpless, with the tears building up in his eyes. His father groaned again as he tried to turn over. Barny reached for the candle that was on the table and put it down by his father's side. He then noticed that there were cuts on his father's face. 'You have fighting marks on your face,' Barny said, as he bent down closer to his father, 'tell me who did this to you, Dad.'

'Barny, please, just leave it,' his dad groaned, 'it's not worth bringing any more trouble to our family. I will be all right, son. I just want to forget about it. Just let me be.'

Barny couldn't take any more of seeing his father in so much pain and returned to the hall where his mother was still standing in the same spot against the wall and still crying. With all the concern and anger he felt for his father being hurt, he hadn't realised that his mother had been injured as well. He put his arm around her shoulder. 'Please, Mum, just tell me who it was, tell me who has done this to Dad?'

His mother turned her head to the wall in silence.

'Mum,' Barny shouted, 'we can't let this go, we need to get it sorted out tonight.'

She turned round and put her hands on his face. 'Please, Barny, please, leave it. If you go looking for them you might get hurt.' She pleaded with him not to cause any more trouble.

The Move to Wilford Road

Barny could take no more. He held her hand and kissed her face.

'Come with me, Mum,' Barny said, 'come into the scullery and take care of Dad. I'll be back in a short while.' He made sure his mother was safely in the scullery, then he took the key and told them he was going to lock the door and they didn't have to worry about anything.

He then ran up the stairs to the landlady's room and started to bang on the door.

'All right, all right, I'm coming,' she shouted.

Barny was so worked up that he stumbled over his words. 'My father, from downstairs, do you know what happened to him? Do you know who the scum were that hurt my father? You had better tell me if you do know, for your own good.'

'Yes, I do,' the landlady replied, 'I saw everything and it's all your bloody fault. This is a rough area round here, lad, and you don't go picking fights with any of the lads who live here. You are a marked man now. They won't rest until you are in the infirmary or worse.'

'So it was the young man I hit this morning. I thought as much,' replied Barny.

'Look, I promised your mother I wouldn't tell you but, yes, it was him and four others. They came knocking on your door looking for you. They were swearing and shouting for you to go out and face them like a man, but of course you weren't here so your poor old father went out. All he wanted to do was to get them away from the house, so as not to upset your mother. He tried to speak to them and calm them down. He was trying so hard to sort things out without any fighting. He pleaded with them to go away.'

'Yes, and what happened then?' Barny asked.

'Listen to me, you have got to realise that some of the people around here don't care who they beat up or who gets hurt, it can be a young woman or an old person.'

Barny started to raise his voice. 'What happened next?' he shouted.

'Your father told them that you were not in and that there was no point in them waiting around for you to return, you might be away for days and he didn't want any trouble on the first day in the house. He told them he just wanted a quiet life. The boys started to talk amongst themselves. I think your father thought he had done it and they were going to go away. So he turned back towards the house and started to walk away from them. It was just then that one of the King brothers grabbed him by the collar and pulled him back out into the road. The look of shock on his face, I will never forget that, and then another one of the lads came up and took hold of your father's arm and they both lifted him off the ground, laughing.

'They then threw him in the air and let him go. He fell to the ground with a thud and he hit the side of his head on the kerb stone. I was nearly sick. I could see his ear splitting open. Then one of them pulled him up by his hair while one of the others struck a blow in your father's face. He hit him so hard, his head just kept moving around, I thought his head was going to leave his shoulders. Your father was then on the ground groaning in pain and the boys started to walk away. That's when I thought they had finished, but they only went a little way and then turned around and came running back up to him and they all took turns in kicking him all over his body. It was then that your mother came out. She was shaking with fear, but I suppose she couldn't just stand there and see her husband get kicked around. She started to shout at the boys to leave her husband alone and then tried to pull one of them away from him. Then they stopped and stepped back. I felt so sorry for your mother. It took all of her strength to try and help your father up but, before she could get him back into the house, the boys came back over. Two of them grabbed hold of your mother and took her to one side and laid her on the ground. One of them had a horse whip that he had taken from a passing cart and he started to whip her across her back as she lay on the ground. Your poor father could see what was happening to his wife. He then tried so hard to get over to her, but he just never had the strength to help her, he had to just lie there and cry.'

Barny's face screwed up with anger. 'Do you mean my mother is hurt as well?' he said.

'Yes, your mother took a right old beating across her back, did you not know about your mother?'

'No, she never told me. Was there no one there to help them get back in the house?' Barny asked.

'Oh yes, there were plenty there watching, but no one was going to help – they were all too afraid. Then two men came along, I think they had just come out of the Queen's Arms, anyway they ran up and took the whip off one of the lads and told them to be on their way. This started another argument between the two men and the boys and whilst this was all going on two of the neighbours and myself quickly brought your parents back into the house. After I had locked the door I took a look out of the window and the boys had gone.' The landlady then pointed her finger up to Barny's face. 'Where were you when your poor mother and father were being beaten?' she said. 'You should have been here. You must have known them boys would be back for you. Was that the reason why you were out?'

Barny pushed her hand away. 'Come on, tell me, where do they live?' he asked, as he held her hand tighter.

'Let go, you're hurting me,' she said. 'I have promised your mother not to tell you and I won't, but be sure they will be back and when they do return, make sure you are in. Please don't let your parents take another beating.'

Barny pushed her back into her room. 'What is your name?'

She looked up at him. 'It's Doris Brown. You can call me Mrs Brown.'

'Well, Doris, I thank you for helping my parents and don't worry, I can promise you that those boys won't return to this house.'

He returned downstairs, and when he turned the key in the door to the kitchen, both his parents jumped. 'It's all right, it's only me,' he shouted. He walked in and looked down at them both sitting on the floor in front of the fire. His eyes filled with tears, a lump came to his throat; it made it hard for him to swallow. His father's head was resting on his mother's lap and she was stroking his face, both their eyes were red and sore from all the crying they had done. It was a sight that would break the heart of anyone, especially a son who felt the guilt of causing his parents so much pain. He stood by the door with his head bowed.

'Come in, son,' his mother said, as she wiped away the tears with her hanky. 'Sit down, son, and I will do you some food.' She knew that if she could keep him at home then she could keep him safe and he would not go out looking for the animals who caused all of this suffering.

'Please, Barny, stay in, don't go out looking for them,' she pleaded with him again and again, but Barny couldn't rest until he had found revenge for his parents.

He walked across to the fire and put his arms around his mum and kissed her on the forehead.

'Mum, you know I have got to sort this out, if I don't everyone will think they can walk all over us and our lives won't be worth living. In the end they will force us to move again and this is the only place we can afford. Don't worry, Mum, I won't do anything stupid.' He lifted his father off the floor and placed him down in a chair with a pillow. He made sure they were both comfortable and told them he wouldn't be too long. 'Don't answer the door to anyone,' he said. 'Not even to that noisy old cow from upstairs, do you understand?'

'Yes, all right, son, but please be careful,' his mother said. Barny walked towards the door. As he was wiping away the tears from his eyes, he stopped and took a deep breath, turned and winked at his mother.

When Barny shut the front door, he leant back against the wall and burst into tears. He knew he couldn't break down in front of his parents, they needed him to be strong, but now they were out of sight and he couldn't hold back any more. He thought about his revenge, but first he had to find them. He knew they were local, but he did not have a clue who they were or where they came from, but he did remember that they knew Violet. There was nothing for it, he would have to go and ask her, whether her father liked it or not. He made his way across the road to Violet's house and walked up to the front door. He was thinking to himself she must know where the boy King lives. He knocked on the door. By this time everyone respectable was in bed, but he kept knocking harder and harder until he saw a flicker of a candle coming towards him through the glass of the door. When the door finally opened, he saw a tall upright man in his night shirt standing there looking out at him.

'What do you think you are doing over here, knocking on my door and making all this racket at this time of night?' he said abruptly.

'Look, I am sorry to get you out of bed, but I must speak to Violet. It is very important,' Barny said.

'Who do you think you are?' he replied. 'I'm not letting you anywhere near my daughter, let alone speak to her, not now or at any time, she doesn't mix with scum like you. Now be off with you before I call a constable and have you put inside,' he said, slamming the door in Barny's face.

Barny kept his temper. It wouldn't do any good hitting him, he thought, and he walked slowly down the road. Who else would know where those animals came from? He then remembered the two women who were over the other side of the road, talking to Violet when he was unloading the cart; they might know something. So he quickly made his way to the two houses where they were standing and knocked on the first door. He didn't have to wait long. A man, who was worse for ale, answered the door.

'What are you after, boy?' he said.

'I need to speak to the woman of the house,' answered Barny.

'Oh, is that right? Well, you come with me, boy,' he said, as he grabbed Barny by the collar and pulled him out into the road.

'Now tell me, why do you want to see my old woman?' the man asked.

'Look, I only need to speak to her for a moment. I just want to ask her something that's all,' Barny said.

'Well, let me tell you something, boy, my misses don't speak to anyone unless I say so. Now hear what I'm saying to you. Think yourself lucky tonight, I'm in a good mood so I'm not going to beat the life out of you, but I am going to count to two and if you're not running down the road, like a dog with his arse on fire, I will beat you to the ground and then I will go and get my axe, come back and chop your bloody legs off. Do you understand what I am saying boy?'

'Look, hold on just a minute,' Barny said. 'Please just come with me to the front of your house and take a look in the window.'

'What are you talking about, you fool. Why do you want me to look through my own window.?'

'Please just have a look inside and then you can do what you want with me.'

The man's curiosity got the better of him and he made his way to the window with Barny close behind him. The man pressed his nose against the glass. 'What am I supposed to be looking at? I can't see anything,' the man said.

'Well, why don't you let me help,' Barny replied. He grabbed the man's hair, pulled him back and then pushed his head through the window, pulled it out and then pushed it through the next window. The man started to scream as Barny hit him to the ground and pulled him out to the middle of the road. He lifted him off the ground and held him there.

'So you're going to chop my legs off are you?' he said to the man just before he placed two punches in the man's ribs and one in the mouth. The man's legs turned to jelly, but Barny was still holding him up and, as he was just about to place the last blow on the man's chin, he heard a scream. He looked behind him and saw a woman in the doorway of the house – the same woman who was talking to Violet earlier. He threw the man to the ground and walked towards the house. When the woman saw that he was coming towards her, she quickly ran indoors. Barny was too quick and before she could close the door, Barny was behind her and half way down the hall. He grabbed hold of the woman's hair.

'Hold on,' he said, 'I'm not going to hurt you, I just want to ask you something.' Barny let go of the woman's hair and she turned round.

'What do you want from me?' she asked.

'Did you see a fight across the road, some lads beating an old man and woman up?'

'What if I did?' she replied.

'They were my parents and I'm looking for the animals who did it. Now did you see them or not?'

'Yes, I did,' the woman replied, 'and it was a shameful sight.'

'Do you know the boys and where they live?' Barny asked, as he grabbed her arm.

'Listen, I don't know who you are and I don't care, but I will give you a warning, you don't want to go round to their house, they will kill you for sure and then they will come back and beat your parents again and again until they drive them out. You can't fight with that family. I have seen it all before. They are animals. The only thing you can do now is to move away tonight: that will be the only way you can finish this for good.'

Barny took hold of both her arms. 'Tell me, woman, where do the boys live?'

Just then the woman looked over Barny's shoulder and Barny looked behind him to see who was coming. He looked down and saw the woman's husband crawling on his hands and knees through the front door, his face dripping with blood. He looked up at his wife and stopped to get his breath.

'Tell him what he wants to know, you stupid woman,' he shouted, 'tell him now.'

The woman looked at Barny. 'They live in Princess Road,' she said, 'left at the bottom of this road and it's the first house on the left.'

'What floor do they live on?'

'They have three rooms on the ground floor, the boy King who beat your parents up, he is the youngest, but keep your eyes open – he has three older brothers and then there is the father and they are all monsters. Please don't tell them I was the one who told you where they live.'

Barny let the woman go and stepped over her husband as he made his way out of the house. He walked to the end of Wilford Road and crossed over the road. He stood opposite the Kings' house and waited for ten minutes. He then crossed over and stood by the door that was ajar. He could hear a lot of laughing coming from the downstairs rooms and wondered how many men were in there, but he knew what he had to do for the sake of his parents. He couldn't get the picture of his parents out of his mind, both of them sitting on the floor crying. He stepped back and gave the door an almighty kick. It smashed open against the inside wall with the glass crashing everywhere. Barny stood there waiting, but he didn't have to wait long before a man appeared from one of the rooms.

'What's all this about, what's happened to our door?' the man asked.

'Are you one of the King brothers?' Barny asked.

'What if I am? Who wants to know?'

'I want your younger brother out here now.'

The man walked closer to the door. 'Look,' he said, 'I don't know who you are or what you're doing around here, but let me tell you, for breaking our door you are going to get the biggest kicking you have ever had.'

Barny looked him in the eyes. 'I have told you, I have no argument with you. Fool, just bring your younger brother out here now.'

'What do you want him for?' the man asked.

'The dirty little scum bag beat my parents up this evening, round at Wilford Road.'

The man stepped back. 'So you're the bastard who hit him this morning. Well let me tell you something, son, you're dead.' With that the man pulled the door back and pulled out a shovel from behind it and ran at Barny, with the blade of the shovel pointing at Barny's face. Barny was too quick for him and moved to the right. The man overbalanced and fell to one side with the shovel still in his hand. He tried to get to his knees in an attempt to get up. Barny gave him an almighty kick in the face, which sent him spinning out into the road. Then he walked over and picked the shovel up and then slowly walked over to the man, who was still rolling about on the ground holding his head. He raised the shovel up and brought it down, once on the man's head and then on his legs, again and again until he heard the sound of the man's bones breaking. He then stepped back and threw the shovel down on the ground. The man was unconscious - he wasn't going to cause any more trouble. Barny then heard a noise behind him. He looked up and saw the boy King standing in the doorway. He still had the marks on his face from the last encounter with Barny. 'Come here,' Barny shouted. The boy knew what was coming.

He slammed the door and ran, but in his panic he tripped and before he could get himself up, Barny was on him. He grabbed him by the hair and pulled him out into the road. He then lifted the boy off the ground by his collar. 'Tell me, boy, was you the one who beat my parents up this evening?'

'No,' the boy replied, 'it wasn't me.'

'Don't lie to me,' said Barny as he pulled the boy's collar tighter. 'Tell me if it was you or not.'

'All right, all right,' the boy shouted, 'it was me, but we came after you and we thought you were hiding in your rooms and if we knocked your parents about a bit you would have to come out.'

Barny lifted him higher off the ground and then threw him down. He moved forward to give the boy a beating, but was stopped by two arms around his neck. It was the other brother. Barny was choking and had a job to get his breath and the brother was shouting to the boy on the ground. 'Get up, get up, and hit him across the head with something.' But the boy had frozen to the spot with fear.

The man with his arms around Barny's neck had waited too long. Barny turned his head to one side, so he could breathe a bit easier. He then took hold of one of the brother's fingers and pulled it back until it broke. This made him lose his grip around Barny's neck and as he did, Barny bent forward slightly and lifted the brother off his feet, at the same time moving backwards until he had rammed the man against the front of the house.

Squashed between Barny and the wall, the man's arms fell limply to his side. Barny raised his right arm up and pushed his elbow back into the man's face; this broke the man's nose and also split open the back of his head where it had hit the wall. Barny then turned around, placed four punches into the man's ribs, grabbed him by his hair and pushed his face into the wall. He stood and watched as the man slowly fell to the ground, without an ounce of life left in him.

He then turned and looked over at the boy – he was the one he had come for, he was the one who had beaten his mother and father. Barny

The Move to Wilford Road

walked up to him. The boy was rigid with fear and unable to move. He just sat on the ground shaking and crying with untold fear. The boy had never seen anyone get the better of his brothers before and he knew this giant wouldn't stop until he had killed him.

Barny asked him again if he was the one who had beaten his mother and father senseless. The boy looked up and started to sob. 'It was me,' he cried, 'and some others.'

That was all Barny wanted to hear. He did no more but picked the boy up and gave him four almighty blows to his face as he held the back of his head. The boy was knocked senseless, but Barny wasn't finished, not by a long shot. He wanted him dead. By this time a crowd had gathered, but no one was saying anything, they all just stood with their mouths open, wondering where this young boy had come from. He had taken on the most vicious family in the area and he had beaten them. They had never seen anyone with such strength.

A woman from the crowd shouted, 'His eyes have fallen into his head,' but it was just the swelling that made his eyes disappear into their sockets. Barny was just about to give him the final blow that would have finished him off, when he heard a frail old voice coming from the crowd.

'Come away, Barny, that's enough,' he heard, 'you've paid them back, now come home, son.' Barny let the boy drop to the ground and looked up. He saw this small feeble figure standing at the front of the large crowd. She walked over to him. 'Come on, son, there's no more to be done. Let the boy go.' His mother took hold of his hand and the crowd moved to one side as they both walked through the middle of them, their heads held high. Barny had beaten the King brothers. He would certainly have no more trouble from them and nor would anyone else for a very long time, but he forgot about the father, for he wasn't at home that night. When the father had left his house, he had a family whom everyone feared, even the police, but now people were laughing at the King family. Would he be able to live with that or would he go looking for Barny and take his revenge?

Chapter 2

Trouble in Forster Road

The next morning Barny was up bright and early. He hadn't slept too well, for it was his first night of sleeping on the floor. They only had three rooms – the scullery, his parents' bedroom and the sitting room, which was the best room and only used on special occasions. Barny was to spend his nights on the sitting room floor, but that never bothered him. Violet was the only thing on his mind, he never stopped thinking about her and the time they had spent together in the railway carriage. He made his way to the scullery without making a sound, for fear of waking his parents up. He lit the fire and poured some water from the jug into the bowl and had a quick wash. He looked on the table to see if there was anything to eat, but there was only a small amount of bread and cheese, which he left for his parents. He crept into the hall and opened the bedroom door quietly, to make sure his parents were all right. He stood there for a moment looking in; his mother was resting in her husband's arms; her eyes were still red and sore from all the crying from the night before. His father's face looked sad and still bruised and marked from the beating he had received. Barny stood there staring, he couldn't believe what his parents had been through. He wiped away the tears from his eyes. I've got to look after them, he thought to himself. I have got to be there for them, when they need me. He slowly walked up to the bed and kissed his mother's forehead. He wanted to hold and kiss his father, but that was something you never ever did. He just took his hand and held it tight. After spending five minutes with his parents, he then left the room and closed the bedroom door behind him slowly and quietly. He put his coat and cap on and made his way to the coal yard. As he passed by Violet's house, he stopped and remembered all that had happened the day before; he smiled and carried on walking. When he reached the yard, Fred was waiting outside the gates.

'Hello, Darky,' he said, as he was trying to remove a drunken man from the gate. 'Take a look at him, Darky.' He opened the man's coat and showed Barny half a dozen silver spoons which were sticking out of his inside pocket.

'What do you think we ought to do with him?' Fred asked.

'Well, we can't leave him here, if a copper comes along he'll be nicked for sure,' replied Barny.

'Yea, you're right, we'll have to try and wake him up and get him on his way.' Fred buttoned the man's jacket back up and then gave him a hard kick up the back side. The man still never moved.

'Do you think he's all right?' asked Barny.

'Yea, he just put a lot of ale away last night, that's his only trouble.' 'Give me a hand, Darky, we'll drag him over to that old barrel, we'll soon have him on his feet.' They both took an arm each and dragged the man across the yard to an old ale barrel that was full of water. They then lifted the man up and dropped him head first into the cold water. There were only half his legs showing out of the top of the barrel, from his knees to his feet, which then started to move and kick about frantically.

'Here you are, I told you he was all right,' Fred said.

'His getting a bit lively now,' replied Barny. 'Do you think we ought to get him out?'

'Yea, I think he's had enough now, grab a leg and we'll pull him out.' As they pulled the man out, the cold water was running out of his mouth, nose and from everywhere and, as they let him drop, he fell to the ground and collapsed.

'He doesn't look any better to me Fred,' Barny said.

'No, don't worry, he's all right, just a bit shocked by the cold water that's all. I'll lift him up and you give him a good slap on the back, that should clear his pipes.' As Fred lifted him up, Barny gave him a good hard slap on the back. The man started coughing and choking and more water came out of his mouth; it was like a fountain. 'I think we might have saved his life there, Barny,' said Fred. When the man came round, he asked why all of his clothes were wet. Fred explained to him that he was trying to walk on top of the barrel and fell in.

'I think you may have had too much to drink last night,' said Fred, with a smile on his face. 'Do you know what? If we hadn't come along when we did, you would have died in that barrel.'

'Well, I never,' the man, replied. 'I don't know how to thank you both'.

'There is no need to thank us,' replied Fred. 'That was just our good deed for the day, now you had better be on your way before you catch your death of cold.'

They watched him drag himself out of the yard, both laughing. Barny then turned to Fred. 'Here, I bet all of them spoons came out of his pocket when he was in that barrel!'

'Yea, you could be right there, Barny, so the poor sod has been through all of that for nothing,' said Fred.

'Still, at least we saved him from going to prison and we saved him from drowning in the end, now that's not bad for a day's work. I'll suppose that I will have to get the spoons out later and try and sell them to someone, never mind,' he said, as he looked down into the barrel. They both made their way back over to Fred's office.

Fred nudged Barny's arm. 'Here, you have certainly made a name for yourself now, Darky,' he said, 'beating them King brothers senseless like that.'

'How did you find out about that? It only happened last night.'

'Well, by the time you and your mother were back in your house, it was all round the public houses; it doesn't take long for something like that to get around, Barny, everyone was talking about it. I am really sorry about your parents though. I hope you gave that family what they deserved. By the way, how are your parents now, were they badly hurt?'

'Yes, they were, but I think they will be all right,' said Barny. 'Listen, Fred, I have got to earn more money now, do you think there will be any chance of some extra work for me around here?'

'You know, Darky, I would love to help you out, but at this time of year our work slackens off a bit.'

'It's all right, Fred, I understand, I will just have to take on more fights and get the money that way.'

Fred looked at him and shook his head. 'That won't be so easy.'

'Why is that?' Barny asked, looking shocked.

'Well, you have gone and made a name for yourself now and you won't find many men around here wanting to fight you, not unless they're full of ale, of course. So I'm afraid your fighting days, at least around here, are finished.'

Barny sat down on an old coaster's barrow. 'What can I do now, Fred? There's hardly any food in the house and the rent is due next week, then there is Violet. I know she's used to having a good time and I don't want to lose her by not taking her out and spending money on her.'

'Well, it sounds to me like you have fallen for that girl good and proper,' smiled Fred.

'Well do you know, Fred, I have never met anyone like her before, when I'm with her all my problems go and life seems worth living again.'

'Yes, that's all well and good, but always remember, Darky, your parents must come first before any bit of skirt, don't matter what.'

'No, of course, I would never forget that, Fred, they mean more to me then anything else in the world,' Barny replied.

'And has this Violet heard about your little bit of trouble, that you had last night?' asked Fred.

'No, I don't think so, not yet, but I had to go over to her house to try and find out where the King brothers lived and her dad came to the door. Cor, he is a right miserable old sod, he opened the door and looked at me as if I was dirt and then when I asked him if I could see his daughter, you would have thought I had asked to borrow £10 off him. In fact the ignorant git slammed the door in my face, quite abruptly. Without a doubt, Fred, I would have given him a good slap if it wasn't for his daughter Violet. You know just thinking about what happened to my parents is bad enough and then you go and see someone like him, who wouldn't even give you the time of day.'

'Yes, I know what he's like. I've had dealings with him before. Do you know I was taking some sacks of coal round his back yard one day and he had the cheek to go through all of the sacks to see if I had put any stones in with the coal.'

'Do you mean to say that he thought you would do something like that and try and diddle him? I don't believe it, Fred!' said Barny laughing. He knew that Fred was always putting stones in the sacks of coal.

'I know,' said Fred, 'that's what I said to him, but he didn't listen, he still went through the sacks. Here, Barny, I've just thought of a way that you can earn more money.' Fred sat down beside him. 'But it will mean that you will have to travel up to Nottingham and you will be fighting the big boys, but you can earn good money. This man I used to know, he organises all the fights up there. We used to be partners years ago in the fight game and I'm sure he will be able to sort you out.'

'But how will I get to Nottingham?' Barny asked. 'I can't afford the tram fare home, let alone the train fare to Nottingham.'

'Don't worry about that, we can sort that out,' he said, as he took some papers out of his pocket. 'Look, these are the timetables for the coal train. An empty one leaves here at six o'clock on Friday evening going to Worksop. Now I know it stops at Nottingham to take on water and if we can get you in one of the empty wagons, it will take you straight to Nottingham without costing you a penny. Mind you, it might be a bit cold and uncomfortable, but it will get you there.'

'That's all right,' replied Barny, 'I don't mind that, but how do I get back?'

'That's easy, there's a loaded train from Worksop that stops in Nottingham at twelve o'clock on Sunday night to pick up the pigeons. The only thing is the wagons will be loaded so you will have to travel back on top of the coal, but it will bring you right back into this yard.'

'Well, I don't like the thought of leaving my parents alone all weekend, but I suppose that I have no choice. Do you think you will be able to arrange it for me?'

'Of course, meet me here at 5.30 on Friday and I will get you on the empty wagon and give you the address of the public house where my mate lives, he will sort you out then. But, whatever you do, don't go telling your parents I had anything to do with it. Your mum will go mad if she knew it was me who had arranged for you to go away and fight at weekends.'

When Barny had finished unloading the coal train, putting the coal into the sacks and loading them on the carts, he grabbed some bread and cheese from Fred's office and made his way to the public wash house. He had an arrangement there with the caretaker. Barny would stoke the boiler up and then move the stack of coal forward so it was closer to the boiler and in return the caretaker would let him have a free bath. The public baths were in the same building as the wash house, where all the women went to wash their clothes. Barny had been going there for some years, so he knew what to expect from the women.

He had taken his Sunday best jacket with him to change into, just in case Violet was at home when he arrived back.

Barny stoked the boiler, moved the coal and by the time he was getting out of the bath, the women of the area were starting to bring their washing in. The same women went to the wash house every day so they were quite used to seeing Barny walking about drying his hair, in fact it was one of the highlights of the day for some of them. They were not used to seeing many men in the wash house because keeping clean wasn't the most important thing in the men's lives and they never went up there until they couldn't stand their own smell. So the women used to look forward to seeing Barny, all washed, cleaned and fresh looking, and as he walked out of the men's changing room, they were all there waiting for him.

'Barny,' one shouted. 'When are you going to make a decent woman of me, you rascal?'

Barny smiled with his face turning bright red, as he always did. Another woman shouted out from behind him. 'Here, sexy, how about five minutes behind the boiler house with me, darling. Don't you worry about this lot, they'll do you no good, I'm all you need.' The women were all laughing, but any one of them would have gone with Barny if he had held his hand out to them.

'Come on, sweetheart,' shouted another one, 'I've thrown my old man out this morning and the bed's still warm, ready and waiting for you, handsome.'

Barny turned and smiled. 'I'm afraid you're too late now, I'm already spoken for.'

'Really, so who's the lucky bitch then?' asked one of the women, who was old enough to be his mother, but still fancied him all the same.

'Her name's Violet, Violet Blake,' Barny replied.

One of the women put her washing down on the floor and walked up to Barny. 'Do you mean the Violet Blake from Wilford Road, the one with the stuck-up parents?' she asked.

'I don't know about the parents, but yes, that's the one.'

'Listen here, Barny, you want to be careful of her, my boy,' the woman said. 'She is well known all around the public houses, a bit of a lady's man by all accounts. Now, don't be taken in by her good looks.' The other women started to move in closer to find out more.

'So how long have you been going out with her then, Barny my boy?' asked one woman.

'Not long, we have only just moved into Wilford Road and we spent our first time together last night.'

'The lucky cow!' one woman shouted. The old woman moved forward again, looking at Barny.

'Were you the one who sorted out the King brothers last night?'

'Yes, it was me, but they got what was coming to them,' Barny replied.

'Well, I must say you have certainly made your mark in the road now, but be aware of that girl Blake, she doesn't seem like she's a good one. You don't want to rely on her too much.'

Barny left the women to their washing and their gossiping and, as he left, he got the normal offers of marriage and his bum pinched, but he was always glad to get away from there, he never knew what the women were going to get up to next. He made his way home and, as he approached Wilford Road, he could feel the people staring and talking about him. He knew what they were thinking, but he never cared, he knew what he had done the night before was the right thing, he was only protecting his parents. He held his head high as he walked down Wilford Road, but then the people started to smile in a friendly way. But he never took much notice, he wasn't bothered about them, all he was thinking about was Violet and hoping that she would be at home when he arrived. He pushed the front door open and walked through to the scullery where his mother was sitting down at the table sewing.

'Have you seen Violet this morning, Mum?' he asked, as he walked up to her and placed a kiss on her cheek.

'No, and I want to have a word with you about that girl later,' she said.

'How are you feeling this morning, Mum?' Barny said, cutting her off before she could say any more about Violet.

'Yes, I'm OK, son, a bit sore, but nothing to worry about.'

'Where is Father? Is he any better this morning?'

He's not saying much, he's out there in the yard cleaning his tools. I told him not to go out there, but no, he wouldn't listen to me. I think he is missing his work so much. You know he wants to teach you some more carpentry today. He keeps going on about when he's taught you enough, then you can take over his tools. You know, Barny, he was one of the best carpenters around and he wants you to follow in his footsteps.'

'Yes, I know, Mum, but I have to do anything at the moment just to bring the money in. That's why I need to talk to you about my fighting,' Barny said, as he sat down next to his mother. 'I won't be able to find any fights around this way now, not after last night, so I am going to go further out where no one knows me, but it will only be at weekends, so I will be with you and father through the week.' His mother got up from her chair; she never liked talking about his fighting.

'I have been speaking to Doris the landlady,' she said, changing the subject. 'She came down this morning to see if we were OK, you know after last night. She told me all about that girl Violet. Did you know she was seeing a sergeant from the army?' Barny stood there in silence. 'Was she the cause of the trouble last night?'

'No, it was nothing to do with her, it was just some of the scum who live around here.' You don't want to listen to that woman, she just a nosy old – '

'That is enough. I'll have no bad language in these rooms.' Just then there was a knock at the door. Barny's mother opened it to find a rough-looking man standing there.

'Is the boy Sturt in?' the man asked, as he was trying to look over Mrs Sturt's shoulder and into the room.

Barny left his chair and pulled his mother back in from the doorway.

'Go and sit down, Mum, I will sort this out.' He turned and looked at the man. 'I'm Barny Sturt,' he said, as he pulled the door to, 'and what do you want?'

The man stepped back away from the door. 'I've got a message from some girl called Violet, she said she wants to see you right away.'

'I hope she is not in any trouble? Where is she?'

'She is in the stable behind the house next to hers, I will take you there, but you must leave now,' the stranger said. Barny told the man to wait and then shut the door. He then went back into the scullery and gave his mother some money. 'Here you are, Mum, take this and buy some food and there is a little bit extra, so you can treat yourself to a new apron. I know you've been wanting for a new one for ages.'

'Thank you, son, you do look after your old mum,' she said.

'You're worth it, Mum, it's not much, only what I earned this morning. I'll be back a bit later.' He followed the man across the road and, when they reached Violet's house, Barny pulled at the man's arm. 'What's she doing in the stable? She hasn't got any horses.'

The stranger turned and moved away from Barny. 'She's looking after someone's horse, it's not too good,' he said, in a frightened voice. They both walked between the houses, and when they reached the stable, the stranger opened the door and walked off to the other side. Barny walked slowly in. He knew something wasn't right. All he could see were two horses and a cart, but no Violet. As he walked in a bit further, the door slammed behind him. Barny turned and there, standing in the doorway, were the boy King's father with three other men. They stood there smiling and all had lead pipes in their hands.

The father looked at Barny. 'We have some unfinished business, Sturt. You made my sons look fools last night and we are here to even the score. You are going to get the biggest beating of your life and then when we are finished, we are going to drag you out into the road and leave you there for everyone to see that the King family always pays its debts.'

Barny looked around quickly but could see no escape; there were no doors or windows. This is it, he thought to himself, I will never be able to fight four of them especially when they have lead pipes. When he turned back round, he saw the men walking slowly towards him, swinging the lead pipes around. There was nowhere for Barny to go, he started to walk slowly backwards until he felt the wall of the stable against his back.

One of the men stopped. 'Hold on,' he said. 'I just want to find out something before we beat the life out of him.' He looked Barny in the eyes. 'Here, Sturt, is it true that you have been seeing the girl Blake?'

Barny's face changed from fear to anger. 'Don't you mention her name, she is too good for scum like you to even talk about her. You want me, you come and get me, but leave Violet's name out of it.'

The man carried on. 'Sturt, did you know I have been seeing her?' he said smiling. This turned Barny's blood cold.

'Yes,' he said, 'I have been out with her quite a bit. We have slept together many times.'

Barny could take no more. If the man had not brought up the subject of Barny's love, then he would certainly have been given a good beating, perhaps he would have even lost his life in that stable, but hearing someone from the gutter talking about the girl he loved made his body repel all fear, he could now see no danger.

The men started to move towards him, lifting the pipes up ready to bring them down on Barny's head. Barny moved slowly along the wall until he could move no further. And then he just happened to look up and noticed a chain which was hanging over the beams of the stable. He reached up, before the men could move any closer, wrapping the chain around his hand and pulling it down. The four men stopped dead. It was a fearful sight for them. A giant of a man holding a six-foot chain which was wrapped around his hand. Barny felt more confident now and he could smell the fear coming from the other men. They knew what he was capable of, with only his fists to fight with, let alone a heavy chain.

One of them turned to run out of the stable, but he was pulled back by the other three. The man King shouted out to the others. 'Come on, he is on his own and there are four of us, he can't take us all at once.' But who was going to be the first one to move towards Barny and risk getting a six-foot chain around their heads? They all looked at each other. Barny knew he had to make his move now before the men gained enough courage to run at him. He started to swing the chain around his head. When the men saw this, they all dropped their lead pipes and tried to duck out of the way of the swinging chain, but it was too late. The chain caught one of the men on the side of his face and this knocked him into the other three. They all stumbled to the ground. Barny was now in control, but he had to move fast, if the chain got caught around one of the wooden posts of the stable, it would give the men enough time to get up and jump on him. He carried on swinging the chain around in all directions, hitting the men across their bodies and legs. It wasn't his intention to finish them off, but he wanted to make sure that they would never ever come back looking for him or his parents again.

The men were lying in a heap on the ground, all of them defenceless against this fighting machine with a six-foot chain. The one thing Barny had learnt from all his days as a bare-knuckle fighter was that you never stopped until the other man was lifeless on the ground and you knew he wasn't going to get back up. The chain came down with ferocious force upon the men's bodies and blood spurted everywhere. And, finally, out of sheer exhaustion of swinging a six-foot chain around his head, Barny dropped to the ground. Three of the men were lifeless and the other one just lay there, groaning in pain from the injuries Barny had inflicted on him. No more would this feud go on, this would be the last time Barny would draw blood from the King family.

It took Barny ten minutes to get his breath back, he then pulled himself up and made his way to the door. And, as he opened it, he saw a small crowd had gathered outside and standing in front was Violet's father. Barny walked up to him and asked if he knew where Violet was. Her father gave him a dirty look and just replied. 'You stay away from her, boy, she's promised to a sergeant and she don't want nothing to do with you.' He then turned and walked away, pushing his way through the crowd.

Barny returned to his rooms. There wasn't a scratch on him so his mother and father were none the wiser of what had happened. His mother asked him if he knew why the crowd had gathered across the road, but Barny just shook his head and lay down on his mother's bed. Thinking how close he had come to losing his life, for there was no doubt in his mind at all that those four men wouldn't have stopped until all the life was beaten out of him.

Four days went by and Barny still hadn't seen Violet, but she was always on his mind, every minute of every day. He would lie awake at night watching the embers of the fire slowly die away. He would walk by her house a hundred times a day in the hope of seeing her. He even asked Doris, the landlady, if she knew where Violet might be. She told him, reluctantly, that Violet would often disappear for a few days at a time; she thought it might be because she was staying over in the big house where she worked.

On the fifth day, Barny went up to the local shop, just at the top of Wilford Road, to buy some tobacco for his father. As he was walking out of the shop, he saw Violet walking along on the other side of the road. He ran across and took hold of her arm. 'Violet,' he said, 'where have you been? I've been looking for you everywhere.'

'I've had to sleep over for a few days in the big house,' she said. 'The nanny's been off sick so I've had to look after those bloody kids on my own. I meant to leave a message with your mother, but I must have forgot. Anyway, I can't talk to you now, Barny, I have to get home.'

'When can I see you?' Barny asked, as he pulled her arm and stopped her from walking off.

'You can take me for a drink tonight,' she replied. 'I haven't been out for the last four days and those bloody horrible kids have driven me round the bend!'

'Do we have to go to a public house?' Barny asked reluctantly.

'Well, that's where I want to go. I know you don't drink, but I like it in the public houses and there's nowhere else around here we can go. Look, I have got to go now, meet me at seven o'clock at the bottom of Wilford Road and we'll sort it out then.' She gave him a quick kiss on the cheek and then ran off down Wilford Road, leaving Barny standing there, wondering if all the stories about her were true. I will have to ask her tonight, he thought.

Just then a man in a suit walked up to him. 'Are you Barny Sturt?' the man asked.

'Why, who wants to know?' Barny replied.

'I'm Detective Sharp and I want to speak to you about seven men who have turned up at the infirmary over the last few days, with some serious injuries. Do you know anything about them?'

'No, not me guvnor,' Barny replied, as he turned to walk away.

The detective took hold of his arm. 'Wait a minute. I haven't finished with you yet.'

Barny stopped and looked the man in the eyes. 'Take your hand off me now. I don't know anything about any beatings. Now I'm telling you to keep away from me.'

'Listen to me,' the detective said, 'I don't care if you lot around here beat each other to death, it will do us a favour if you did, but the infirmary sends a report to my guvnor and he's on my back now to get this sorted out. No one has told me it was you who gave those men the beatings, but your name's been mentioned a few times. I hear you're a street fighter, handy with your fists, but you will go too far one day, my boy. I've have seen it all before and when you do, I'll be there to put the cuffs on.'

'It will take more than you to put the cuffs on my hands, copper,' Barny replied.

'Don't you worry, boy, I won't be on my own when the time comes and believe me I have seen your type before and your time will come.'

Barny pushed him to one side and walked off, he was more worried about Violet. Would she be straight with him tonight and tell him the truth?

At the Precipice of Poverty

At 6.45 Barny was standing on the corner of Wilford Road and at 7.30 Violet turned up. She ran straight up to him and kissed him on the lips. 'I've missed you Barny,' she said.

'Well, you never said that earlier,' he replied.

'No, well I couldn't,' she said. 'My parents might have seen us, you know they don't like you, Barny.'

'No, I know they don't, but I don't want to walk out with them. Do you know I have only met your father twice and both times were bad occasions?'

'Yes, I know. My father told me about the fight in the stable. You will have to be more careful, you'll kill someone one day and where will that leave me then?'

Barny put his arms around her. 'I will never leave you, Violet, you can be sure of that.'

'Come on, let's go up the Four in Hand public house and you can tell me what you have been doing with yourself for the last few days.'

They walked up the road hand in hand, talking about the fight in the stable and, as they walked up to the door, Barny looked through the window. It was packed and it looked as though most of the people in there had been there all day. Barny opened the door for Violet and as she walked in, one young man shouted out.

'Well, what do you know, here comes Violet Blake. Come over here sweetheart and sit on my lap.'

Barny then followed Violet in, and the young man soon stopped shouting at her and silence loomed over the whole room. It was only broken by a few drunken men falling about and the landlord looking at Barny and saying, 'I don't want any trouble in here tonight, son.'

Violet walked over to him. It gave her a great sense of power knowing that she was the only one in the room, apart from the drunks, who wasn't afraid of Barny. 'It's all right, George,' she said, 'he's with me and there will be no trouble tonight. Come on, Barny, what are you having to drink?' she said as she held his arm tightly.

'You know I don't drink, Violet, I don't like these places.'

'All right, Barny, just have a ginger beer then and I'll have a few ales and then afterwards we will go for a walk,' she said.

Barny sat down and looked around him; he could fill the tension from the other men building up. The drunks were all looking at him, just waiting for the chance to take him outside and prove that they could beat the young man who had sent the King family away, but Barny knew he had his first fights up north this weekend and couldn't take the risk of getting hurt, if he could help it, for he needed the money for his parents. Violet got the drinks and came and sat down.

'I want to ask you something, Violet,' he said, as he moved closer to her. 'I have heard you are seeing a sergeant from the army; is it true?'

'Well, I have been seeing a sergeant, but he is away for most of the time. It's my parents who want me to marry him. He has good prospects in the army.'

'Do you love him?' Barny asked.

'I like him of course I do, but I've got you, haven't I?' she replied.

'That's OK then, I've been really worried about it for days, especially after what happened between us.'

They carried on drinking, but it wasn't long before trouble reared its evil head. Two men walked over to their table.

'So you think you're hard, do ya?' one of the men said to Barny.

'No, I don't think I'm hard and I don't want any trouble tonight,' Barny replied. He could be as gentle as a baby as long as no one bad mouthed or hurt the people he cared for.

The two men carried on. 'We would like to take you outside. Just to see if you're as good as they say you are.'

Violet looked around her and saw the people looking at them and she was in her glory – everyone in the public house was waiting to see what Barny would do.

'Go on, Barny, take them outside,' she said, 'and give them what for.'

Barny looked at her and smiled, 'You take them outside and sort them out,' he said jokingly.

She didn't know where to put her face and sank slowly down in her chair. Everyone started to laugh. The two drunken men started to get a bit loud, throwing their arms around. One of them picked up a match stand and threw it on to the ground, just missing Violet's leg. Barny was just about to get up to push the man away from the table when the landlord and his two sons came over. The two sons took a drunk on each arm and led them to the bar. The landlord picked the match stand up and said to Violet, 'Come on, you two, you had better go before there's any more trouble.'

'What about those two men?' Violet said, feeling a bit shaky now. 'They are bound to follow us outside.'

'No, they won't,' said the landlord. 'I will give them some more ale and I know they won't leave here until that's finished.' Violet and Barny both stood up together and walked to the door. Violet held her head down low, feeling a bit ashamed of her new boyfriend.

They walked away from the house and Barny went to hold Violet's hand, but she pulled away. 'Why didn't you sort them two out? I know you could have done it with one arm behind your back. Why did you have to make me look like a fool?'

'Look, I don't fight for the fun of it, Violet. If I had thought you were in danger I would have done something, but they were harmless.'

'I don't know what people will think of you now, one day you're beating four of the hardest men in the road and the next day you're walking away from two old drunks. We won't be able to go back in that public house this weekend.'

'We won't be going in any public house this weekend.' He explained why he wouldn't be around at weekends.

'Well, I won't be sitting indoors on my own waiting for you to come home,' she said.

They turned into Forster Road, the next road down from Wilford Road and just as rough. Half way down the road Violet stopped. 'What was that?'

'I never heard anything,' Barny replied.

'It was a woman screaming I'm sure of it,' Violet said, as she held Barny's arm tighter. 'Listen, there it is again.'

'You're right, and it's coming from across the road.' They crossed over and stopped outside 34. 'That's old Mrs Effingham's house, someone's in trouble in there.'

'Come on let's go, it's none of our business,' he replied, as he pulled at Violet's arm.

'No, Barny, someone's shouting murder, you've got to go in there and find out who it is.'

Barny agreed to go in the house and find out what was going on, just to shut Violet up.

'Now you stop here. I don't want you going in there until I know it's safe.' He walked up to the door and pushed it open. It was dark, but he could just about see a figure lying on the floor, at the bottom of the stairs.

'Are you all right?' Barny shouted, as he walked through the door.

'No, I've been stabbed,' a voice said. 'Please help me, my husband has gone mad. He's in that room there with a knife and I don't know what he is going to do next.'

Barny tried to see through the darkness, he could just make out that there were three doors leading off the hall, but which one was the man behind? Just then he heard a woman shouting from behind the door of the room facing him: 'Murder, murder.'

He walked up to the door and then stopped. I better not just walk in there, he thought to himself, if the man's standing by the door with the knife, he'll go for me. I'll have to take him by surprise and kick the door in. So he started to walk backwards to take a run up at the door. When all of a sudden, he felt someone behind him. He jumped and shouted and the person behind him jumped and screamed. It was Violet, she had crept into the hall without him knowing. 'What are you doing in here. I thought I told you to stop outside until I called you.'

When Violet had calmed down and her eyes were getting used to the darkness, she looked down at the woman on the floor. 'That's Kate Carn. Is she hurt?'

'I don't know,' he replied. 'Now go back outside and get a constable,' he said. He pushed her out of the front door and returned to the room and kicked the door open. 'What's going on in here?' he shouted.

An old woman came running over to him. 'Quick,' she said, 'George has gone mad, he has already stabbed his wife and his friend Bert and he is going to cause more trouble.'

Barny looked down on the floor and saw a man lying there, moaning and groaning with his head covered in blood.

The woman took hold of Barny's arm. 'He has gone completely mad.'

'Well, where is he now?' Barny asked.

'He's run out in the back yard to get a chopper. He says his going to do away with his wife's legs. Quick, you have got to stop him.'

Barny pushed her away. 'Can't you help that poor man on the floor?'

'I don't know what to do with him. He has been stabbed in the forehead and the neck, I'm no doctor. What am I supposed to do with him?'

'Well, go and get some bed sheets and wrap them around his wounds and try to stop the bleeding.' Barny said. He then left the woman and made his way out to the back yard. As he made his way to the back door he was thinking about Violet coming back in the house and he didn't want her to be in any danger from the man, so he had to make sure it was safe for her. He kicked open the back door that led to the yard, but it was pitch black out there and he couldn't see a hand in front of him. He shouted out, 'George, you had better come out and let me see you. You're in big trouble now, don't make it any worse.' He started to walk slowly forwards, but then all of a sudden, he felt someone push him from behind violently and then, he felt a sharp pain in his right shoulder.

Barny fell to the ground. George had come up behind him and tried to pull his head back by his hair, so he could thrust his knife into Barny's throat, but his hand slipped and he accidentally pushed Barny forward and on to the ground. Barny was stunned for a few seconds, but then he rolled over and looked up. And, as he did so he saw a figure of a man just about to come down on him with a chopper. Barny rolled over again. The man's arm came down, but with no target to hit, he stumbled and overbalanced and fell to the ground. Barny quickly moved his legs round and kicked the man in the face. The skin of the man's forehead split open and the blood started to run down the man's face. While the man was dazed Barny got to his feet. He couldn't see the chopper anywhere, but the man was still holding the knife. Barny placed his boot on the man's forearm and twisted it until the knife dropped from his hand. He then picked the knife up and knelt down on the man's chest. He held the man's head back by his hair, that was now covered in blood, and pressed the knife against his throat; it pierced his skin and he started to bleed. 'Is this what you want, old man?' Barny said. 'Do you want to die?'

'No, of course I don't,' the old man said as he was trying to catch his breath and stop choking on his blood.

'Listen, son, this is not your fight so be on your way and let me do what I have to do.'

'You made it my fight, old man, when you jumped me. Tell me, were you really going to chop your wife's legs off?'

He looked into Barny's eyes.

'Yes, I was going to do it, I thought it would be the only way to have stopped her walking out on me with that Bert, the dirty bitch.'

Barny released his grip and pulled the man to his feet. 'Come on, old man, you're too old for all of this.' They began walking to the house, but the man stopped Barny before they reached the door and said to him.

'If she leaves me for Bert I will have nothing. She brings the money in from charring and I will end up in the workhouse.'

Barny looked round at him. 'And where will you end up if you kill them both?' he said, as he pushed the man through the door. He looked down the hall and saw Violet kneeling down by the woman and a constable standing next to her rubbing his head. Violet looked up at the man. 'You bastard, look what you have done to her.' Barny gave the man to the constable and he marched him out of the house. 'This man needs the police doctor. I'll take him to the station and then I'll be back later to take some statements.'

Barny lifted Violet off the ground. 'Look what he's done to her, Barny, he has stabbed her in the top of her legs, on her buttocks and around her waist. She's like a bloody pincushion. It's a good job they are not deep cuts, but we had still better get her to the infirmary.'

'There's some man called Bert in the other room whom he has stabbed too,' Barny said.

Violet walked through to the room and saw the man on the floor. 'We need someone with a barrow. Go outside and see if there's someone in the crowd with a barrow who would be willing to take them to the infirmary.'

Barny found someone and helped put the man and woman on to the barrow.

'Where is Mrs Effingham?' Violet asked.

'She's in the kitchen having a drop of stout,' Barny replied. They walked back into the house, where the floor of the hall was covered in blood. 'Don't tread in that, you've got enough of it over yourself already.'

Barny then remembered the sharp pain he had felt in his shoulder when the man had jumped him. He looked down and saw that it was his own blood running down his arm. He never told Violet, he didn't want her to worry. He put his hand over the wound and they both walked through to the scullery.

'Mrs Effingham, are you all right?' Violet asked.

'Me nerves have gone a bit, but a few more of these and I will be all right,' the old woman said. They sat around the table and Mrs Effingham started to tell them of the day's events. 'We all met up this morning outside the fishmongers. I said to Bert, "If you would like to get a few jugs of ale we can all go back to my room and have a drink," which we did. At about two o'clock the ale ran out and Mr Carn suggested that we all go up the Fisherman's Arms and have a few drinks and then bring some jugs back with us. By the time we got back home we were all worse for the drink. You know what old Bert's like. He got up and started to have a jig about, he then pulled Mrs Carn up and they were dancing together and then suddenly Mr Carn got up and started shouting at his wife about her sleeping with Bert and when I looked around, Bert had his hand up Mrs Carn's dress. Mr Carn ordered his wife to go home, but she said, "No I'm not going, you will only beat me." Mr Carn then went to the table and picked up a knife. He walked across to his wife and slapped her across her face. "You will go home, lady," he said. She then ran out of the door and up the stairs. Mr Carn followed and the next thing I heard was someone falling down the stairs. I poked my head around the door and saw poor Mrs Carn on the floor at the bottom of the stairs – she had blood all round her middle.'

'What happened next?' Violet asked. 'Where was Mr Carn?'

'I don't know,' Mrs Effingham replied. 'I was so frightened I quickly slammed the door and put a chair against it. A few minutes later Mr Carn started to bang on the door. I shouted for him to go away, but then he started to kick at the door and by this time old Bert was over in the corner, he was quite frightened. The door smashed opened and Mr Carn came in. He pushed me to one side and went for Bert. Bert made a run for the door, but Mr Carn punched him on the side of the head as he went by and he fell to the ground. Mr Carn then jumped on him and began stabbing him in the head, but the knife was only an old kitchen one and it kept bouncing off Bert's forehead. He then stuck it in the side of his neck and that's when I started to scream and shout murder. Mr Carn left Bert and came over to me and said, "Shut up, woman, or you'll have some of this." He asked me where the chopper was and I said to him, "What do you want that for?" He replied, "To chop her bloody legs off, I'll teach her," he said. I was so frightened I just told him there was one in the back yard. He then pushed me to the ground and left the room for the yard and that's when you both appeared.'

'Well, I never,' Violet said, 'it's a good job my Barny was here, he soon sorted him out.'

'Do you want to wash that blood off your hands, duck?' Mrs Effingham said, as she brought a jug of water over to him.

Violet got up and left the table. 'I had better go now, Barny. Give me five minutes in case my father's out there in the crowd. I'll leave by the back door. You know he will go mad if he knows I've been in here.'

Violet left and Barny stayed with the old woman. She was still the worse for drink and kept rubbing Barny's head. 'You're a good boy,' she kept saying. 'I wish I had a boy like you.'

Barny thought it was time to go and left the house. The crowd looked at him as he walked down the road. There is more trouble in the road and Barny Sturt is in the middle of it, they all thought.

When Barny got home his father was in bed. His mother saw the blood and nearly fainted. 'What have you been up to, Barny?'

'It's all right, Mum.' He began taking his coat and shirt off, while he explained what had happened. His mother looked at his shoulder.

'That's a nasty cut. It looks like it's touched your muscle. Stay there and I'll get some water and bathe it for you. Have you had anything to eat?'

Barny remembered that the money he had to get some pies for himself was spent in the Four in Hand. 'Yes, it's all right, I had something earlier.' But really he was starving hungry.

'Well, if you feel a bit hungry later, there's some mutton left over on the stove, just help yourself.'

'I tell you what, Mum, I might have that mutton now, if you don't mind.' Barny walked to the stove.

'You haven't eaten today have you?' his mother said. 'What happened to the money you had for food?'

'I took Violet for a drink.'

'You have got to look after yourself; don't worry about that girl, she is going to be well taken care of.'

Barny sat down next to his mother and they were talking for about half an hour when there was a knock on the door. 'Come in,' his mother shouted. It was Doris, the landlady. 'I've only popped in to see how you are,' she said.

'Yes, we're fine now. Do you fancy a cup of tea, Doris, while you're here?'

'Well, yes go on then, I'll have a quick one. Here you won't believe this, but I did a good deed last night,' she said.

'Oh yea,' Barny replied, 'have you found somewhere else to live?'

'Now shut up,' Barny's mother said. 'Go on, Doris, you tell us all about it.'

'Well, you know I went to visit my sister last night. Well, she did me a bit of tea and then she realised she had run out of ale, so I said that I'd pop down the public house and get a jug; it was only down the road you know the one, the Jolly Bleachers. Anyway, I was standing there waiting for the landlord to fill the jug and a young girl came in. I found out later that she was only fourteen years of age. She walked up to the bar and ordered a jug of ale to take away. A barmaid went to get the young girl's ale and the landlord, who was serving me, was called round to the other side of the house. I think he had a bit of trouble round there, anyway the barmaid came back with the girl's jug and I noticed that it wasn't sealed. I said to the woman serving that the jug wasn't sealed and she replied that she had put a cork in the top of the jug and that was sufficient. I knew it wasn't because I have worked behind a bar before, so I went outside to find a constable. I was lucky there was one just walking past. I told him what had happened and he grabbed the girl and took her back into the house with me.

'He called the landlord over, who had just finished filling my jug. He came over and asked what the trouble was. The constable told him what had happened and showed him the unsealed jug. The landlord said that the girl couldn't have bought the ale from him, he wouldn't have sold it to her without it being sealed. That's when I piped in, I told him I had seen one of his barmaids sell it to the girl. Do you know what he said to me then?'

'Thank you for helping me,' Barny said sarcastically.

'No, he never said that at all, he told me that I should mind my own business. The bloody sauce, I had a right to report him.'

'Of course you did, Doris,' Barny's mother replied. 'What happened next?'

'Well, he went and got the barmaid who had served the young girl and she admitted that she gave her the jug without sealing it. She said that they had run out of sealing wax and labels, but she pushed the cork in the jug really firm.'

'What did the constable say?' Barny asked.

'He arrested him, of course,' replied Doris.

'Do you know, I have known that landlord for several years,' said Barny. 'He's a really good friend of Fred's from the coal yard and I know he has had his licence for the last ten years without any trouble and now you have gone and got him nicked, he could even lose his licence over this.'

'If he has done wrong then he has to pay for it,' said Doris. 'That Fred's no better, did you know he got summoned last year?'

'What was that for, Mrs Know-it-all?'

'For having sacks of coal on his cart with short weight in them. Yes, and he got fined 20s and 5s 6d costs and he deserved it as well.'

Barny couldn't take any more of this; he stood up and left the room, but only to return five minutes later. He walked back into the scullery and told Doris that someone in the greengrocer's was looking for her. He said the person told him that they had some very important news for her.

Doris stood up. 'I wonder who that can be? I must go and find out.'

When she left, Mrs Sturt asked Barny what the person looked like.

'I don't know, there's no one up there who wants her, I just made it up to get rid of her, she gets on my bloody nerves. She's always running someone down. You mark my words, Mum, someone will teach her a lesson one of these days.'

'You shouldn't do that to her, I know she's a bit of an old gossip, but there's is no harm in her. Where do you think she is now?' his mother asked laughing.

'I never thought I would see the day when you would be laughing at old Doris.'

'No, I'm not. Well, it was funny, I have never seen her move so fast, she was up and out of that chair like I don't know what. I bet she will be walking up and down that road for the next hour or so, you sod.'

Chapter 3

The Killing of a Best Friend

After Barny had eaten and his mother had dressed his shoulder as best she could, they both sat back in their chairs. 'Would you like a mug of tea?' his mother asked.

'No not now, thank you, Mum,' Barny replied.

'What's wrong with you, son, you look worried about something, it's not the fighting this weekend is it?'

'No, I'm not worried about that, it's that bloody court case tomorrow. It's really getting to me, knowing that I'm going to be in that room with all those coppers. It gets me really worried.'

'You know you've done nothing wrong and it's not you on trial, you're only the witness. Something terrible must have happened that day, what with one man dead. Would you like to talk to me about it now? You never know, it might help you when you give your story in court and you never did tell me the whole story or how you got involved. I don't even know what you were doing there in the first place.'

His mother had asked Barny many times in the past what had really happened, but he had always changed the subject. It seemed like he just wanted to forget about what happened that day which, of course, was unlike Barny, he normally told his mother everything that was going on, but he never wanted to mention this to his mother. She had heard the usual rumours of Wilford Road and everyone adding their bit to the story.

'Well,' he said, 'I suppose I will have to talk about it in court, but I don't like you hearing things like that, it's not nice.'

The Killing of a Best Friend

'It's all right, son, you couldn't shock me. I've lived round this way for too long now and have seen too many things. Now tell me, how did you get involved?' his mother asked.

'I don't know, Mum,' he said. 'I was just doing a few jobs for Fred that day, delivering a few sacks of coal, and I remember dropping three sacks off in Whitehorse Road and the next address was in Princess Road, so I thought, instead of going all round the houses, I'd take a short cut down Wilford or Forster Road and that would bring me out in Princess Road, right where I wanted to be.'

'But you know they don't like strangers down there,' his mother said, interrupting. 'You took a bit of a chance being on your own with all that coal on.'

'Yea, I know, I lost four sacks while all the trouble was going on outside the house and Fred wasn't too happy about that when I got back to the yard,' Barny carried on. 'As I left the house in Whitehorse Road, the horse started to play up a bit and that's what made my mind up, that I would take the short cut. Anyway, as I pulled into the top of Wilford Road the horse went lame on me, so I kept him going until we got half way down and then pulled over. I took a look at his hind leg and found that he had lost a shoe. I then waited a few minutes, wondering what to do. I knew I couldn't leave the cart there and go and get help, because by the time I had come back, all the coal would have been stolen. So I put the nose bag on the horse and I was just standing there stroking his back, when I heard a lot of commotion and shouting coming from the back yard of one of the houses, number 81 it was.'

'Do you know the boy's wife still lives there in that very house where her husband died?' his mother said. 'I really don't know how she could, after what happened. I don't think I would be able to stay there, it would bring back too many sad memories. Sorry, son, you carry on.'

'I thought to myself I can't just stand here, not knowing what was going on. I'll have to leave the cart and go and see what's happening round the back of the house, someone might be getting attacked and need some help. So I slowly walked up the yard, and as I poked my head around the end of the house, I saw two men having a heated argument. I recognised both of them from a few weeks back. We were sorting through some rubbish in the coal yard and we had a pile of old iron to get rid of. Fred asked me to go out on to the road and wave down an old totter to come in and pick up the iron. I was only out there a couple of minutes when two carts came along. I shouted out to one of the drivers and they both followed me back into the yard. As soon as Fred saw them he knew who they were. We helped them load the carts up and they paid Fred some money and then went on their way.

'I later asked Fred why the two totters went around together. I said surely they would do better if they worked on their own. And Fred then told me that they had been all through school together, started work together as general dealers, both got married at the same time and now had rooms in the same house, down Wilford Road; he said they were never ever apart.'

'What were they like?' his mother asked. 'Did they seem like good boys?'

'Yea, they never said a word to each other all the time they were loading the cart, but they were talking to Fred and myself. They were only young lads,' Barny replied. 'One was about 25 and the other 26, I think the younger one was Hugh Goodidge and the other one's name was Fredrick Plest.'

'So what was all the trouble about?' his mother asked.

'Well, I stood there for a moment in the alley, listening to the argument, and what I could make out was that Plest was having a right old go at Goodidge for telling the police that his wife was not going to surrender to her bail. Apparently it all started when they were having a drink in the Fisherman's Arms sometime ago. As this woman walked past their table, she accidentally knocked into it and spilt some of their ale. Plest's wife started to have a go at the woman and then a fight broke out between them. The other woman got the better of Plest's wife and while she was on the floor the other woman walked away from her, but as she was walking up to the bar, Plest's wife got her bag from the table and took out a carving knife and then ran up to the woman and stabbed her in her neck. The police were round her house the same night and took her away, but when she appeared in court, she got bail and this is what the argument was about.'

'Do you know what, Barny, that bloody drink causes more trouble then anything else? I'm glad you don't drink,' she said. 'Now I like a drink, don't get me wrong, but some people, it just goes straight to their heads and they lose all of their senses.'

'The two men weren't drunk when they were having the argument,' said Barny, 'they knew exactly what they were doing.'

'Did Plest hit Goodidge then?' she asked.

'No, they just carried on with the argument for a short while with Plest still blaming Goodidge for telling the police, but all the time he denied making such a statement. Goodidge then shouted back at him. "If that's the sort of man you think I am then we had better take a lump of iron each and sort this out once and for all." And with that he pushed the boy Plest away, turned and walked into the kitchen, picked up a poker and came back out towards Goodidge.'

'What did he do then, when he came out with the poker, just stand there?'

'He looked at him and then ran off, past me and out to the road, where they had parked both their carts. Goodidge followed him with the poker resting on his shoulder and by the time I had got out there, they were facing each other by one of their carts. Goodidge stood there, looking Plest in the eyes. He then raised the poker above his shoulders, as if to bring it down on Plest's head, but then he stopped, he stepped back and said. "No, I won't hit you with this poker; we won't fight like this, we will fight the proper English way with our fists." But before he could say any more, Plest picked up a piece of lead piping from the cart and brought it down on Goodidge's head.

'He struck him on the left side of his forehead with the piping saying, "Take that you bastard." And Goodridge gradually sank to the ground near the cart wheel. I could have stopped him, I was that close to them when he hit him. When the pipe hit his head, it seemed to fold round to the shape of his head and the noise it made! I have seen men being hit with pipes before, but I have never heard a sound like that. Goodidge was on the ground and I don't know where Plest ran off to. I walked up to Goodidge and helped him back into the house and sat him in a chair. I asked him if he was all right and he replied in a faint voice, "No, my head hurts and I feel sick." I didn't know at the time if I had put him in his own room or the other man's room, but I thought I can't let him be sick all over the floor if it's not his room and I thought it might make him feel better if he was in the fresh air.'

'You did the right thing there, son, it's always best to get them out in the open.'

'So I took a pillow from the bed and carried him to the backyard where he vomited. I then laid him down, resting his head on the pillow.'

'Were there no other people around who could have helped you? You normally get a crowd around here when there's a fight going on.'

'There were some people watching, but they never went up to help him, they just stood there looking. I couldn't just leave him there. I could tell he was really hurt. I stayed outside with him for about half an hour, but he seemed to get worse and he looked so ill, I thought I will have to take him back indoors and lay him on the bed.

'A woman from upstairs came down and I told her to go and fetch some water, but when I tried to give it to him, he couldn't even swallow that, so I then told the woman to go and fetch the doctor and we waited for over an hour for him to get there. When he did arrive, all he said was that this is a serious one, he's got concussion of the brain and recommended ice. He looked up at me and said that we need some ice now. So I replied, "Hold on, I'll go and see if there's a bucketful under the bed,"'

'Barny, you shouldn't have said that, not to a doctor,' his mother said. 'You don't want to say that in court or you will go down in the cells yourself.'

'How did I know where to get the ice from? It's not the sort of thing you get every day is it?'

'So what did the doctor say then?'

'I think he was a bit lost for words. He stood up and started to rub the back of his head and then he asked me if I was a relative of the injured man. I told him no, I wasn't, but there was no one else here, apart from the woman upstairs. "Oh," he said and then he stood there looking at me again and then asked me if I knew the fishmongers up Whitehorse Road. I said yes I did know where it was and then, I think he was trying to be a bit sarcastic, he told me if I was to walk up there and ask the man in the white coat for some ice, he would most probably turn round and give me some. I had just about had enough of him then, he was getting right on my nerves, so I was glad I was going out to get the ice. Just as I was opening the door, the doctor called out to me. "Have the police been informed yet?" he asked. "No, I don't think they have," I replied, "and before you ask me to bring one back with me I suggest you ask the woman upstairs, because I don't talk to the coppers." I put on my posh voice then, Mum, just to let him know that he wasn't any better than me.'

His mother raised her eyes and looked up at the ceiling. 'I will have to have a talk to you, Barny, there are some people you have to have

The Killing of a Best Friend

respect for, and doctors are one of them. So did you get the ice in the end?'

'Oh, I had a right old game up the fishmongers, first they wouldn't give it to me unless I paid for it and then, when I told them that a doctor had asked for it to give to a dying man, they said there was some out the back I could take. But when I went and had a look, it was all mixed up with old fish heads and tails. I asked them if they had anything I could put it in and they gave me an old sack. So I started to sort the ice and fill the sack and did it stink, as I began to move the ice so the smell started to rise. In the end I had sorted enough ice out from the other stuff and put it in the sack and carried it back to the house. When I put it down on the floor the doctor told me to put some in a pillowcase and place it round the man's head, which I did, but as the ice melted, it mixed with the dirt on the pillow case and dripped down the man's face. The woman from upstairs said that the bruise was coming out on his face now. It did look like his face was black and blue, but it was only the dirt from the pillowcase.'

'What was the boy Plest doing while all this was going on?' asked his mother.

'I remember when I took the man out in the back yard, I looked up and saw Plest standing by the stable door, I asked him if he could give me some help to take him back indoors, but he never gave any answer and I never saw him after that. But after I had put the ice around his head, his wife Jane came into the room with Plest following her. As she was looking down at her husband, Plest took her arm and said. "I am very sorry, Jane, that it happened." He then turned and walked out.'

'Was the young boy dead then?'

'Yes,' Barny said. 'The doctor told them in front of his wife. That's it, he's gone. I looked down at him, I don't know if it was the dirt from the pillowcase and the blood mixed together, but he started to go a funny colour. It was then that the constable came in; he said that he wanted to question everyone.'

'I suppose that's when you left. I don't know why you are so afraid of the police.'

'Mum, you don't know what they are like. Some of them are just looking for an excuse to put me away.'

Barny's mother left the room to check on her husband and when she came back Barny was asleep in the chair. She fetched a blanket and wrapped it around him and kissed him on the forehead. 'You're a good boy, Barny,' she whispered in his ear; she then turned the gas lamp down and retired to her bed.

The next morning Barny was up at five o'clock. There was no work at the coal yard, so he just spent an hour sitting in the kitchen alone thinking about Violet. He was holding his shoulder, which was still hurting, and when he tried to lift his arm up it would go no further than his shoulder, but he put the pain right out of his mind. He knew today was the day he had to leave for Nottingham and he knew the fight, where he could earn a lot of money, was getting closer and closer and he had to look 100 per cent fit. Even if he couldn't raise his arm up, he had to look as if he could. He waited until 6.30 and then made his way to Violet's house and stood opposite, waiting there until 7 o'clock her head appeared out of the front door. She looked out across the road and saw Barny waiting; she put her hand up and gave him a sign to tell him to meet her on the corner of the road. He walked away and waited anxiously for her to appear. She finally came around the corner and Barny walked up to her and put his arms around her. 'I've really missed you,' he said.

'Yes, and I've missed you too, Barny,' she replied. He told her that he had to be in court as a witness that morning and wouldn't have enough time to come back to see her before leaving to go up north. That didn't bother her, she said. 'That's all right because I wouldn't be able to see you anyway.'

'And why is that?' Barny asked. 'Are you working all day today?'

'No,' Violet replied and carried on, 'look, I know you're not going to be too happy about this, but I don't have no option, the sergeant has 48 hours' leave, which starts tonight, and my father's invited him round to stay with us.'

'Right, that settles it,' Barny said, as he pushed Violet away. 'I'm stopping here and I'm going to sort him out once and for all and make him understand that you're my girl now.'

'No, you can't do that, it would ruin everything we have,' she said. 'My father would never accept you if he knew you had come between us.'

'Why is your father so fond of him?' Barny asked, as he put his arms around her again.

'He serves in the same regiment as my father did during the war and my father thinks he is a good upstanding young man and wants me to marry him,' she replied.

'Do you want to marry him?'

'It would get me away from Wilford Road, but I do love you, Barny,' she said.

'That's all that matters to me, Violet. I will go away tonight, but you must promise me that you will think about leaving him.'

'It's very hard, Barny, you know I can't upset my parents, but let's just wait and see what happens,' she said.

Violet said her goodbyes and made her way to her mistress's house to look after the children for a few hours and Barny made his way to the court house. His nerves were getting the better of him now and he stumbled as he walked through the door. When he turned around, he saw Detective Sharp, the copper who was always on his back, standing in the hall way. Barny walked the other way to avoid him, but Sharp noticed him and shouted for him to stop. 'Sturt, we have finally got you good and proper now, you won't be walking back out that door if I have anything to do with your case.'

'Yea, well that's where you're wrong, I'm only here as a witness in the murder case,' Barny replied.

'That's a shame, that's ruined my day,' the detective said, 'but give it time, boy, the day will come when you walk in and you won't be walking out again. I'll have you behind bars before you're much older, believe me.'

Barny waited nearly all day before he was called. He gave his evidence and quickly left the court house. By this time he couldn't move his injured arm at all and wondered whether he would be able to go to the fights, but then he remembered his parents and with no money coming in, there would be no food. So he had no other option, bad arm or no bad arm, he had to make the fights and he had to win.

On the way back to the coal yard, he saw his old mate Bert, selling flowers from a basket on the footpath. 'Hello, Bert, how is it going mate?' Barny asked.

'Yea, I'm not too bad. I hear you're fighting up north this weekend,' Bert said, as he put the large basket down. 'You know, Barny, if you were to get hurt or have a bit of trouble, it's a long way from home up there and you won't have anyone to fall back on to help you out.'

'I know, I've thought about that a lot, but there is nothing I can do about it and it's a chance that I'm just going to have to take,' Barny replied.

Bert stood there thinking. 'Well, how would you like me to come with you?' Bert asked. 'I could watch your back and then help you if there's any trouble.'

'That's good of you, Bert, but I was going to ask you to keep an eye on Violet for me. That sergeant boy is going to be around this weekend and I wanted you to tell me how they were together.'

'You have been told what she is like and there won't be much more that I'll be able to tell you,' said Bert, 'and I have got a good reason why I want to go with you.'

'Why is that?'

'I don't know if you have heard or not, but for the last three months I've been seeing that Fanny from Forster Road.'

'Everyone knows about that, you dirty old codger,' replied Barny.

'No, it wasn't anything like that, Barny, I was only keeping her company while her husband was away,' he said.

'That's not what she has been telling everyone; she's saying you had quite a thing going together.'

'Let's forget about that for now. The thing is, her husband is released from prison today and I don't want to be around when he's walking the streets. I bet he's already round her house now and you know what they are like down that road, somebody's bound to tell him that I've been popping in to see his old girl, so I know that sometime over the weekend, if I stay around here, I can expect a good hiding. I don't mind that so much. You know me, I can take a good pasting as good as the next man, but he's a nutter. He's been inside for cutting some bloke's fingers off and the bloke only said to him that he had a face like a pig's arse. What will he do to me when he finds out I've been keeping his Fanny company? If he chops my fingers off, that's bad enough, but what if he doesn't stop there and keeps going down. And I was thinking, if I lose my fingers, how would I, you know, Barny, what I'm talking about, how would I, you know, afterwards.'

Barny started to laugh. 'You would find out who your best friends were!'

They both started laughing as Bert put his hands in his pockets.

'Look, I don't mind you coming with me, Bert, but if I'm in trouble and you're with me, they will give you the same beating.'

'Yea I know, but I will still have me fingers, won't I?'

'All right,' said Barny, 'but we will have to leave now. What will you do with all these flowers?'

'Don't you worry about them, my son, they're nearly all dead anyway, I'll just leave them here,' Bert replied. So Bert threw his flowers up an alley and hid his basket in an old empty shop and walked off with Barny heading for the coal yard. They couldn't see Fred in the yard, so they started to look for him in the many sheds which were scattered around the yard. After a while they found him in the stone shed; he was putting some stones in the sacks with the coal to make them weigh more.

'Caught ya,' Barny shouted, 'I hope that sack doesn't end up round my house, Fred.'

'Hello, Darky, you frightened the life out of me then, I thought it was one of those inspector blokes. You wait and see, it won't be long before they put a stop to all the fiddles.'

'They will have to get up early to catch you out, Fred, and what poor sod's going to end up with these sacks?'

'The big houses, the ones with the money, you know how they like parting with their money,' said Fred jokingly. 'You know you have to make a bit where you can nowadays. How have you been keeping Bert? I didn't expect to see you here today.'

'Yea, I'm not too bad, Fred, I'm going along with me old cocker for the weekend, keeping an eye on him and making sure he keeps out of trouble,' Bert answered.

'That sounds like a good idea, but who is going to keep an eye on you?'

'What do you mean?'

'Do you know a man called Charlie Ede?' Fred asked.

Bert quickly looked around him. 'I might know him,' he said in a quiet voice. 'He's not here now, is he?'

'No, you're all right, mate, but he did come through the station this afternoon, he had just got off the train from Ashford – you know, where he has been for the last year.'

'Did he say anything about me?' Bert asked.

'Funny you should say that; he did ask if you had been about. I think, by what he was saying, he's heard the rumours about you and his wife Fanny.'

'He couldn't have done, he's only just come home. Who could have told him?'

'Do you know what, Bert, they reckon that there are more people locked up in prison who come from Wilford Road and Forster than there are still living down there. Someone must have told him who has just been put away.'

Bert looked round at Barny. 'Don't you think it's time we went?'

'Don't worry about him, Bert,' Barny said.

'You know, every man has his weakness and I think a good kick in the head will be Charlie's. What time is the train due out?'

'Not for another hour, but come with me and I will show you where you will have to wait and you must remember you have got to make sure you get on the back of the train. That's the only part that doesn't stop near the platform, so no one will see you getting out. I've put some old sacks by for you to cover over yourselves. You know it's going to get bitter cold during the night.'

'Thank you, Fred, would you like us to give you a hand with anything before we go?' Barny asked.

'Yea, it would be handy if you could give me a hand to load some of these sacks on to the cart outside, I'll be very grateful.'

'Come on, Bert,' Barny said, 'we need to build you up before you and Charlie Ede have a meeting.'

'Don't say that, Barny, you're tempting fate, all I want to do is to get away from here.'

Barny put his arm around Bert's shoulder and looked over at Fred. 'Here, Fred, if you see that Charlie Ede over the weekend, let him know that Bert will meet him here in the yard on Monday, midday, to sort things out man to man.'

Bert's face dropped as he pushed Barny's arm away and replied in a high-pitched voice.

'Don't be a fool, I don't want to see him and there's no way he's getting hold of my fingers.'

Barny and Fred started to laugh. 'Oh yes, that's right, I forgot that was his third time in prison for chopping someone's fingers off,' Fred said, laughing.

Barny had a bit of trouble loading the sacks on to the cart; his arm was giving him a lot of pain, but he never let it show. They finished loading the cart and then made their way over to the train that was to take Barny to his first fight up north. Little did he know that if he had looked just across the tracks to the station, he would have seen his loved one Violet, waiting on the platform for her Sergeant Bylett to arrive from Aldershot, but Barny was too frightened to look over the side of the wagon in case one of the guards saw him and ordered him off.

The train finally moved off at a slow pace and the cold wind started to blow around the inside the wagon. They covered themselves over with the sacks that Fred had given them, but these were no protection. By the time the train reached Nottingham, their bodies were blue with the cold. When the train stopped, they rubbed their arms and legs frantically until they could feel the blood flowing again. Barny stood up and looked over the side of the wagon. There was no one around, so they both climbed up the end of the wagon and over the side, but because their bodies were still numb, they fell to the ground. They tried to stand up, but the pain was too much, all they could do was to crawl on their hands and knees, away from the tracks. After a short while lying on the ground, which was warmer then the cold steel of the wagon, Barny began to feel his legs again and started to look over the bushes; he could see the light of some flames in the distance. 'Come on, there's a fire over there, I don't care who's sitting around it, we need to get warm.' As they crawled closer to the glow of the flames, they could see that the fire belonged to a night watchman. He was sitting just inside the gates of a goods yard and had a fire burning in a wheelbarrow.

They both tried to stand up, but their legs were too stiff with the cold. They held on to each other tightly and when they finally found their feet, they slowly made their way towards the fire. As they carried each other closer towards the fire, they heard a voice shout out. 'Stop there, you two, and don't come any nearer. I have a piece of lead piping here and I will use it on you if you come any closer.'

Barny shouted back, 'We only want to warm ourselves up by your fire.'

'Are you drunk?' The night watchman shouted out.

'No, we have just travelled up from London and we don't know where we are, we only want to sit by your fire for a while and warm up before we carry on.'

The night watchman was hesitant, but in the end he shouted back. 'All right, you can come on over, but I warn you, any trouble and I'll use the pipe on yer.'

They both sat around the fire shaking uncontrollably, steam starting to rise from their clothes that were wet from the cold, damp night air. After about fifteen minutes, they started to thaw out. Bert looked up at Barny. 'Sod this for a game of soldiers. I've never been so cold, I thought I was a goner at one time out there.'

Barny turned to the night watchman and asked him if he knew a public house called the Fighting Ring.

'Yes,' he said, 'it's only about two miles away just outside of town. Are you two fighting boys?'

'I'm not,' Bert said, 'I'm too bloody cold, but Barny is.'

'You'll have your work cut out up here, my boy, we've got some big lads, off the farms, you know, and strong as horses they are.'

When Barny's body started to feel the warmth of the fire he could feel the pain from his shoulder again; he put his hand up and held it.

'Have you got an injured shoulder, boy?' the night watchman asked.

'No,' Barny replied, 'just stiff.'

'Let me give you a bit of advice: if you're not feeling 100 per cent fit, I suggest you jump on the next train back to London, because the boys up here show no mercy and, if there's one thing they love more than anything else it's to knock the life out of a London boy.'

Barny stood up. 'Did you know, old man, fighting's not just about brute strength and brawn. You need to know what the other man's thinking, whether he's scared, over-confident or just stupid. Being a winner takes brains as well as muscle and that's where your lot up here fall down.'

'You're right, Barny,' said Bert, 'I've never seen a turnip with a brain before.'

'You see, that's where you London boys go wrong,' the night watchman said. 'You're too cocky for your own good.'

'We will see. Come on, Bert, let's go and find this public house and then we will get ourselves ready to plant some turnips.'

Meanwhile, back home, Violet met her soldier friend from the train and they walked arm in arm slowly back to her house. 'I want to ask you something this weekend, Violet,' the sergeant said.

'What's that?' she asked.

'I can't tell you now, not in the street. I want to pick the right moment.'

'Well, you can take me out tonight for a drink and then perhaps you can tell me what you have to say then,' she said.

'Yes, of course, I want to spend as much time with you as I can, while I'm on leave.'

When they finally arrived at Violet's house, her father already had the door open and was waiting inside with open arms to welcome the soldier into his house. 'Come in, my son, you're looking well. Is the old regiment still looking after its men?' They walked through to the best room. 'Violet's mother has cooked us a nice meal so, while they're preparing it, we can sit down in here and you can tell me all that's been happening in the old regiment.'

After a short while Violet called out to them and told them that the meal was now ready. They were still talking about the army as they sat down, during the meal and when they returned to the best room. After Violet had helped her mother to clear away the table she joined her father and Percy, but she was only with them for a short time before she was bored stiff with all the talk of the regiment. 'Are we going out Percy?' she said, interrupting his conversation. 'If we leave it much later it won't be worth going out at all.'

Her father put his hand on Percy's arm. 'Go on, son, you go out and enjoy yourself, you deserve it.' As they were about to leave the room, her father stood up. 'By the way, Percy, when are you going to make an honest woman of my daughter?'

Percy looked back and laughed, but Violet was not amused. She pulled his arm and walked him out to the front door. 'Shall we go up the Four in Hand?' Percy asked.

'No, it's getting a bit rough up there, let's go to the Fish instead.' Violet remembered the embarrassing time she had there with Barny only a few days before and she didn't want to take the chance of anyone saying anything to her while Percy was at her side.

When they arrived at the Fisherman's Arms they looked through the door and could see the usual drunks rolling about on the floor and the usual gambling going on at the corner tables with fights breaking out when someone lost or someone cheated. But this is what put a smile on Violet's face; this is what Violet enjoyed, the danger, the excitement and, of course, the attention she received from the men. It wasn't very long after they had arrived that she was approached by a man who was the worse for drink. He walked up to her and in front of Percy, put his arm around her and asked her to go outside with him. She immediately slapped him round the face, bringing more attention to herself.

'My, you're a plucky bitch,' the man said.

Percy heard this and walked up to the man ready to bring a blow down on the man's head, but he was a soldier – he could attack an enemy line with a rifle and bayonet but, in a street fight, he wasn't at his best. He was a gentleman and gentlemen never got involved in street brawls, but this time he had no choice. Violet's honour was at stake. As Percy's blow came down near the man's head, he easily ducked away from it and, as Percy's arm swung past him, the man took hold of Percy's hair and grabbed him round his neck. 'Now,' he said, 'what shall we do with you? Firstly, I think we might have to teach you a little lesson.'

He turned Percy around and with one hand behind Percy's head he put two almighty blows straight into Percy's face.

Violet screamed. 'Let him go, you animal!'

But he had no intention of letting Percy go. He knew he could beat Percy with one hand tied behind his back so he wasn't going to let an opportunity like this pass him by.

Percy was half conscious after the two vicious blows to his face and the man was in charge. He could do whatever he wanted to and with everyone around him laughing, shouting and egging him on, he was enjoying every minute of it. He took Percy by the hair and dragged him around the tables, allowing some of the women to take the opportunity to give Percy a quick slap round the face. Luckily for Percy, two constables were walking by and, as always, they took a look in through the window and saw what was going on. They came into the bar and took hold of the man and pulled him away from Percy, who then fell to the ground. A crowd in any of the public houses at that time never liked the police invading their ground and this crowd were no different. They started shouting at the two constables, telling them to go home and leave things alone; they could sort this out themselves, but the two constables were determined not to leave without a prisoner. Out came their truncheons and a few hits into the crowd soon pushed them backwards and slowly they marched the man to the door, and off to the station.

Violet was left there on her own with Percy out cold on the floor. She asked for help, but no one wanted to know, although most of them were Violet's friends. None of them liked Percy, he was a different breed to them and they only helped their own kind. Violet knew she couldn't take him home on her own, so she ran outside and stopped a passing dray. She shouted up to the driver and offered him a penny if he would help to take Percy home. 'It's only round the corner,' she cried.

'Why can't he walk it then?' the man asked.

'He's fallen over and hit his head,' she replied.

The man agreed to help and they both struggled to pull Percy out of the bar and on to the back of the cart. Violet walked by the side of the cart until it reached her house. She then ran inside crying to fetch her father who then helped the man bring Percy into the house and they laid him on Violet's bed.

'What on earth's happened to him?' her father asked.

'We were just walking down Forster Road and two men jumped Percy from behind; he never stood a chance. They overpowered him and just kept kicking him.' She couldn't dare tell her father that it happened in a public house.

'You will have to sleep in the chair tonight, Violet,' her father said 'and Percy will have to take your bed.'

Violet sat back in a chair. Oh, how I wished Barny had been with me tonight, she thought. But he was a long way away and having troubles of his own.

Barney had found the Fighting Ring public house and he was arranging the fights with Fred's mate but, unknown to Barny, Bert was up at the bar getting drunk. He tried to put his arm around a young lady who was sitting near to him and then tried to kiss her, but she was with her husband that night. He was only over the other side of the bar and could see what was going on. He immediately ran over to Bert, picked up a chair and brought it down across Bert's head. Bert fell to the floor and the man then placed kick after kick into Bert's body.

All this time Barny was unaware of what was happening. There was always trouble breaking out and he took no notice; he was still talking to the man about the fights. 'I want three fights a night.'

'That's not on,' the man replied, 'two fights are the most you can have.'

Barny leaned across the table. 'Look, I've come a long way and it's not worth me travelling up here if there's only two fights on offer.'

The man looked over Barny's shoulder. 'It looks like your mate's in a bit of trouble over there.'

Barny turned round to see what the man was going on about. He then saw Bert on the floor with the man standing over him with one foot on his head. Barny rushed over to help his mate. He grabbed the man's arm and pulled him off.

At the Precipice of Poverty

He then turned the man around, picked a bottle up from the bar and pushed it, with some force, into the side of the man's face. The bottle broke and cut right through the man's ear. A small piece of his ear flew through the air and landed on the bar beside two ladies, who screamed as it fell next to their drinks. The man was stunned, but before he could get himself together, Barny put both his hands behind the man's head and brought it down hard and at the same time bringing his knee up to meet the man's face. The force of Barny's strong arms and his muscle-bound thigh smashed the man's nose across his face and blood spurted every way and this time people moved away from the bar.

Barny threw the man to the ground and picked his friend up. He walked him to the door and, as he passed the man who was arranging the fights, he stopped and said, 'I want three fights, do you understand me?'

The man looked up. 'All right, you win, you can go in for the three fights.'

'Where do we go?' Barny asked.

'Go left, down the lane outside of here and, about five miles down, you will come to a farm. Go through the farm gates and walk down the dirt path for about half a mile and there you will see a field on your left with a barn in it. Be there at ten o'clock and I'll see what I can do.'

Just then Bert started to come round. 'What happened, Barny?' he said looking shocked, 'I can't remember anything.'

'Don't you worry, mate, you're safe now.'

Barny knew he had to find somewhere for Bert to rest for the night, not just to get over the beating, but also to get over the drink. He started to make his way down a few alleys until he came across an empty outhouse. He made sure no one was around and took his friend in and laid him down. 'You're going to have a sore head in the morning, my old son,' he said, but Bert never heard him; he was out for the count. It was cold and damp in the outhouse so Barny looked round to find something to keep them warm. All he could find was some old canvas sheeting, so he covered it over Bert and then he lay down beside him, closed his eyes and thought about Violet. He pictured her asleep in her warm bed with sheets that were freshly washed and smelling of lavender. Little did he know that her bed was occupied by the sergeant and Violet was awake sitting in a chair, crying.

The Killing of a Best Friend

Back home, Violet had been awake all night thinking about Barny, whom she loved, but knew he could never take her away from the depressing life of Wilford Road. Then there was Percy. He earned good money, was due for a good pension from the army and his parents lived in a nice house in a nice area. How was she going to decide which one to stay with? If she kept seeing both it would just end up in tears and she might lose both of them. She knew she had to make up her mind and quickly.

The following morning she was up early and made Percy a cup of tea and took it in to him. He looked terrible, his face was cut and bruised and he looked really drawn. She put her hand on his head and stroked his hair. 'How do you feel this morning?' she asked him.

'A bit sore,' he said, 'I hope you never got hurt last night, did you?'

'No, I was fine,' she replied. 'Listen, Percy, I need to talk to you about us.' She sat beside him on the bed.

'Hold on, Violet,' he said, as he tried to pull himself up, 'I told you last night there was something I wanted to ask you. This isn't how I planned it, but it will have to do. Will you marry me?'

She looked at him in surprise. 'Marry you?'

'Yes, I know it's a bolt from the blue, but I really want to marry you and I think the time is right. I can take you and your parents away from all the scum around here. It's not safe for a girl like you, last night proved that. Say you will.'

Violet got off the bed and walked to the window, looking across the road at the house where Barny lived. 'Please, Percy, let me have time to think about it.'

She turned and looked at him lying pitifully on the bed. Just then the door opened and her father walked in.

'Congratulations, both of you,' he said.

'How did you know?' Violet asked.

'I told your father last night before we went out. I thought it only right to ask his permission first,' Percy said, looking a bit worried.

Violet turned and walked to the door. 'I'm going to the wash house for a bath.' She didn't know what to say, but she knew she had to leave that room before she said something she might regret later. I must have time to think this out, she thought to herself. If I marry Percy I will leave this road and the people in it behind, but that will mean I will never see Barny again.

Before she reached the front door, Percy called out to her. 'Violet, I thought we could take your parents to my house tomorrow. My mother said she would lay some tea on and we can tell them the news.'

'Good idea, son,' Violet's father said. 'I haven't seen your father for some time now and it will be nice to catch up on things.'

Violet walked out and slammed the door, making out she never heard.

As Violet walked to the top of Wilford Road, she noticed Barny's mother waiting for the butcher's shop to open. 'Good morning, Mrs Sturt,' Violet said.

'Hello, love,' she replied. 'I wish I could afford a nice joint of pig. That would go down a treat with my husband.'

'Do you know when Barny will be coming home?' Violet asked.

'Sometime Monday morning,' she replied, turning round and looking Violet in the eyes. 'You know he thinks the world of you, he would do anything for you and you know he's not just fighting up north for us. He told me he wants money to buy you things and take you out.'

'I know,' Violet replied.

'But what do you do? The first night he's away, you're walking out with another man, that sergeant boy. Now I don't think that's very fair, Violet, do you?'

'He's just a very good friend of the family's, I can't just stay away from him when he's on leave.'

'If that's all it is then, that's fine, but let me tell you, Violet, don't ever mess Barny about, he won't stand for that and nor will I, do you hear me?'

'Yes, I know,' Violet replied. She stood there for a while thinking about what Barny's mother had said and then slowly made her way back to her house.

'That was quick,' Percy said as she walked through the door.

'I know, I decided not to have a bath. Look, Percy, I do want to marry you, but can't we just wait a little while?'

'I'm sorry, Violet, it's too late for that now. Your father's already on his way round to my house. He's going to tell my parents the good news and start to make the arrangements. The parish church I think he said. He wants a big wedding and I don't think there is any way we can stop him now.'

Violet sat back in the chair.

'You do want this, you do want to marry me, don't you?' Percy asked.
'Yes, I do,' she said, holding back the tears.
By this time Barny and Bert were awake and had left the outhouse. 'We need some food,' said Bert, as he was trying to clean the dried blood off his face. Just then a farmer with a flock of sheep was coming down the lane. Barny shouted over to him, 'You off to market then, mate?'
'That's right,' the farmer replied in a funny voice.
'And where is this here market then?' Barny asked, trying to copy the farmer's accent.
'It be in market square, in middle of town. If you want to go there, you best follow me behind the flock.'
'Come on, Bert, we're going to get some breakfast,' Barny said as he pulled Bert into the middle of the sheep.
'What we going to have, lamb for breakfast are we?' said Bert.
'Did that bloke kick all your brains out last night? Where there's a market you will find some stalls and where there's stalls there is always someone who is selling pies and that's what we are having for breakfast.'
'I'm right behind you, Barny, me old cocker,' Bert said. When they reached the market they looked around trying to find a pie stall. 'There it is,' Bert said, 'and there's only two men looking after it.'
'Good. Now here's what we do, I will go up and try to get the two men away from the stall and while I'm doing that, you grab as many pies as you can, right?'
'How are you going to get the men away from the stall?' Bert asked.
'Don't worry about that, I will think of something, but just be ready to take as many pies as you can. Grab them and put them in your pockets and run and I'll meet you over the other side of that church.'
They strolled innocently up to the stall. Barny then pushed Bert to the side of the stall and told him to go around to the back. He then walked up to the two men and took hold of the first man's arm. 'I've been looking for you,' he said, as the man turned round to face him. 'You've been walking out with my young lady, you bastard.'
The two men looked at each other. The first one pushed Barny's hand away from his arm. 'Go away, young man, we don't know what you're talking about.'
'You will do now,' Barny said, as he punched the man in the face.
The other man moved forward and jumped at Barny. He took hold of him by the collar but, before he could do anything, Barny kicked him

in the shins. He then looked over at Bert who was dropping more pies on the ground then he was putting in his pockets. 'Come on, Bert, hurry up.' He then turned and gave each man another blow on the head and ran off down the road, behind Bert. After five minutes they stopped running. 'How many pies did you get?' Barny asked. 'I don't know, I was too busy looking at you,' Bert replied. 'Hold on I'll take a look.'

He took four pies out of one pocket and put his hand in the other pocket. 'Oh no, I forgot this pocket was ripped, they've all fallen out. Still we've got two each, that should see us through until you win tonight, then perhaps we can have some proper food.'

They jumped over a fence and finished off the pies and then made their way to the barn where the fighting was going to take place. 'We'll get there early,' Barny said, 'so we can see the other fighters arrive, I'll know what I'm up against then.'

It was just starting to get dark when they reached the barn. They sat down behind some bushes and both fell asleep, and were only awakened some time later by the sound of horses' hooves. They looked round and could see outlines of men coming from all directions.

'My God,' said Bert, 'look at the size of some of them! I think I would rather face Charlie Ede with his chopper than fight some of them men.'

Barny looked round at him, 'I will remember that on Monday morning. Come on, let's go inside and take a look.' They followed the other men in through the big wooden doors. It was packed with just a small empty circle in the middle.

'There should be some good money here tonight with all this crowd,' said Barny. He then pulled on Bert's arm. 'Listen, Bert, the money I win on the first fight, I want you to put it all on the second fight and the same for the third.'

'Surely you can't be having three fights in one night,' Bert said, 'you'll never be able to handle three.'

'Don't worry about me. Just make sure you do what I told you to do with the money.'

'Why three fights? You're just asking for trouble. You could be badly injured or even killed,' said Bert.

'Look, this is what I need the money for: the money from the first fight is for my parents, the second fight is for Violet and the third is to put by just in case anything happens to me. I don't want my parents to end up in the workhouse if I'm not around. Come on, it looks like I'm on first.'

Barny removed his coat and cap and Bert helped him tighten his belt and as Bert was doing up Barny's waistcoat he saw the knife mark on Barny's shoulder. 'What's that mark on your shoulder?' he asked.

'It's nothing, just an old cut,' Barny replied.

'Just an old cut, it doesn't look like an old cut to me.'

Barny looked up at Bert. 'Look, just do what I have told you and leave the rest to me. Remember what I told you; if I get beaten, they will come straight after you. They don't like our sort around here, so be on your guard.'

Bert took a quick look over at Barny's opponents and then shut his eyes and shuddered. 'Please, Barny, make sure you beat them whatever happens. I don't even think I could outrun them, let alone fight them. If anything does happen to you, I will have to put on one of those country bumpkin's voices and make out I'm one of them.'

'Well, that shouldn't be too hard for you, not the way you lost all those bloody pies.'

Barny walked into the circle, while Bert sat there with his fingers, arms and legs crossed, praying that Barny wouldn't have to be carried out.

Chapter 4

The Vicar's Daughter

In a barn, in the middle of a field far away from home, Barny was sitting alone and waiting to be called. He knew he had to win the three fights that were on tonight. He looked at his opponents; they were big and strong, but that didn't frighten Barny. He knew it wasn't just strength that won the fights, it was knowing when to hit and when to duck, it was a strategic game, one that he had mastered. As Barny was waiting, the man who had arranged the fights and whom Barny only knew as 'the guvnor' came up to him.

'Now look,' he said to Barny, 'I've put you up for three fights, that's if you're still standing. Now, let me give you a bit of advice: can you see those three men over there, standing down at the front with the suits and hats on?'

'Yes, what about them?' Barny replied.

'They run all of the fights in the East Midlands and along the east coast and if you're any good, they will try and get you to go and fight for them. They will offer you everything you want in return, but don't be taken in by their sweet talk. You will only end up owing them money and all the fights you have will be for nothing.'

'Why are you telling me all this?' Barny asked.

'I'm only telling you because you're one of Fred's mates and he was a good friend to me in the past, helped me out when I had no one to turn to. So be on your guard and don't believe a word they tell you.' The guvnor took Barny down to the centre where the fight was to take

The Vicar's Daughter

place and then left him standing there on his own waiting for his first opponent.

He stood there looking all around him but he could see no friendly faces. Everyone in the barn wanted blood and the way they were looking at Barny, they wanted the new boy's blood. Just then a small figure appeared and walked up opposite Barny. This was his first opponent. He was a short, thin young man and the crowd began shouting: 'Get the kid off, it will be a walk over,' but the young man never took any notice and stood his ground. Barny looked round at Bert, who was giving him the thumbs up. 'Go on, Barny,' he shouted, 'take him out.'

Barny never took anyone for granted, no matter how small or how big they were. He had seen too many fighters knocked out by a much smaller, quicker man than themselves.

The fight began and Barny walked around the young man with caution and then he moved towards him with a right hook that would have knocked a carthorse out, but it missed. The young man was quick on his feet, he saw Barny coming and ducked to miss his blow. At the same time Barny overbalanced and, as he went past the young man, he received a vicious punch in the kidneys, which made him fall to the ground, doubled up in pain. The young man took his opportunity and jumped on Barny's chest and then put his arm down across Barny's throat. Barny started to choke and found it hard to get his breath. The young man put his other hand across Barny's mouth to finish him off, but this was his first mistake. Barny sank his teeth into the man's arm. The man screamed as the blood run down his hand and his grip loosened. Barny then brought his left knee up and forced it hard into the man's back which made him overbalance and gave Barny the opportunity to push him off. They both got up together, the man holding his right arm where Barny had bitten him. Barny quickly moved forward and placed two ferocious punches to the man's face, which knocked him back into the crowd. The crowd were screaming for more. Barny walked towards him, picked him up and then threw him to the ground. That was it, the young man was out cold and the fight was over. The crowd suddenly became silent, apart from Bert, who was at the back, waving his arms and shouting.

Two men came in and pulled the young man out of the barn and Barny walked across to Bert. 'Well done, my son,' Bert said. 'You made that look easy. I felt as if I could have gone in there and done that myself.'

At the Precipice of Poverty

'I was lucky, Bert, I nearly lost it,' Barny replied. 'One punch off that small man and I was down and he nearly had me, he knew what he was doing all right, a good fighter. I was just lucky to have got the better of him.'

'Well, it doesn't matter now, he's out of it,' Bert said. 'Let's go and pick our winnings up.'

Barny quickly pulled Bert back. 'Now, remember what I told you Bert, it must all go on to the next fight.'

'Yea, I heard you, Barny, but I still think you're silly. If it was mine, I would pick the money up, leave here and go back to the public house and enjoy it.'

Barny's next fight was not over as quickly as his first one, but Barny had the upper hand. All he received was a cut eye and a split lip and it was over in twenty minutes. Again his opponent had to be carried out from the barn. Barny knew he had been lucky; all of his opponents' punches had just clipped him, apart from the one in the kidneys. He was asking himself whether he would be so lucky in his third fight. He knew he had a lot of money riding on this one and so did all the people in the barn. At first they never thought he could win three fights, not in one night, but now they were all betting on him in this fight and, of course, they hadn't seen Barny at his best. His shoulder was still playing him up, but up to now his opponents hadn't noticed.

'It's all down to this one now, Barny, my boy,' Bert said. 'If we win this one we will have more money than I could earn in a month selling flowers. I tell you, Barny, if you win the next one I will run over to you and give you a big kiss on the lips.'

'If you do that, my friend, you will be the next one they will have to carry outside, mark my words. Anyway what's all this "we"?' Barny asked.

'You know what I mean,' said Bert. Barny was sitting in a chair bathing his face when he felt a tap on his shoulder. It was the guvnor. 'I'm not happy,' he said, 'I told you three fights were too much. Everyone's betting on you for the third fight and unless we can come up with better fighters, it just won't be worth you coming up next week.'

Barny looked up at him. 'I thought all the turnips up here were strong, good fighters.'

'They are,' he replied, 'but they don't seem to have the luck you have. You know you would make a lot more money if you lost the next fight, but you would have to let me know first.'

'What did he mean?' Bert asked.

'Well, if everyone bets on me in the next fight and I lose, then the guvnor makes a lot of money and he won't have to pay out much.'

'That sounds good to me,' Bert said. 'You'll only have to take a dive after the first punch and Bob's your uncle, money for old rope.'

'Listen here,' Barny shouted, 'if you think I'm going to take a fall then you've got another think coming. I have never lost a fight in my life and I'm not going to start now, do you understand? So stop trying to talk me in to it.'

'Yes, of course I do, mate, I don't blame you, I would do the same thing,' Bert said shaking his head.

To everyone's surprise the next fight was touch and go for Barny. It started off with a few punches being exchanged. Barny's opponent was built like a horse with a powerful punch, but he was slow. Barny knew as long as he kept his distance from him he would be all right. Half way through the fight an accidental blow caught Barny's cut shoulder and it started to bleed. Of course the other man noticed this and kept going for the cut. Every time he went for Barny's shoulder, Barny would come back with some vicious blows to the man's face, which was now covered in blood and he could only just about see. A lucky blow from the man came down on Barny's shoulder, right on the cut. Barny screamed with pain and the blood started to run down his arm. The man started to move quicker; he knew this was his chance, his fists moved faster, one-two in Barny's face.

No one in that barn that night knew how Barny kept on his feet. He was still moving around, ducking from most of his opponent's punches, but the ones that did hit him, did untold damage around his eyes. He could now just about see where his eyes were swollen and blurred with the blood running into them. All the time he was thinking to himself, I could end up a beggar on the streets with no sight. With one last effort that took all his willpower and strength he gave one almighty kick. He couldn't see, he could only hear the panting of his breath. He just hoped that the kick would make contact and do some damage. Luck was with Barny that night. His boot landed right between the man's legs, the barn filled with the sound of a painful scream and the man then fell to the ground. Barny was swaying from side to side trying to find where the man had fallen. He finally walked into him and fell on to the man. He raised his arms to feel for the man's face and when he found it, placed four blows on and around his head. He then rolled over and lay next to the man, totally exhausted. But he had won the fight, although he never realised it at the time The other man was out cold and done for, he had no more fight left in him. It then took five men to drag the giant out of the barn.

Bert came running down to Barny, who was still lying on the ground. 'You've done it!' he shouted. But Barny couldn't see him, his eyes had swollen right up now and he couldn't see anything. He heard Bert's voice and reached out for him. 'I'm here,' Bert shouted, as he held on to his hand.

'Bert, now go and pick up the money and then come back and get me out of here.'

Bert did what Barny had asked, he collected the winnings. He couldn't believe his eyes, he had never seen so much money. He folded it and placed it in two of his pockets and then went back for his old pal. They both walked out through the big wooden doors, Barny being dragged on Bert's shoulders. He could only carry him a little way, so he went through some woods and down a bank and then he stopped and laid Barny down. 'We should be safe here, he said, 'no one will find us down here.'

While Barny was asleep, Bert moved down the bank a bit further and came across a stream. He tore the bottom half of his shirt off and dipped it into the water and went back up to Barny. He carried on wiping Barny's face with the cold wet cloth for the next four hours until Barny came around. The swelling was starting to go down as Barny opened his eyes. He looked up at Bert. 'Where are we? Did I do it, did I win and did you get the money?'

'Yes, you done it mate, you won and I got the money, but you nearly got killed doing it, you bloody fool! How's your head and shoulder, do they feel any better?'

'They still hurt a bit, but I'm feeling a lot better now, now that I know we have the money.' Just then it started to rain hard.

'We had better find some cover,' Bert said, 'will you be able to walk now?'

'I think so,' Barny replied. 'Wasn't there an old church we passed on the way to the barn?'

'Yes, I think you're right. Come on, let me help you up and we'll go and find it, and shelter for the night.'

They walked back about half a mile down the lane and could see the church across a field. 'There it is, but I don't fancy sleeping in there tonight – look at all them graves, Barny.'

'At least we'll be under cover and out of the rain,' Barny said.

Bert walked round the church to see if a door had been left open, but they were all locked. 'Shall I break in?'

'No, you can't do that,' Barny replied, 'you can't break into a church, that's not right.'

'I'm not staying out here amongst all the dead and you can't go on much further, we have got to find somewhere.'

'Listen, you go across that field and see if there is an old barn nearby and then come back and get me, I'll wait here for you.'

Bert had been gone about ten minutes and then came running back. 'I've found somewhere,' he shouted, 'an old church hall and there's a window open. Only trouble is, it's surrounded by graves, the same as this place. Why are there so many graves around here? There's not that many people in the village: where have they all come from?'

'I don't know and I don't care,' Barny replied. 'Come on, help me up. I don't care if the hall's full of bodies, I just want to get out of this rain.'

As they walked slowly over to the church hall, Bert looked round at Barny. 'You don't think there will be any in there, do you?' he asked.

'What and in where?'

'Bodies in that church hall – you don't think there will be any inside?'

'I don't know. They have some funny ways, these turnips, you don't know what they get up to out here in the sticks.'

When they reached the hall, Barny looked through the window. 'Yes, this will do for tonight, you climb through and then help me in.'

Bert looked through the window. 'Are you sure? It looks a bit scary in there. Look at them big curtains down the other end, you don't know who could be behind them. Come on, can't we sleep under those trees tonight?'

'Don't be a fool, we can't sleep out in the rain. At least we will have some shelter in there.'

'Oh all right, but once I'm in there don't you go walking off and leaving me, I don't like this at all.'

Bert climbed through the window and helped Barny in. As they walked a bit further into the hall, the window slammed shut behind them. 'Jesus, what was that?' Bert shouted.

75

'It's all right, it was only the window. Now stop shaking, you're supposed to be looking after me.'

'I don't like this one little bit,' Bert said. They carried on walking through the big hall. It was scary; the wind was blowing, the branches of the trees were hitting against the glass of the windows; the floorboards were creaking and the air was ice cold.

'Barny, let's go back outside, something's not right in here, I can't stop myself shaking.'

Barny stopped, and whispered in Bert's ear: 'You know this is where they bring the bodies before they bury them, you know that's the time in between, when they say the spirit leaves the body.'

'Don't mess about,' Bert replied, 'I don't like it in here. Come on, let's get out.'

Barny continued, 'I wouldn't be surprised if the bodies are not behind that curtain right now, waiting to be put in the ground tomorrow. If they are there, I wonder where their spirits are now?'

Bert froze to the spot. 'That's it, I'm out of here, you stop in here if you want, but I'm off.'

But before he could move, Barny grabbed his hand. 'Come on, it's all right, I was only joking, we'll sleep in this corner tonight.'

'Sod you, I'm out of here, there's no way I'm sleeping in this hall tonight, not when there might be bodies behind that curtain.'

'All right, let's try that door,' said Barny. They walked across the hall and opened a door to a large cupboard which was full of curtains and blankets. 'This will do,' he said.

Bert started to pick up the curtains and placed them against the closed door. 'You sleep here, against the door so no one can get in.'

Barny jumped in pain as he started to laugh, pulling the skin around his swollen face. They both settled down for the night, Bert with the curtains over his head and Barny wedged up against the door and after a while they both fell asleep.

The next morning Bert was awoken by the sound of an organ playing. 'What's that?' he shouted, 'Barny, Barny, wake up.' It took him a short time before he emerged from under the curtains, and crawled over to where Barny was lying. He started to shake at his leg. 'Wake up!' he shouted.

'What's wrong?' Barny said, rubbing his eyes.

'Can you hear that noise? I knew we shouldn't have stayed in here last night, we've had it now.'

'Shut up and listen,' Barny said. They sat still and quiet and tried to make out where the noise was coming from. 'We will have to go out and take a look,' Barny said.

'Well, you go on your own,' replied Bert. 'No, wait a minute, I'm not stopping in here on my own, I'll be behind you.'

There were no windows in the cupboard, so Barny had to feel his way around until he found the door handle. He opened it slowly, just enough to poke his head round to have a look. Bert was so close to him that Barny could feel his hot breath on the back of his neck. Barny could now see a lot better in the hall, as the daylight was shining through the windows. 'There's nothing in the hall,' he said.

'Where the bloody hell is that noise coming from?' Bert replied.

'It must be behind the curtain, that's the only place it can be coming from.'

'Oh my God! Let's just make a run for the door and break it open, I can't stop in here any longer.'

'No, hold on, I want to find out what's behind that curtain.' They opened the door slowly and crept across the floor.

'I don't believe,' said Bert, 'we've had it, I know we have. You can't fight this sort of thing, someone told me about these sprits. They can pick you up and carry you off and you can't do anything to stop them. All this money and the only spirit around here is going to kill us or worse.'

'Shut up, Bert,' Barny said.

They were just about to take another step when they heard a sudden loud bang. Bert grabbed Barny's arm and screamed, 'They have got us, Barny.'

Just then the curtain opened just a fraction and a face appeared between them. That was the last straw for Bert, he let out another scream, pushed Barny forward towards the curtain, turned and ran towards the unlocked window as fast as his legs could carry him. But, in his panic, he never noticed the coil of rope on the floor in front of him and ran straight into it. He screamed again. 'Barny, they got me, they got me. Get them off me!'

Barny was still on the floor after Bert's push from behind. 'There's no one there you fool, get up,' he said. Bert stopped shaking against the rope. He finally got himself together and untangled the rope from his legs, pulled himself back up and on to his feet. He looked back round at the curtain and then made a run for the window, and he was gone out of the window and away across the fields. Barny got himself up and then shouted out to whoever was behind the curtain. 'Come on out now from behind that curtain.'

The curtain moved again more violently this time. Barny began to walk backwards towards the window. 'Come out or I'm coming in,' he shouted. Just then the curtain was pulled apart and standing there was – a vicar.

Barny stopped and took a sigh of relief. 'You frightened the life out of me, Father,' Barny said.

'Yes, and you gave us a bit of a scare too, my son.'

'Have you been up there all night, Father?'

'No, not at all,' and, as he spoke, six young lads appeared from behind the curtain. 'This is the church choir. We always practise here early on a Sunday morning before church and we were having a bit of trouble with the curtain.' Barny walked up to him. 'We never had nowhere to sleep last night and as we walked past the hall, we saw a window open.'

'What happened to the other chap?' the father asked.

'I don't know, he's most likely half way back to London by now.'

'Those injuries look quite bad. Have you been in a fight?'

'No, they're not as bad as they look. I must be going now, it was nice to have met you, Father,' Barny said, as he turned to walk away.

'Wait a minute, you'll need to get those cuts seen to. Come back to the vicarage with me and I will get you some food and my daughter will see to your face. I have two hours before church starts,' the vicar said.

On the way to the vicarage Barny told him all about Wilford Road, his parents and Violet, the girl he was going to marry ,and the reasons why he had to leave London to make some money.

'It sounds a very different way of life down there, my son. Here we are,' the vicar said as he opened the door for Barny. As Barny walked into the kitchen he saw a young lady at the table chopping vegetables. 'This is Beth, my daughter. She was a nurse during the war, so she's used to patching up cuts and bruises. Beth, this is Barny from London. I found him in the church hall and I told him you would take care of his injuries for him while I go and get him some food. Sit yourself down, Barny.'

Beth walked over and took a look at his face. 'You have certainly been in the wars. Were you up at the old barn last night?'

'Yes, then we got lost and ended up at the church hall. We needed to shelter from the rain so we spent the night in there and your father found us this morning.'

'We,' Beth replied. 'Was there someone else with you?'

'Yes, my mate Bert, he got a bit frightened in the church hall; he thought it was haunted and ran off.'

'And you haven't seen him since?' she asked.

'No, but he'll be all right, he can look after himself.'

She cleaned his face up the best she could. 'Your face is not too bad considering, just superficial cuts, but it's the one on your shoulder that's worrying me, it's quite deep you know and infected. I will treat and dress it, but you will need to keep it covered for the next few days.' She removed his shirt. 'Now, this is going to hurt a bit.'

Barny looked down. 'What's that you're putting on it?' he asked.

'It's only some crushed petals from a flower which grows in the woods, it will help to stop the bleeding and also clean the wound.'

'How did you find out about all of this?'

'My granny used it and her granny before her, so it's been tried and tested many times. Don't worry, it won't kill you. I've dealt with a lot worse than this during the war.'

'What do you mean?' Barny asked.

'The injured soldiers, sometimes they would be brought to me with no arms, some with no legs and they would expect us to perform miracles on them.'

'So what did you do?'

'Just be there for them most of the time, until they died. If they had a hand, we used to hold it, most of them were past any kind of help. They never knew where they were or who was with them, but we would try and comfort them and be there so they wouldn't die alone.'

'What if they never had a hand to hold?'

'Then you would hold any part of their body that they could feel. Most of these soldiers were victims of bomb blasts so, apart from the loss of limbs, they also had a lot of other injuries. I remember one young lad, he must have been about sixteen. A bomb landed not far off from where he was standing, it killed three of his mates. Anyway, when they brought him in, he was barely alive, but he was still conscious. I was asked to stay with him until he died. I will always remember his face, he was looking up at me all the time and mumbling some names which must have been his family. His arms were still there, but they were shredded, you couldn't recognise them. I placed my hand on his face, which was covered in blood. I started to pray and as I did I could feel my hand slowly sinking into his face. The bomb had ripped half of his cheek away, it was just hanging there by a piece of skin and my hand was slowly going under it. He lasted for about ten minutes and then passed away.'

'That's really terrible,' Barny said. 'I think that would have sent me round the bend.'

'You became used to it. The times when I really got upset were when the young lads thought I was their mother and they would look up at me and say ... "please don't leave me, Mum, and help stop this dreadful pain" ... I know God was helping me through it all, I used to pray all the time that the fighting would stop and these young boys could go home to their families, and of course it did. There, that's finished. I can bring you a jug of water now if you would like to wash before you eat.'

'Yes please, we've been sleeping rough for the last few nights.' Barny had a quick wash and had his food. 'That was very nice, he said, 'thank you.'

Her father walked back into the room. 'We had better go now, Beth. You can stay here if you want until we get back.'

'No, I'm all right, thank you, I had better be going. I had better try and find Bert before the train leaves, can't leave him up here on his own.'

'Well, perhaps Barny would like to come to church with us, Father,' Beth asked as she put her coat on.

'Yes, would you like that, Barny?' the vicar asked.

'I don't know,' he replied.

'Oh come on, Barny, it won't hurt you,' she said, as she held his arm, 'it's not that bad.'

'All right then, I will if you're sure I won't be in the way.'

So they all left the house and made their way down the lane and into the churchyard. Barny looked around him. 'There's no one here,' he said.

Beth laughed. 'It doesn't start for another half an hour, we have to get things ready before the people arrive.'

'If I can help, I don't mind.'

The Vicar's Daughter

'Right, if you're offering, you can put the hymn books on the seats and change the numbers of the hymns to the ones we are having today.'

Barny had never been to church before, he looked around trying to see what numbers Beth was talking about. What numbers, he thought and where do the books go? He walked up to the vicar who was in the back room and asked him about the numbers and where they went.

'Oh yes, these are the hymns we are having today, so you can put them up there on that board and the hymn books, put one on each seat.'

By the time Barny had finished the people had started to arrive. He felt someone pull his arm. 'Come on,' said Beth, 'you can sit with me at the front and share my book.'

Barny started to worry, he could read, but not too fast and he had never ever sung before, only to himself when he was in the coal yard on his own, but it all went well and they both had a laugh at the way some of the old girls were singing. But he took notice of Beth's father giving his sermon and he did relate to a lot of what was said, remembering the soldiers Beth had told him about. On the way out Barny said goodbye to the vicar, who was staying behind to get the church ready for the evening service, and thanked him for his help. 'You must come and visit us again, any time,' he said.

On the way back to the vicarage, Barny asked Beth where her mother was. 'She died when I was six. We were in Africa and she caught a fever and never recovered.'

'I'm really sorry about that, Beth. Anyway I had better go now, it's a long way back to London. Thank you again for all that you have done for me, you know, the cuts and that.'

'That's all right, make sure you come back and see us, but please, not in the state you were in this time.'

Barny walked down the path, then he turned round and waved. 'I hope you find your friend,' she shouted. Barny laughed and made his way to the station.

While all of this was going on, back home Violet and her parents were just stepping off the tram outside Percy's family home. They owned a big house with four floors, and a big garden with an orchard. A far cry from the small back yard in Wilford road where the Blakes lived. Percy's family were quite well off, owning five drapery shops in and around the town. But Violet's mind was still on Barny. Earlier that day she went across to Barny's parents and asked them if they would tell Barny, when he arrived home, to meet her in Fred's yard at twelve o'clock the next day. She decided it was time he was told of her plans to marry Percy, which was something she wasn't looking forward to.

There was a warm welcome at Percy's house for the Blake family; both the fathers had served in the same regiment and remained good friends since leaving the army.

'We've got something special for dinner,' Percy's father said, as he poured the drinks.

'Now, anything for you, Violet?' he asked.

Her father looked across at her. 'I think just a ginger beer for her, that will be sufficient,' he said. 'So what are we having for dinner, Frank? A nice joint of pig?'

'No, something better today, seeing as it's a special occasion. My brother sent me down a nice plump pheasant off his farm.'

'That was very good of him and how is he doing these days?' John asked.

'Not too good. Come along to the study, John, we'll have our drinks in there until dinner's ready. I'm sure these two love birds would like to be alone.'

Violet looked across at Percy and then left her seat. 'I'm going out to the kitchen to see how your mother's getting on with the dinner.'

'Don't you want to stay with me and talk about the wedding?' Percy asked. 'You know there is still a lot to be sorted before the big day.'

Violet raised her eyes to the ceiling. 'I don't think there will be much left for us to do, Percy. Our parents seemed to have taken over all the organising of it.' As much as she liked Percy, she couldn't stop thinking about Barny, he was the one she really loved, but how could she spoil her parents' dream? They would never forgive her, would never talk to her again, and she had too much respect for them to break their hearts. She knew she would have to go through with the wedding. She would have to tell Barny and try to convince him that this was what she really wanted.

Back in the study both the fathers were still talking. 'Yes, as I was saying, my brother's having a bit of a bad time at the moment; in fact I have had to lend him quite a substantial amount of money to get him out of trouble.'

'Really,' replied John, 'and I thought farmers earned quite a good living.'

'Normally they do, but he's had so many crop failures in the last year or so, due to the weather and the mites, that if I hadn't put money into the farm he would have lost everything by now. And seeing as he was the one who gave me the capital to get my businesses off the ground when I left the army, I couldn't really refuse to lend him the money, but it has hit me really hard. So hard in fact that I have two of my shops on the market at the moment. That's one of the reasons why I want to get this wedding over and done with as soon as possible before things get really bad and I don't have the money for a nice wedding.'

'Well, I had no idea, I'm really sorry to hear that, Frank. I only wish I could help out more, but we've only got a small amount that we have saved in the bank and that's about it.'

'No, don't be silly, I wouldn't think of it. You have had a rough time since leaving the army, what with your accident, losing your position and having to move to that road, you'll keep what you have got and keep some dignity. We'll get the two young ones married off and settled down in a nice house, that's my main concern.'

All through dinner the conversation was about the wedding plans. Violet didn't know if it was the pheasant that made her feel sick or the talk of the wedding day, but she had never seen her parents so happy so she put on a brave face, even though her eyes were full of tears.

Back up in the country, Barny was walking through the goods yard looking for Bert, but with no luck. As he walked across the lines he noticed an old canvas sheet at the bottom of a bank. There were two feet poking out of the end of it and Barny recognised the holes in the soles of the boots – they were Bert's. He was fast asleep under the old canvas. Barny crept up quietly and then grabbed both of his feet and gave them an almighty pull, at the same time shouting as loud as he could, 'They've got you, Bert, they've got you.' Bert didn't know where he was when he opened his eyes. He screamed and got tangled up in the canvas. Barny could hold on no more, he had to let go of his feet, the tears rolling down his cheeks. In the end he was laughing so much, he fell to the ground and rolled over on top of Bert. Bert poked his head up from under the canvas and was relieved to see it was Barny rolling about on top of him. 'You'll end up killing me,' he said, in a relieved voice. 'A heart attack, that's what you will give me, a bloody heart attack, you dozy sod.'

When Bert had calmed down and Barny had stopped laughing. Bert asked him what happened in the hall after he had left. 'I thought you were behind me, when I ran out.'

'You bloody liar, you knew that I couldn't run because of my injuries, you just left me on my own to face them spirits.'

'You're joking, were they really there?' Bert asked.

'No, all that was behind that curtain was a vicar and his choir.' Barny sat down beside him and told him the story about the vicar and his daughter.

When he had finished Bert shook his head. 'I don't believe it. I've been out here for hours on my own, freezing cold, wet and starving hungry and all the time you've been in a warm room, having tea with the vicar and his daughter.'

'Come on, soppy, cheer up,' Barny said. 'We'll go and get you something to eat and then I'm going to buy two tickets for the passenger train, we are going home in style today. I've had enough of roughing it for one weekend. Beth told me there's a train that leaves for London today and we have got about half an hour before it comes in.'

Bert nudged Barny with his arm. 'Beth? That's a funny name for a vicar in it?'

Barny turned and slapped him around the head. 'I told you his daughter lives with him and she was the one who cleaned up my face.'

They carried on walking until they came to the village and found a shop that sold pies. Bert's eyes nearly popped out of their sockets when he saw all the different types of pies, he was so hungry. As they walked into the shop Barny asked him how many pies he wanted.

'I could eat about thirty,' he replied, 'but I don't want to be greedy, half a dozen will do.'

Barny walked over to the shop assistant. 'Three pies, please, to take away.'

He then looked behind him at Bert standing there shaking his head again. 'That will fall off one day,' he shouted across to Bert.

'What will?' Bert asked.

'Your bloody head, you, keep shaking it all the time.'

'But you don't know how hungry I am, three pies are not going to fill me up.'

'It's all right, I was only joking, give us another six pies please, love.' They started to eat the pies on the way back to the station and were only just in time to catch the London train.

As they boarded the train, Bert looked up at Barny. 'This is nice, I've never been on a train before, well not in the passenger carriage.'

'No, nor have I,' Barny said. 'I'm going to sleep now,' and he put his feet up on the seat opposite. 'I've never laid on anything so comfortable before, I could live here in one of these carriages very easily.'

As the train pulled into the station, after the journey, Barny asked Bert where he could buy some flowers.

'Mine should still be there, you can take them.'

'If you think I'm giving them to my mum, you've got another think coming. I want some nice ones,' he said, 'she deserves the best.'

'Well, old Harry should still be out selling, you know, down the high street, he normally sells some nice bunches,' Bert said. 'But let me go and get them, he will let me have them a bit cheaper.' So before they got off the train, Barny gave Bert some money for himself, for going with him for the weekend, and some money for the flowers. Barny waited for him at the front of the station and when Bert returned, he had the biggest bunch of flowers you had ever seen. 'Here you are, mate, and I've got some change for you.'

'Thanks, Bert. I'm going home now to see my parents. I suppose you're going to spend your money in a public house?'

'Yes,' replied Bert, 'but not around here. Not with that Charlie Ede about. I'll see you later.' And he started to run for a tram. Barny walked home and as he got to the top of Wilford Road, he stopped and looked down the road. I can't believe two places could be so different, he thought. I would love to take Violet and my parents away to live in that village.

He walked down the road slowly, looking across at Violet's house and wondering if the sergeant was still in there. He was tempted to go over and find out, but he had promised Violet he wouldn't go near the sergeant, so he walked on until he came to his own house. The kitchen door was open and he could see his mother making some tea. He walked up to her and put both his arms around her. 'Hello, Mum, are you all right?'

She looked up at him. 'Yes, I'm fine, it's really nice to see you, Barny.' She looked down at the flowers. 'Have you brought them for me?' she asked.

'Of course I have, just to let you know that I still love you.'

'You're a good boy and you certainly know how to look after your old mum. Thank you, son, they're beautiful, but look at your face, it looks really sore.'

'No, I'm all right, it's not as bad as it looks and I've had it looked at by a nurse.'

'What you mean? Have you been in an infirmary?' she asked.

'No, it was a nurse from the war. I've got so much to tell you and Father; by the way, where is he? Is he in the back yard?'

'No, he's gone to visit your uncle Billy at work,' she replied.

'I don't know why he has to go round there to see him. Who in their right mind can sit and talk in a mortuary? He should go and see him when he's at home.'

'But he can't,' his mother replied, 'it's too far to walk and we can't afford the tram fare, and anyway they sit in Billy's office, so they are nowhere near any bodies, although it's only in the next room. I wouldn't fancy it myself, but don't let your father know I said that.'

'Come and sit down, Mum.' He pulled a chair out for her. 'Look, here's some money for the rent, gas and coal and this is for next week's food and I want you to put this money in your pocket, it's to buy you that new shawl you wanted.'

'Oh, you're a good boy, son. My old one's falling apart. Thank you,' she said, as she gave him a kiss.

'Now listen,' Barny said as he leant across the table, 'this place where I've been, it's so beautiful, Mum, you wouldn't believe it. It's all countryside with miles and miles of lanes and as you're walking down them, the cows are right next to you in the fields.'

'You're joking, son,' his mother said.

'No, it's true and some of the lanes go right through the middle of the farms and as you're walking through them, you can see the pigs in their pens.'

'No, I wouldn't fancy that. I don't mind them on the plate, but having them right next to you, no, I don't think so.'

'But it's so quiet, you can hear the birds sing and there's no trouble at all, no fight and no drunks. It's just so peaceful; that's where I want us to live, I want to take you, Dad and Violet and move up there.'

The Vicar's Daughter

'Oh that reminds me,' his mother said, 'Violet came round this morning, really early it was, and said she will meet you at Fred's yard at twelve o'clock tomorrow.'

'Good,' Barny replied, 'I have missed her so much.'

'This lovely place you've been talking about, I bet there's no work there, except maybe on the farms and I don't think you'd like that.'

'No, I've sorted that. I had dinner with this vicar and his daughter.'

'You never did,' she said.

'Yes and I went to church,' Barny said, with a smile on his face.

'Well done, son, I'm proud of you.'

'Anyway, I told Beth all about Father.'

'Hold on, who's Beth?'

'She's the vicar's daughter and I was telling her about Father being one of the best carpenters in the south and how he's teaching me the trade. She reckons that the nearest coffin maker is about two hundred miles away and if we could rent a cottage and make the garden into a workshop, we could make the coffins and a few bits of small furniture to sell to all the surrounding villages. What do you think, Mum?'

'Well, I couldn't have coffins in the house, but it's worth thinking about. This Beth, is she the nurse who cleaned you up?'

'Yes, she is really nice, kind and gentle.'

'And is she married or walking out with anyone?'

'I don't know,' he replied, 'I don't think so, she never said, anyway what's that got to do with it?'

'Nothing, I was just wondering, you seemed to have taken quite a fancy to her, that's all.'

'No, I haven't,' he replied, 'I've got Violet, and that's all I want.'

His mother made his bed up and Barny retired for the night. She waited in the scullery for her husband to come home; she always worried if he wasn't home before dark. There were always lots of drunks about and she knew if one of them started on him, he wouldn't walk away, he would have a go back. I'll give it another hour, she thought and then I will get Barny to go and look for him.

Chapter 5

Death from Lockjaw

The next morning, Barny was awoken by his father making the tea.
'Do you want some?' his father asked.
'Yea, I will have a mug, if you have got one going spare,' Barny replied, as he folded his blanket up. 'You were late home last night – was everything all right, Dad?'
'Yes, your mother was worried sick, but I just lost track of time, Billy and I were talking for hours.'
'How is uncle Billy keeping?' Barny asked.
'He's all right, he's been really busy round the infirmary. He was telling me the morgue is packed full.'
Just then his mother walked into the scullery and looked across at Barny. 'You're up then,' she said, 'what, no work this morning?'
'No, Fred's not very busy at this time of year so I'm only doing three mornings a week.'
His father poured the tea and they all sat around the table. 'It makes a change us all being here together. I was just telling Barny how busy Billy is around the morgue. You wouldn't believe some of the things that go on around there, it's enough to make your hair curl. Do you know what part of his job is now? He has to go round to the workhouse every second day and sort the bodies out. They are having so many deaths in there that they don't bother taking them to the infirmary any more. They have even put a new gate in the cemetery opposite the

workhouse so they can carry the dead straight across the road without having to go up to Queens Road.'

'I wonder what they will do when that one's full up?' his wife asked.

'They don't bury the ones from the workhouse in their own graves. Sometimes they wait until there are four or five bodies together and then put them in one grave. Sometimes they wait until there's a funeral and when all the people have left the grave side, then before they fill it in, they put a couple of bodies in the same hole.'

'When I die, Mum,' Barny said, 'I want to be buried up north in that little village.'

His father quickly interrupted him. 'Well, will you tell me how you would like to be taken up there? Would you like me to carry you across my shoulders or perhaps you would like your mother to push you all the way on a barrow?'

'All right,' Barny said, 'I was only dreaming.' He looked over at his father. 'Can you guess where I'm going to put you when you go?' he said to his dad, smiling. 'In our back yard, you know underneath all that horse dung.'

'I don't care, you can stick me in the corner of the bedroom with a plant pot on my head if you like, it won't bother me when I'm dead.'

'Now shut up, both of you,' his mother shouted, 'all this morbid talk, you shouldn't speak about death like that. You don't know when it will happen to any of us; it really makes my blood run cold, thinking about it.'

Barny's father left the table and made another pot of tea. 'Billy was telling me last night,' he said to his wife, 'do you remember old Doris from upstairs saying about that young child from Forster Road dying from lockjaw?'

'Yes, that was little James, he was only two years and ten months old. I used to talk to his mother up the wash house. Her name's Kate, but I haven't seen her since the little boy's death.'

'Well,' her husband continued, 'Billy was saying that on the day the accident happened she was out in the back yard using the wringing machine, when the little lad put his hand up and crushed his finger in the cog wheels. Apparently his mother never knew anything about it until the child walked round to the side of the machine and put his hand up to her.'

'My God, I would have fainted if I had seen that poor little mite with his finger crushed,' his wife said, 'what did she do when it happened, rush him round to the infirmary?'

'No, she picked him up and ran with him up the road to the shops and went in to old Mr Cooper's, you know, the hairdressers. He took the child off her and bound his finger up with some linen. He told the mother to go back home and get her hat and coat and then return to shop. Mr Cooper then advised her to take him straight to Dr Murdoch.'

'I don't know why she didn't take him there in the first pace,' Barny asked. 'It would have saved a lot of time.'

'You know what some people are like,' his mother replied. 'They are really afraid of doctors, they think they are going to do more harm than good. Especially the people from around here, they would rather go to a shopkeeper to get advice and leave the doctors till the last resort. Anyway, what did the doctor say?'

Her husband continued. 'The doctor removed the sheeting from his finger and advised her to take him straight to the infirmary; there was nothing he could do, the lad's finger was too badly damaged.

'She already had her hat and coat on, so she left the doctors and went straight to the infirmary. Billy was there when she brought the child in. He said a nurse took the child off his mother and told her to go home and come back later, which she did. She came back in the evening and inquired about her child, but was told by another nurse that she couldn't see him owing to an infection being in the ward. But the nurse also told her that the finger had not been amputated yet, but would be done the next day. His mother asked why it had not been amputated straight away, as the doctor said it would have to be taken off before an infection set in. The nurse replied that the child had a cough and the finger that was crushed was practically amputated anyway. "We have cleaned the wound as best we could under the circumstances," the nurse said, "but we had not surgically cleaned it and the doctors could not remove the damaged structures until the child could stand up to the anesthetic." The mother left the infirmary that night and returned the next morning, still being told that she could not see her child, but they did tell her that the finger would be amputated that afternoon or the next morning.

'She retuned again that evening and was told the operation would be performed the next morning. Billy said he felt so sorry for the woman,

Death from Lockjaw

she didn't know where her child was or what was happening and she was crying every time she left the infirmary without seeing the lad.'

'Is this story going to take long?' Barny asked, smiling. 'Only I have to go back up north in four days' time.'

'Look, I'm not talking to you, dirt box, I am telling your mother about it,' his father said.

'No, you go on, I was only joking,' Barny said.

'Well, the woman, what was her name again?' he asked his wife.

'Kate,' she replied.

'Yes, that's it. Well, she came back on the Thursday evening and was told it had been done and the child was quite comfortable and she was allowed to see him. She returned every evening until the Tuesday, that's when she received a postcard asking her to go and fetch the child and take him home the next morning. Billy said that was the first time he had seen her with a smile on her face. She walked up to him in the main hall and said, "I'm going to take little James home today." "Good," he replied, "I am so happy for you." Billy stayed with the mother until the nurse brought the child out, but when she saw him, she remarked to Billy how bad the child looked. She told the nurse she didn't think her child looked well enough to go home. Even the nurse remarked that the child seemed to have adenoids and advised her to have him attended to later on. The mother left the infirmary with her child but, when she got the child home, he never looked at all well and apparently he was spluttering over his food, and he kept fretting and crying. When Billy saw her the next time, she was telling him that her child seemed very hungry but would not take any food, and then he started to have spasms and this frightened her so much that she took him back to the infirmary that afternoon.

'The house surgeon examined the child and he was admitted. Billy said that he was on the ward at the time and another doctor was called who said that the child was very ill and must be closely watched. They then told his mother that the child was worse on the Thursday and during the evening he died.'

'The poor little mite, I bet his mother was going mad when they told her.'

'Yes, well she knew something was not right that afternoon so she had called for some of her family to be at the infirmary with her and Billy said that there was uproar when they heard of the baby's death.

There were eight of them screaming and shouting and in the end one of the nurses had to send for a constable.'

'Did they not know that he had lockjaw when they sent the poor little mite home?' his wife asked.

'No, apparently not, they never knew until the mother returned with the child later on in the day. There were no symptoms of lockjaw until the doctor examined him and whilst they were trying to open the child's mouth, he had a spasm, which indicated lockjaw. When they saw this, they injected him with an antitoxin, I think that's what Billy called it, but then he died a short time later.'

'I bet the mother and father had some questions for the doctors,' said his wife.

'Billy said it was murder. A large crowd gathered in the main hall and they were pushing the doctors around. The father was shouting out and asking the doctors if the operation could not have been performed without an anesthetic being given, at least that way his son might still be alive. Although the doctor replied, he thought it had nothing to do with his death considering the age of the child. It was then that the mother started shouting at the doctor. "Why wasn't the wound cleaned properly when I brought my child in?" she asked. The doctor said it was, but the father shouted at him that the nurse told his wife that it had not been surgically cleaned. The doctor then said he could not explain any more than that. Another doctor walked up to the father and said. "If your wife had been more careful, then the child would never have had his finger crushed in the first place." He said that was the cause of the child's death, not anything the doctors had done.'

'Bloody sauce,' Barny's mum said,' fancy saying that just after the child had died. The poor mother.'

'Yes, but just as things were getting really hot, the senior house surgeon came down. He took the mother and father to one side and told them that they were sorry at the death of their child, but no one could tell if lockjaw would develop in the child. The operation had gone very well and the risk of tetanus was not thought of in a case of a clean crush like the one the child suffered. The symptoms sometimes develop very rapidly.'

'Those doctors are a law unto themselves,' said his wife. 'They can do whatever they want in that operating room and no one ever knows.

That's why people don't like going to the infirmary, it's such a terrible thing to happen to such a small lad.'

'So, was there a fight in the end?' Barny asked.

'No, Billy said that once the surgeon started to explain things, it all went quiet. He remembered the father asking the surgeon if the child was eating in the infirmary. The surgeon replied that he thought the sister had given him a cup of bread and milk, but he didn't know if he had taken it. He held the mother's arm and said that they all regretted the child was sent out, but no one could foresee what was going to happen and as far as he was concerned, on one was to blame.'

'Well, Mum, you had better run upstairs to tell Doris,' Barny said. 'She's the local newspaper around here, but she won't be too happy that you know something she doesn't.'

'You leave her alone, she's all right,' his mother said, 'at least she is friendly.'

'Don't you mean nosy?'

'Have you not told him about Doris?' his father asked his mother.

'No, I won't tell him because he will only laugh.'

'What's that, Mum, come on tell me, what has she been up to then?'

'Your father went to see Billy at the infirmary at the beginning of last week and Billy gave him one of the old newspapers to bring home for me to read.'

Barny started to laugh. 'Now don't tell me Doris the nose was in the paper! What did she do? Something really bad, I hope. Come on, where is the paper, I want you to read it out to me, word for word.'

'Right, now you must promise you won't take the mick out of her when you see her, I don't want her to find out that we know about it,' mother said.

'No, of course I won't, go on, what's has she done?'

'Well, pass my glasses then, I can't see without them. Now let me see, where is it. Ha yes, here it is. Now this is the reporter from the court house who has written this.'

'Don't forget, word for word,' Barny said.

'All right, I will start from the beginning.

'Doris Green, of Wilford Road, was charged on remand on a warrant with unlawfully wounding Traisette Hall by stabbing her with a knife. Mrs Hall, also of Wilford Road, stated that on Saturday evening, 16 May, her father and another man were quarrelling outside the Crown and Sceptre. Both were drunk. She tried to get her father away and got him as far as Union Road, when they began fighting again. Doris Green's sister came up and struck Mrs Hall and then she struck her back. Whilst they were fighting, Doris Green, who had a knife, stabbed Mrs Hall in the back and on the head, causing her to fall to the ground, and she did not remember anything more of what occurred. She said she had never associated with Doris Green, and had never given her any provocation. Cross examined, Mrs Hall said she liked a glass of beer, but she worked hard, she had been charged with being drunk only once. She did not try to hit Doris Green's father with a boot and she was not aware that Doris had a cut on her arm. She also stated that it was necessary for the residents of Bangall (Wilford Road) "to look after themselves". She saw Green raise her hand with the knife in it. She denied having thrown a tea pot through the Greens' window, sometime ago or having thrown a chopper at her, and also last Christmas, being a time of goodwill, she did not throw a sugar basin at her and was not aware that her father and the Green's father were continually fighting about once a week.

'Dr C. Soundamore, from the infirmary, who attended Mrs Hall afterwards, said that her head and face were covered with blood. She had an incised wound two inches long over the right ear, penetrating not quite down to the bone; another wound above and behind this one, two inches long; a superficial wound on the right cheek and one just under her nose, both about an inch long. When he saw her again the next day she told him she had a wound in her back, and on examination he found an incised wound over the right shoulder blade three inches long and about an eighth of an inch deep. There was a cut in her clothing corresponding with the wound. The wounds could have been caused by the knife produced.

'Cross examined, he said that when he saw Mrs Hall she was perfectly sober and did not even smell of drink. He would say the wounds were caused by a not very sharp instrument. He did not think the wounds were caused in a struggle for the possession of the knife, unless the person fell on it. It was possible that Mrs Hall might have fallen on the knife three times during the struggle.

'Susan Smart, aged 13, said that she saw the prisoner stab Hall with a knife like the one produced. She dropped it on the ground and the witness picked it up, wiped it on her frock and gave it to the constable. In reply to

Death from Lockjaw

the clerk, she said that the frock she was wearing at the time was at home. It had since been washed.

'Mrs Williams who, the girl said, washed the skirt, was called and denied having done so. She had not washed any skirts for her since the affair. PC 694 said that whilst Mr Hall was being attended to by Dr Soundamore the girl Smart handed him a knife. There was no blood on it. Nothing was said to him about it being wiped. At this point the case was adjourned for a fortnight in order that witnesses might be called.'

'That's it, the end of the story,' his mother said. 'Now you mustn't say anything to her, Barny. She was only protecting her father at the time,'

'Well, I never,' Barny said, 'I would never have believed it. She's preaching to me about fighting and she is out there sticking a knife in another woman. But I won't say anything, the last thing I want to do is upset her. Anyway I've have got to go now and meet Violet.'

He kissed his mother on the forehead and left the room. But before he reached the front door, he could not resist going upstairs to see Doris. He banged on her door. 'Who's that?' she shouted.

'It's me,' Barny replied. The door opened slowly and Doris poked her head round.

'What are you doing knocking on my door? Come on, tell me what you were after,' she asked.

'I was just wondering,' he said, 'since you know most of what goes on around here, I just wanted to know if you have heard anything about poor old Mrs Hall, you know the one who lives just down the road. I heard she was attacked with a knife by some mad woman and I have been trying to find out who it was. No one seems to know, do you have any idea?'

Doris pulled the door back hard and hit a coat stand which was behind it, knocking it over. She then moved forwards towards Barny and looked him straight in the eyes and said, 'I don't care how big you are but, if I was you, I would turn around and walk back down those stairs as quick as you can, before I push you down there. I know what your game is, you evil little sod. You're just trying to wind me up. Now you had better start running, my boy.'

Barny started walking backwards down the stairs, laughing on his way. 'My God it's you,' he shouted. 'You're the mad knife woman. Don't you come near me!' he shouted jokingly.

At the Precipice of Poverty

Doris turned back into her room and then picked up a vase and threw it at him.

Barny stood there laughing as the vase flew past his head. Well, 'I suppose a vase is better then a knife in my back,' he said, as he ran down the stairs.

'I will have you, my boy, mark my words,' she shouted, 'I will have you, you cocky little sod.'

Barny ran out of the house and was still laughing to himself as he walked through the gate of the coal yard. He looked round for Violet, but again she was late. He turned a barrow on its side to sit on and waited for the love of his life to arrive. He waited thirty minutes and at last he could see her walking down the road towards him. He walked up to her and met her half way. 'Hello,' he said, as he put his arms around her. 'I've missed you so much this weekend, Violet.'

'Yes, and I have missed you too,' she replied. They walked down the road, arm in arm.

'I have so much to tell you,' he said. 'I've saved enough money from the fight so I thought we could catch a tram to Shirley Hells for the afternoon.'

She stopped and turned towards him. 'I need to talk to you, Barny,' she said, as she held his hand tighter. 'There is something I must tell you.'

Barny lifted her head up. 'What's wrong? You're crying. Has anyone been upsetting you?'

'No, not at all. There is something I need to talk to you about, but not here. Let's go to Fred's office and talk, that's if he's not there?'

'Ok,' Barny said, 'I know he's not there, he's always down at the market this time of the morning, but we can still get in there, as I have a key to the front door.'

They made their way to the carriage and sat down on the same bench where they had spent their first night together. Barny turned to her. 'OK, now tell me what this is all about.'

'Well, Barny, I know you wouldn't hurt your parents, don't matter what the situation was, you wouldn't hurt them because you love them, don't you?'

'Of course I do, I wouldn't hurt them, not intentionally,' he replied.

'Well, what my parents want, more than anything else in the world, is for me to be married off to a respectable young man and I told you on Friday that the sergeant was coming to stay with us this weekend. He asked me if I would like to marry him, but what made it worse was that he also told my father that he was going to ask me. It all happened so quickly from then on. It seemed like one day he was asking me to marry him and the next day everyone was arranging the wedding.'

'So what did you say?' Barny asked.

'I'm so sorry, Barny, but I had to say yes. I had no option.' Barny stood up and walked to the end of the carriage. He felt his body go numb. He wanted to turn round and try to change Violet's mind, but he couldn't move, he just stood there. His eyes began to ache as the tears built up and his throat felt like someone had cut it, he found it very hard to swallow. This was his worst nightmare. It was nearly as bad as seeing his parents on that night after they had been beaten. He stood there for a while and then felt a hand on his shoulder. 'Barny, please hold me,' Violet said.

He couldn't, he was to choked up; he just stood there staring out of the window. He then felt her arms around his waist.

'Barny, I am so sorry,' she said. She rested her head against his back and he could feel her tears rolling down his skin, through a rip in his shirt. 'Please hold me, Barny, I love you so much. I don't want to lose you, but there is nothing I can do about it.'

He wiped his eyes with the sleeve of his shirt and turned round. 'Please stay with me, Violet,' he said, 'I have so many plans for us and I know I could make you happy and you know I would never let anyone hurt you, not even your parents.'

'I know you would make me happy,' she replied, 'but I just can't go against my parents' wishes, it would break their hearts and I know my father would disown me if I let him down now.'

'That don't matter,' he replied, 'you could come and stay with me, at least that way we would still be together. I just don't think I could go on without you, Violet, I know I can't.'

'Barny, you're a kind and generous man, you will find someone else, someone who will love you like I do and can give you what you want.'

'You know I don't want anyone else, you were my first love and I know you will be my last.'

'It's too late now, I have got to go through with the wedding, there's no other way, but please don't be angry with me, I will always love you.'

Barny knew by the sound of her voice that this was the end, he knew deep down inside that she couldn't go against her parents' wishes, no matter what he said to her. The same as he wouldn't go against his parents. He put his arms around her and held her tighter than he had ever done before. He wanted to make the last few moments with her last as long as possible. The tears were streaming down Violet's face. Barny could not take in the thought of not being able to hold her any more and he couldn't stand the thought of someone else being with her.

They both pulled away and looked at each other and as they went to kiss, there was a loud bang on the door. 'Who's that?' Violet asked, wiping the tears away from her eyes.

'I don't know, but don't worry about that now, just hold me,' he said. The banging on the door continued, getting louder and louder.

'Please see who it is.' She was worried in case her father had followed her and was standing outside banging on the door.

Barny walked over and opened up the door and saw a stranger standing there. 'What do you want?' he asked abruptly.

'I am looking for some bloke called Bert the flower seller,' the stranger said. 'I've heard he sometimes calls down here.'

'Well, he's not here now,' Barny replied. 'Now just be on your way.' Barny stepped back and went to shut the door, but the stranger stopped him by putting his foot against the door and then he looked Barny in the eyes. 'It looks like you've been crying, boy,' he said.

Barny pulled the door back open. 'Look, you fool, I have no argument with you so just leave me alone and go on your way.' He then turned to walk back inside again. Without Barny knowing, the stranger followed him in. He looked across the carriage as he walked through the door and saw Violet sitting on the bench over the other side of the carriage. 'Hello, darling,' he said, 'my name's Charlie Ede, now what's yours?'

Barny stopped; he now knew who the stranger was – Charlie Ede; it was the man his friend Bert had been so scared of. The one whose wife he had been seeing and the one who carried a small chopper in his inside pocket. He was now coming up against Barny Sturt. Barny felt at his lowest at this point of time, but he knew how dangerous this man Ede was and he couldn't take any chances, not with Violet sitting in the carriage.

Death from Lockjaw

Barny walked back out to the door and pushed past the man, but he was too busy looking at Violet, sitting at the back of the carriage. Barny stood outside the carriage and shouted in to the man, who was well known for chopping people's fingers off. 'If you're looking for Bert, I've just seen him coming into the yard.'

Charlie looked at Violet. 'You stay where you are, my beauty and I won't be long,' he said to her. He turned and ran back out of the carriage but, as he did, Barny was waiting for him and caught him with a blow on the back of the head and knocked him to the ground. 'Don't ever call my girl darling again,' Barny shouted at him, and then kicked him in the chest, as he was rolling around on the ground.

Violet was now standing in the doorway and started to scream. 'Leave him, Barny,' she shouted.

Barny knew the man wouldn't walk away; he would have to make certain that he would have to be carried out of the yard or else he would keep coming back until he had taken Barny's fingers off. Barny stopped and was looking up at Violet crying. Charlie was just about on his knees, trying to get up. But Barny saw him first and walked over to him and kicked him in the face, sending him falling backwards with some force. As Charlie hit the ground, a chopper fell from his pocket and Barny again remembered that this was the animal that chopped other men's fingers off, just for a laugh. As Barny looked down at him, he saw something go past him, in the corner of his eye. He looked round, it was Violet, she'd had enough and was running out of the coal yard.

Barny shouted to her to come back and she stopped and looked round at Barny and then screamed out, shouting his name. Barny then felt a heavy blow on the back of his neck and fell to the ground. Charlie had got himself together and made it to his feet. He searched frantically for his chopper, but this had fallen from his pocket earlier, so he picked up the first thing he could find, a fence post and brought it down on Barny. It missed his head and hit him on the side of the neck. Charlie was trying to wipe the blood away from his eyes, which was streaming down his face from a cut on his forehead that he had received from Barny's kick in the face. He then reached down to his boot and pulled out a knife and went for Barny. But his eyes filled with blood again and the knife missed Barny's head and went through the collar of his shirt, pinning him to the ground. Charlie was on top of Barny, but had to release his grip to wipe the blood away from his eyes.

At the Precipice of Poverty

Barny knew this was his only chance to avoid certain death. He reached out for the knife and pulled it out from the ground and then brought it down three times in Charlie's thigh. He screamed with the pain and pulled himself off Barny before he could strike again with the knife. He started to crawl away, holding his leg and not being able to see where he was going for the blood. Barny shook his head, trying to clear his blurred vision and then followed the man. He reached out and grabbed Charlie's arm and then turned him over on to his back. He still had hold of his arm when he noticed the chopper by the side of Charlie's head. He reached for it and then pulled himself on top of Charlie, holding him down with one knee on Charlie's forearm. He placed another blow down on Charlie's chin and then reached the chopper and brought it down across Charlie's hand, taking off four fingers with one blow. 'You'll not be chopping anyone else up, you bastard,' Barny shouted. It wasn't Charlie who had built up all the anger inside of Barny, it was the thought of losing Violet to that sergeant and not being able to see or hold her any more that made Barny so angry.

Although Charlie's injuries were not life-threatening; he looked dead, just lying there on the ground of the coal yard, covered in blood. And that's what Fred thought when he came back through the gates of the yard. 'What have you done, Darky?' he shouted. He went and knelt down by the side of Charlie and put his fingers on his neck, to try to get a pulse. He did not realise that Charlie was still wearing his cravat around his neck that was soaked in blood and this was why Fred couldn't feel any pulse.

Fred looked up at Barny. 'You've bloody killed him!' he shouted. He then grabbed Barny's arm. 'Come on,' he said, 'you have got to get out of here before the police arrive, they will have you banged up to rights for this.'

'No, I can't Fred. I have got to try and find Violet and speak to her. She's just told me she is going to marry that sergeant bloke and I must try and talk her out of it.'

'Listen to me,' Fred said. 'There are so many constables out there on the road today, it won't be long before one of them looks in and sees him on the ground. Now if they catch you in here with him, you've had it. You know how much some of them want to put you behind bars, well, it will be a lot worse than that, my son, I can tell you. If they do you for this, it will be the death sentence for sure, now you have got to get away, if not for your sake, for your parents' sake. Can you imagine your poor old mother when she finds out that you are going to be sentenced to hang, it would be the finish of her. You can't put her through that, Darky. Come on, you have got to be sensible about this, a train leaves in fifteen minutes for Nottingham, you can jump on one of the empty wagons and be long gone, before they start to look for you.'

'All right I will, Fred, but I must just try and find her, she has only just left so she can't be far away. Listen, Fred, when I have gone, go and see my parents and make up some story that I have found a job up north and tell them that I will send them some money down each week.'

Barny then ran out through the gates and down the road, but everywhere he looked the police were there. What he didn't know was that the army had just finished a parade down the high street and the police were there to block off the roads and control the crowds. So when he saw all the police, he started to use the alleys, carefully poking his head round all the corners to see if he could see Violet, but she was nowhere in sight. He ran down one alley and up another and eventually he ran into Bert. 'Hello, Barny,' Bert said. 'Where are you off to in such a hurry?'

'I'm sorry, Bert, I can't talk now I'm going back up north straight away. Here, you haven't seen Violet have you?'

'No, I haven't clapped eyes on her all day. Anyway what do you mean you're going back up north? I thought the fights were only at weekends.'

'Yes, they are, but this is for a different reason. I can't explain now, but I need your help. Look, I want you to come up and meet me next Sunday. I will give you some money to bring back for my parents, do you understand?'

'Yes, I understand, but listen, if you're in trouble, I will come with you and help you sort it out.'

'No, you can't help me this time, Bert, but if anything happens to me, promise me you will look after my parents.'

'Barny, I don't like the sound of this, please let me come with you,' Bert pleaded with him.

'No, I've already told you I've got to do this on my own. Here take this money, it's for the train fare up north next weekend. And don't worry about that Charlie Ede getting hold of you, he's been sorted. I've got to go now, Bert, the train leaves at any time. Look, don't let me down.'

'You know I won't,' said Bert as he moved closer and put his arms around him. 'Look, you take care, Barny, you're like a brother to me. Do you want me to give a message to Violet when I see her?'

'No, don't worry it's too late now. She's left me and is going to marry that sergeant.'

'You're joking! What a bitch she is. Do you want me to duff both of them up for you while you're away?'

'No, don't do that,' Barny said. 'That will only make things worse. I have lost her now, but if you do see her just tell her that I wish her all the best and I will always love her.' Barny made his way back to the coal yard and, as he looked through the gates, he could see the police standing around Charlie Ede on the ground. He ran past the gates, round the back and on to the lines; he could see the train just pulling out towards him. He waited until the last five wagons were going past and then jumped on. He sat down on the cold steel floor of the wagon. He had no sacking this time to cover himself. But that didn't worry him though, he just sat there with his head in his hands and began to cry. I have lost everything now, he thought to himself. I have now lost my parents, my home and my lovely Violet. I have nothing left, nothing to live for.

Barny sat there for over an hour, but the cold was starting to get to him. He stood up; it was getting dark and he couldn't see much. He could feel that the train was going at full speed. He walked up to the front of the open wagon as he swayed from side to side. He reached up and grabbed the top of the wagon and slowly pulled himself up. He looked over the side and could see the large heavy wheels thundering along the iron track. He pulled himself up a bit more and leaned right over. He had a job to fight against the strong wind that was blowing against his numb body. He had now pulled himself right up and was balancing on the front of the wagon. He closed his eyes and all he could see was a picture of Violet in his mind. He took a deep breath and thought, if I let go of my grip now for just one second, it would be all over, I would be under the wheels and my troubles would end. He was just about to let go and end it all, when he suddenly opened his eyes and then the only thing he could see in the darkness, was a picture of his dear old mother, wiping the tears away from her eyes. He tightened his grip on the wagon and pulled both his legs back over. How can I put my mother through all the pain, he thought, she doesn't deserve

Death from Lockjaw

all the suffering it will cause, it would finish her off, and there would be no one to look after them. No, I can't do it, I can't let them down. He turned slowly round and let himself down inside the wagon. He lay on the cold floor with his head in his arms and cried and cried until there were no tears left.

Back at the coal yard the police were just about to take Charlie Ede away to the infirmary and Fred had now realised his mistake, that Barny hadn't killed Charlie Ede. But it was too late, for Barny was already half way to Nottingham, thinking that he was now a murderer and had no future back at Wilford Road. Bert was also in the coal yard. He was walking around as bold as brass now that he was safe from Charlie Ede's chopper.

A detective was walking around too, trying to find out what had happened. He walked up to Bert. 'What's your business in here?' he asked.

'I don't see that that's anything to do with you,' Bert replied.

'OK, well, if that's your attitude, I'm going to be charging you with assault,' he said.

'No, now hold on, I had nothing to do with that man you just took away.' Bert looked over at Fred. 'I was with him,' he said.

'Yes, we were together when we found the man.'

'Right, I'll be checking that and if it's not true, you will be off down the station.' The detective walked away from Bert and as he did Bert turned and ran over towards the wall, on to a barrow and then a cart and up over the wall. He wasn't going to take a chance of being put away and of not being able to meet Barny next Sunday.

He ran all the way back to Wilford Road and as he turned the corner, he bumped into Violet and the sergeant. 'Hello Violet,' he said, as he was staring straight into the sergeant's eyes. 'Where are you off to, trying to find Barny are we?'

'No, don't be stupid, Bert, what would I want to find him for?'

'Well, you have been seeing him for, well I don't know how long,' he said.

'What's he talking about, Violet?' the sergeant asked.

'Nothing, nothing at all, the boy's stupid, come on, let's go.'

'No, wait just a minute, I'm not having him come up and talk to you like that. Apologise, young man, or I'll have your head off with my cutlass,' the sergeant said.

'You can go and take a run,' Bert said he then grabbed the sergeant's collar and pushed him up against the wall. 'I could have you for my breakfast, you fool, but I promised someone that I wouldn't touch you.'

'What are you talking about?' the sergeant asked.

Bert looked across at Violet. She knew what he was talking about, she knew Barny had told him not to harm the sergeant. Bert threw the sergeant to the ground and looked over at Violet. 'You want to be careful, girl,' he shouted. 'Barny's well liked around here and people are not going to like it when they find out that you're the one who has driven him away, so if I was you I would move as far away as possible after you marry that fool.'

The sergeant got himself up and went to walk over to where Bert was standing, but Violet pulled him back by the arm and made him walk away.

'That's right, run off, typical of your type, no guts.'

Violet turned round and shouted back at Bert, 'You want to watch yourself, Bert. Barny won't stand for you talking to me in that way.'

'No, well I wouldn't be too sure of that now, Violet. I think if he was here he would pat me on the back.'

Violet grabbed the sergeant by the arm again and stormed off down Windmill Road.

Bert walked down Wilford Road, mumbling under his breath. I should have knocked his head off and then hers. Never have liked her or her family, the stuck-up bitch; she always thinks her tom tits don't stink, but I bet they do, I bet it smells just as bad, if not worse then anyone else's down Bangall. He carried on walking and mumbling until he reached Barny's rooms. He opened the front door just as Doris was walking out. 'Can I help you, young man?' she asked.

'If you were twenty years younger, sweetheart, you might do something for me,' he replied.

'How dare you talk to me like that,' she shouted, 'go on, get out of my house.'

'Hold on, humpy, I haven't come to see you,' he shouted, 'I've come to see the woman of the house.' He knew this would wind her up.

Just then Mrs Sturt opened the bedroom door to see what all the noise was about. 'Bert, I hope you're not upsetting Doris,' she said.

'Of course not Mrs Sturt, 'as if I would. I've come round to see you and as we passed in the hall, she tried to push herself up against me.'

'You lying little sod, you know that's not true,' she said. 'I wouldn't touch you if you were scrubbed from head to toe with carbolic, you dirty little git.'

'Go through to the scullery, Bert,' Mrs Sturt said as she pushed him past Doris. 'I'm sorry about this, Doris, I'll have a word with him later.'

'Well, I wish you would, I don't know why all the young men around here always have to pick on me.'

Mrs Sturt followed Bert into the scullery. 'I don't know why you and Barny always have to pick on that woman. She has done nothing to you two and yet you always pick on her.'

'I'm sorry, Mrs Sturt, I didn't mean to upset you,' he replied.

'You didn't upset me. It was Doris that you're always upsetting.'

'Oh well, that's all right then,' he replied.

'Sit down. I've just made some soup, would you like some?'

'Cor, yes please, Mrs Sturt, do you know you make the best soup in the world?'

'You can put a stop to that, trying to get round me, that won't work. Have you seen Barny this morning?'

'Yes, just a few hours ago I saw him.'

'He wasn't with that Violet was he?' she asked.

'No, I think he has finished with her now.'

'Oh, that's good. Now, don't get me wrong, I think she's a nice girl, but I don't think she's right for my Barny.'

'No, you're right, Barny deserves better than that. Do you know I think he was quite fond of that girl he met up north the way he was talking about her, he never stopped.'

'Yes, he was telling me all about her,' said Mrs Sturt. 'I do hope she is a nice respectable girl.'

'Well, I should think so,' Bert replied, 'her father's a vicar and she has been trained as a nurse. Now you can't get more respectable than that can you, Mrs Sturt?'

'What about you, Bert? When are you going to settle down and find yourself a nice young lady.'

'Well, Mrs Sturt, there are so many out there who want me, it's very hard for me to pick one out, you know. I would hate to hurt all the others, that's why I just go from one to the other. It's very hard for me sometimes.'

'Now that's your trouble, you're always messing about, everything's a joke with you; you'll never find a nice respectable young girl if you're always joking around.'

Mr Sturt then entered the room. 'I could hear you out in the hall way. Why don't you leave the boy alone, it's his life.'

'No, that's all right, Mr Sturt. Your wife is right.' Bert stood up from the table and walked over to Mrs Sturt. 'Do you know what? Do you know why I can't settle down with a young lady? It's because I love you too much, Mrs Sturt, you've always been like a mother to me and there is not a girl in the world who could compare to you.' He looked over her shoulder and saw Mr Sturt laughing at the table. 'No truly, I am so grateful to you for all you have done for me, since me and Barny were at school. You know I never knew my mother, but you've sort of been there for me whenever I needed you and I will never forget that for as long as I live.'

'Oh shut up, Bert, you'll have me in tears,' Mr Sturt shouted out.

'No, I really mean it, she has been like a mother to me. I am being serious for once in my life, Mrs Sturt. I would do anything for you.'

'I know you would, Bert, now would you like some more soup, love?' she asked.

'That would be really nice, thank you.' Bert looked over to Mr Sturt and winked at him as Mrs Sturt was bringing the soup over. Even though he was always messing about, he did think the world of the Sturts. They had been really good to him. Helped him when he had been in trouble, when no one else would go near him. They were there and they would always take him in when he got thrown out of his room and they always fed him when he was hungry. They were the closest he had ever had to a family.

Mrs Sturt kept asking when Barny would be home, but Bert couldn't answer that. All he could say was that he was working late with Fred and hoped that Fred would call round soon and make up some story as to why Barny had gone back up north again.

Chapter 6

Tales from the Workhouse

After what seemed like days, but in fact was only four hours, the train finally stopped in the sidings at Nottingham. Barny was blue with the cold, as he was on the last journey up there, but this time he could feel no pain, his mind had blocked out everything except his parents and Violet, whom he thought he would never ever see again. It took him all of his strength to pull himself up and over the side of the wagon and then he fell to the ground. After a while, and when he had got himself together, he picked himself up and started to walk, he didn't know where, he never cared, he just walked. Sometimes he would fall to his knees when he lost the strength to walk any more. And so he went on, mile after mile over the fields and through the lanes, getting weaker by the hour. He eventually stopped in some woods and sat down on a fallen tree, he could go no further – he was totally exhausted.

After he had rested for a short time, he leaned back and looked up towards the sky. The stars were so bright. He had never noticed them before, not in Wilford Road, or perhaps he never took the time to look up at the sky. If he had done, most of the people from around there would have thought him mad.

For a short time he let Violet and all of the troubles he had back in Wilford Road drift from his mind. He remembered back to when he was last in this area, to Beth and her father and the words he had spoken in that tiny church, not far from where he was now sitting. His mind went back and he concentrated hard. Believe in God, have faith in him and he will help you through the troubled times and stay with you always, were spoken in that small country church. These were the only words that he could remember clearly and they had stayed locked in his mind. God, if you are really there, I could do with some of your help now, he thought to himself.

With his head lowered Barny fell down to his knees and with his hands grasped tightly together, he started to pray. Please, dear God, please stand by the side of my mother and father and help them in their hour of need when I can't be with them and also forgive me, God, for taking my anger out on that man and taking his life away from him. Please, help me if you can. Barny stayed there for over an hour, asking for God's help and his forgiveness. His knees were slowly sinking deeper into the mud, but he stayed there in that one position hoping that God would guide him through these bad times. He was far away from home and far away from all of his family and friends. He thought he had no one to turn to, apart from this someone whom he had only known for two days, this someone whom he had never spoken to before and never believed existed, but from whom he was now begging forgiveness, this someone whom he couldn't see, and couldn't touch, but somehow he knew he was being heard. This someone who was a stranger to him, but was his last resort; there was no one else who could help him, no one else he could turn to and nowhere left for him to go. He carried on praying, but at times he could feel the guilt and the shame for asking this one person for help and guidance. Why should he help me, Barny thought, I have never prayed to him before, I have never even believed in him before and now that there is nothing left in my life, I am on my knees asking him for help and forgiveness.

Just then Barny began to feel a warm glow come over his whole body, all the anger that was built up inside him was slowly draining from him. He thought he was dreaming, but he started to feel the cold wet pain starting to rise from his knees. He suddenly felt that his father and mother would never be in danger again, there would always be this someone by their side, guiding them and making sure they were kept safe. He also felt that Violet was destined to have a good life and she would be happy – he had to let her go and find his own happiness. It didn't matter if he was sent to prison for taking away that man's life, or if he was sentenced to death, God would always be there, waiting for him, to guide him on the right path. The best thing to come from all of this was that he knew he would never ever be alone again, even if he had no one in life to be there for him, he would now always have God.

After a while Barny stopped praying. He stood still for a moment and completely blanked his mind of everything. He then stood up and started to walk back through the trees. It felt as though a huge weight had been taken off his shoulders; he started to feel the pain from the cold, his hands and feet were numb, but his mind was clear. He carried on walking and after a short while he looked across a destined field and could see the outline of that tiny church where he had said his first prayers. He walked across the muddy field, through the church gate and across the graveyard until he reached the two giant doors, but they were both shut tight and locked. He began to knock hard on the doors with his fists, he wanted to become even closer to God and he wanted this feeling to last. He did not want to go back to how he had felt earlier. He knew if only he could get inside the church then he would be on God's ground and this feeling that he now had would become even stronger.

To his dismay the doors stayed locked. After a while Barny realised he wasn't going to make them move, no matter how hard he tried. So he stopped hitting the doors and slowly turned round. Immediately his eyes focused on all of the stone and wooden crosses of the graves that stood out so clearly in the brightness of the moon. He leaned back against the giant doors and slowly fell to the ground and, with his head in his hands and from just sheer exhaustion, he curled up in the corner and fell asleep.

Back home, Fred was sitting in the scullery at Barny's house, trying to explain to his parents that Barny might not be home for some time. He told them that he had received a message that had come down with the driver of the coal train, saying that a job had become vacant up there for Barny, which he had sorted out the last time he was up north. But he had to leave straight away and go back on the train and had no time to come and tell them himself; the message said that he had to be up there at once in order to get the job. Fred explained to them that Barny would arrange for his wages to be sent down every weekend, so there was no need for them to worry – he had sorted everything out, he said.

'When will we see him again?' his mother asked.

'I'm not too sure,' Fred replied, 'but he will need some time to settle in and find somewhere to lodge and then he said he will come back and see you and tell you all about it.'

At the same time, across the road, Violet was sitting by her window; she could just about see Barny's house and was wondering if he was there or if he was hurt and lying in the infirmary. The last time she had seen him was when he was fighting Charlie Ede, and she did not know what the outcome was.

She was in two minds whether to go over to his house and see if he was at home, but then she thought, if he was at home what would she say to him, especially if his mother and father were there? It would just be embarrassing and make matters worse and it would be even harder to walk away from him again. So she stayed in her room, crying and trying to think of some way to stop the wedding without hurting her parents or her future husband, but she knew, deep down in her heart, there was no way she could get out of it; she knew she had to go through with it and put on a brave face, no matter how much it hurt, losing Barny.

The next morning, just as it was getting light, Barny was woken up by someone shaking his arm, 'Barny, Barny,' he shouted. He opened his eyes and looked up to see the vicar. 'Barny, what are you doing out here? It's freezing cold.'

'Hello, Father, I came down from London late last night and had nowhere to stay and the only place I could think of was this church. I thought I might be able to take shelter in here, but then I found that the doors were locked, so I rested for a while and I must have fallen asleep.'

'You should have come straight to the vicarage, my son, I told you there would always be a welcome there for you, no matter what time of day it is. I'm sorry the doors of the church were locked but just recently we have had some reports of a gang of poachers in the area and the doors of the church have been locked up during the night, in case anything gets stolen. You can't be too careful these days. Anyway, up you get, Barny, follow me inside and we will try to find you some dry clothes, I think we have some from the last Christmas play we held. I don't suppose they will fit you, but it's only until yours are dry and then we can go back to the vicarage. Do you know how long you will be staying this time?'

'No, I'm not sure, Father. I haven't made up my mind yet,' replied Barny.

'So you don't know what you are doing or where you are going. That's up to you, my son, but one thing I'm sure of, you can't sleep on the church steps for another night, you'll catch your death of cold. So, until you have made up your mind on what you're doing, I think the best thing for you to do is to stay in one of our spare rooms at the vicarage. I am sure Beth will be pleased to know you are back.'

'Father, I have no money to pay for my keep,' Barny said, 'but I would be willing to work and will do anything that needs doing, you only have to ask.'

'Yes, that would be helpful, but we will talk about that later,' the vicar replied.

'Tell me, how is Beth?' Barny asked.

'Yes, she's fine, she is working at the infirmary in town today, they have been so short of nurses and she's been helping them out. It's only for a few days, she'll be back tomorrow.'

As they walked off, Barny looked around him and asked if there would be any carpentry work to be done around the church. 'That's right, Beth said your father is teaching you carpentry. If you know how to work with wood then there is quite a lot that needs doing around here and at the vicarage. Things soon become run down if they are not properly maintained.'

'The only trouble is, I have no tools with me.'

'That's not a problem,' the vicar replied. 'One of our villagers died last year, the poor soul, a lovely man, and he used to be a carpenter, and a good one at that. Anyway, he left his complete set of tools to the church, everything you would need. It's a shame, no one has used them since he left us and I certainly don't know how to put them to good use, but I am sure they will be in good hands with you, Barny. Now let me think, I believe they are in the vicarage somewhere, we will have to have a look for them when we get back, but you're most welcome to use them if you want. But before you start, how would you like me to cook you some breakfast? I'm sure you haven't eaten for some time.'

'No, you're right, it was yesterday morning I think, yes, that was the last time I had something to eat.'

'Well, come along let's get going.'

They took a slow walk back to the vicarage and Barny was shown to his room. 'I'm afraid it's not much,' the vicar said, 'but you have a bed and a small chest of drawers, with a jug and basin, so you should be comfortable.'

Barny looked around the room: this was the first time in his life that he had a room to himself; in the past he had always had to share or sleep on the floor. He couldn't believe it.

He spent the next few days doing odd jobs around the church and vicarage and also spent a lot of time in his new room. He couldn't get used to the space and the quietness; all he could hear were the birds singing, something he wasn't used to back in Wilford Road. On the following Friday, Beth returned home. She got the shock of her life when she saw Barny, but was so pleased to see him. 'I thought we would never see you again,' she said, as she kissed him on the side of his face. 'How long will you be staying?'

'I'm not quite sure at the moment,' Barny replied. 'I have been earning my keep.'

'Yes, I know,' she said, 'I have noticed the gate post to the church and the window have been repaired; you've done well.'

'So you have been up to the church already?' Barny asked. 'I thought you would come straight home first.'

'No, when I have been away, I always go back to the church first to pray.'

'I prayed the other night, Beth,' he said, looking down at the floor.

'Did you? And did it make you feel any better?'

'Yes, it did. I have to admit to you, Beth, I did some terrible things before I left home and when I arrived up here it seemed like I had no one to turn to. I was in quite a bad way and then I remembered how much faith you had in God and how you told me that he was always there to help when you were in troubled times, and I remember you saying that you only had to ask for help if you needed it. That was my last resort, my last place to turn, so I prayed and after a while I did find peace.'

'You know, you could have come and spoken to my father or myself, we would have tried to help to you.'

'Well, I wasn't sure about that but I would have liked to have come to you.'

'Would you like to talk to me now about what happened when you left home?' Beth asked.

'I don't know if I should, you might throw me out once you have heard what I have done.'

'Everyone deserves forgiveness,' she said, 'whatever you have done, I can tell that you are truly sorry and that is the most important thing, as long as you know that you have done wrong and you are willing to accept forgiveness.'

Barny looked up at her. 'That's one thing I am sure about. I would like to talk to you about it, Beth, but not here. I wouldn't like your father to walk in and hear me telling you. It's not something that I am proud of.'

'That's fine,' Beth said. 'We will have our tea and then go for a walk and you can tell me all about it then.'

After tea, Beth's father fell asleep in the chair while Beth cleared away the plates and then they left the vicarage and walked along the lanes. Barny tried to explain to her all about Violet and how she was getting married for the sake of her parents and how he had wished that it was him. Beth replied that it was so wrong for Violet to marry this man just to keep her parents happy. 'You can't let her marry for all the wrong reasons, Barny,' she said. 'You must return and try and talk some sense into the girl and stop her getting married. You can't let her go through with it, just because people want her to marry this man. She has to think of herself and it is not very fair on the man. There has to be more than commitment, you need love and devotion or else the marriage won't stand a chance. You must go back there, Barny, and try to persuade her that she is marrying this man for all the wrong reasons.'

'I can't do that, Beth,' he replied. 'Something else happened just before I left, something terrible, something that is haunting me every second of the day since it happened. I can't seem to get it out of my head.'

'Tell me, Barny, you never know, it might help if you get it off your chest.'

He was just about to inform her that he was involved in a fight with this man called Charlie Ede and Ede had died as a result of the fight, when they both heard a loud piercing scream – it seemed like it was coming from behind a group of trees on the right hand side of the lane.

They both looked at each other and started to run and as they turned a bend in the lane, they could see a cottage in the distance. As they ran closer they could see flames and smoke coming from a window. 'That's Charlie Welch's cottage,' Beth shouted. They kept running until they reached the cottage.

'Who's that?' Barny asked, as he pointed to an outline of a man standing by the door.

'That's poor old Mr Welch,' Beth shouted as she ran up to him. 'Are you all right, Mr Welch?'

'Yes, I think so,' he replied. 'My wife – I am sure she is still trapped in the scullery. I have tried time and time again to get to her, but the smoke is so thick and it is so hot in there. I can't do anything to help my wife.'

While they were talking, Barny ran round to the back of the cottage and tried to look in through a window. He couldn't see much, the smoke was too thick. He turned round and saw a milk churn by the side of the wall. He picked it up and threw it through the scullery window. This helped to clear some of the smoke. He then poked his head through the broken window, but the smoke was still choking him. He took a handkerchief from his pocket and wrapped it around his mouth and then looked back through the window again. This time he could see the outline of a woman, lying on the floor. He couldn't tell if the woman was alive or dead.

By this time Beth and Mr Welch had walked round to the back of the cottage and met up with Barny. 'Was your wife in the scullery at the time of the fire?' he asked Mr Welch.

'Yes. Tell me, did you see her through the window, is she all right?'

'I don't know,' Barny replied. 'Your back door's locked. Do you know where the key is kept?'

'I am sure it is in the scullery by the side of the stove.'

Barny looked at Beth. 'We need to get in there somehow, she looks like she is in a bad way.'

He then told Beth to stand to one side and he took a run at the kitchen door and kicked it in to try to get close to the woman, but immediately, as the door fell in, the draught turned the smouldering embers into more flames. He then tried to get to the sink where he could see a bowl full of water, but the flames were to much for him. He stumbled back outside coughing and choking.

'Are you all right?' Beth asked.

'Yes, but we need some water to put the flames out. Mr Welch, where is your water pump?'

'It's down at the bottom of the garden, but there's some water in that old water butt over there,' he said.

'Go and fetch me a pail. Help me fill it up and then pass it to me in the scullery and I'll throw it through the smoke and try to put the flames out that way.'

Mr Welch found two pails and he and Beth took turns in filling them from the water butt and passing them to Barny, who was now leaning through the scullery window and throwing the water around Mrs Welch's body.

After a while Barny managed to put out the fire. He returned to the scullery door and walked in. He looked down at Mrs Welch on the floor and saw she was terribly burnt. After he had a look around to make sure the fire wouldn't start up again, he shouted out to Beth to keep Mr Welch outside. The flames had not damaged the scullery beyond burning two towels hanging on the back door, some soiled linen and charring the paint. He couldn't understand how the woman was so badly burnt and yet there was not much damage to the rest of the room. Barny wondered how such a fire with such intense heat and smoke could do so little damage. He walked around and saw a glass on the copper and a candle nearby, which was still in one piece and had not melted in the heat. He walked to the window and asked Mr Welch what his wife was doing in the kitchen. He said that she normally went down for a drink during the night. Barny said to Beth that it looked as though the woman had gone to get a drink and leaned across to get a glass and the candle must have set her nightdress alight. Barny again looked down at the woman. It wasn't a very nice sight, she was very extensively burnt; in fact every particle of clothing was burnt off her.

Barny left the scullery and went out to Beth. Mr Welch was telling Beth what had happened. He said his wife had not been quite well for some time and she had been attended to by Dr Thompson who, he understood, was treating her for her nerves. He said that, when they went to bed last evening, she had seemed quite as usual. 'I thought she went to sleep before I did, but the next thing I knew, I was awakened by a scream. I thought my wife was still lying next to me and knowing how nervous she is, I put my hand out to let her know I was awake and was there for her. I thought the sound of screaming would frighten her, but to my horror, she wasn't there. I immediately rushed downstairs and could smell burning linen and flannel. As I opened the scullery door, which was where I thought she would be, it was just full of smoke and heat. I couldn't go past the door and that's when I came outside to find a pail and then you two turned up.'

'Did you see her in the scullery, Barny?' Beth asked.

'Yes, she is on the floor. She's, well she is... I think you had better come and have a look for yourself, Beth.' They told Mr Welch to stay there and then they went back in the kitchen.

'She is over there,' said Barny, 'but I must warn you she is not a very nice sight.'

Beth went over and bent down to try and lift her up, but finding her rigid she laid her back down again and asked Barny to fetch a light as the scullery was quite dark and still fairly thick with smoke.

With the aid of a light, she found that the woman was past all human aid. Barny showed her the glass and where the candle was and said that he thought that she may have leaned across the candle and set herself alight. Beth said that if she was wearing a flannelette nightdress, then it would have just burst into flames and she wouldn't have had any chance of putting the flames out, they would have been so intense.

'Are flannelette nightdresses that dangerous?' Barny asked.

'Yes, and the cheaper they are, the more dangerous they are.'

'I must remember not to wear one of them to bed,' he said jokingly.

'What was that?'

'Oh nothing, I was just talking to myself.'

'Come on. We had better go and break the bad news to Mr Welch.'

'But I can't understand how she was so badly burnt and yet most of the scullery was all right,' Barny said.

'I have come across this before. In the battlefields, a doctor once told me that sometimes when a person catches alight, their clothes burn and this starts to burn their body which then releases the body fats and this in turn starts to burn slowly, but very intensely and sometimes that's why the body can be unrecognisable and yet the surrounding area can be untouched.'

'That's really spooky,' Barny replied.

They then went out to Mr Welch and explained to him that the fire was now out, but poor Mrs Welch was no longer with us and the best thing to do was to leave her there until the morning and then send for the doctor and the undertaker. 'In the mean time,' Beth said, 'you had better come back with us to the vicarage and spend the rest of the night there.'

On the way back Barny was telling Mr Welch what he thought had happened in the scullery and how his wife had caught alight. Barny was well known for coming right out with things. Mr Welch replied that she was wearing a flannelette nightdress and she was in the habit of going down for a glass of water during the night.

When they reached the vicarage, Beth went upstairs and woke her father. She explained to him what had happened and he came down and took Mr Welch across to the church, to pray for his poor wife's soul. By this time Beth was exhausted and retired to her bed, but Barny sat down in front of the fire and every time he closed his eyes, all he could see was the charred body of Mrs Welch lying on the floor. He knew he wouldn't get much sleep that night, still, he thought to himself, at least that stopped me from telling Beth about the man I had killed: I'm still not sure how she would have taken it – it might have been the end of our friendship.

The next morning Barny woke up in the chair; he must have fallen asleep at some time in front of the fire. He could remember a nightmare he had during the night. He could see it as clear as day; Mrs Welch was on the scullery floor, looking all burnt and still smoking and when he went up to help her, she suddenly jumped up and grabbed him by the neck and tried to pull him down. What a terrible night I've had, he thought.

Just then Mr Welch walked into the room. It looked as though he had been crying most of the night and he came and sat next to him. Barny felt a bit awkward and wasn't too sure what to say at first although he knew he would have to make some sort of conversation. 'So how long have you and Mrs Welch been married?' he asked.

'Forty-eight years,' he replied, 'but we've been together fifty-two. I don't know what I'm going to do now. I've got no family, no one at all.' Just then Beth walked through the door before Mr Welch had finished talking. 'Now, don't go worrying about that,' she said. 'You have always got my father and myself and lots of friends in the village and you know you can stop here in the vicarage for as long as you like.'

Barny had trouble taking in just how friendly the people were around this way. They tried to help each other out as much as possible, not like

Wilford. If this had happened there, poor Mr Welch would be in the workhouse this time tomorrow. 'Don't you worry, Mr Welch,' Barny said, 'I will give you a hand to get your kitchen back to its old self.'

'No, thank you, son, I don't think I will be moving back to that cottage, it has too many memories for me. I was thinking about it last night and I thought I might get a place in town, it wouldn't be so lonely there. I couldn't stand being on my own.'

As Mr Welch was talking about his wife, the front door opened and Beth's father walked in.

'I have contacted the police and the undertaker. They said they would meet us at your cottage, Mr Welch, so I think we had better go now; we don't want to miss them.'

Mr Welch thanked Barny and Beth for all their help and left with Beth's father. 'The poor man, I feel so sorry for him,' said Beth and then walked over to Barny. 'You did a really good job last night, I don't know what I would have done without you. With all of that commotion going on, you never did tell me about that terrible thing that happened before you came up here.'

'Oh, don't worry about that now. It doesn't seem that important any more, not after what happened last night, but thanks anyway.' As he finished talking he turned to Beth and held her hand. 'Listen, Beth, I know it's not the right time and I do feel sorry for poor Mr Welch, but he did say that he might not be moving back to that cottage and if it was going to be empty, do you think it would be possible for me and my parents to move in?'

'Yes, I don't see why not,' Beth replied. 'I know Mr Welch owns it and I am sure he would be pleased that someone was living in there rather than it going to rack and ruin and I know the rent would come in handy for him. But I think it might be best to get the funeral over with first, before I ask him.'

'Yes of course,' Barny replied. 'Well, I can't sit back here all day, I had better get started. I'm fixing the roof of the church today and someone came up to me yesterday and asked if I could repair their fence posts. I think he said he was the owner of a stoat farm, a few miles up the lane.'

'There you go, you're already getting work in! I told you there is plenty of work around here for a good carpenter; you might even be able to give that fighting up soon,' she said smiling.

Barny spent the next few days doing odd jobs and on Saturday night he got ready for the fights, which he won with ease. He noticed the two men standing at the front again, whom the guvnor had warned him about. They walked over to him after the last fight, but Barny walked out before they could talk to him. The next morning he went back to the barn to meet Bert and after waiting for over an hour, Bert finally turned up. 'How are you, Barny?' he asked. 'You look a lot better.'

'I'm OK, how are my parents?'

'I haven't seen much of them myself, but Fred has been round your house quite a few times and he asked me to let you know that your mother's not too well. She's had a bad chest and I think she has been in bed for the last three days.'

'Right, when you get back, I want you to call the doctor out and whatever he says she needs, you go out and get it for her,.I don't care how much it costs. Here, take this money for yourself for coming up here and give this to my father for the bills, but before you give it to him make sure you get my mother anything she needs and let her know that I will see her soon and I might also have some good news for her when I return.'

'Are you not going to ask about Violet?' Bert asked.

'Well, have you seen her?'

'Yes, she's been around, but she has been very quiet, not her usual self.'

'Has the sergeant been seen with her?'

'I haven't seen him about at all, he must have gone back to his barracks to have a game of soldiers, but I have heard talk that it's going to be a very big wedding.'

'Good luck to them,' Barny said. 'Come on, I'll take you to meet Beth and get you something to eat, your train's not due for two hours.' As they walked up to the vicarage, they saw Beth in the garden, hanging her washing out.

'Is that Beth?' Bert asked.

'Yes,' Barny replied.

'You're living in this place with a lovely girl like that looking after you? She's beautiful. You jammy old sod, you've got it made up here,' he said.

'Keep your eyes off her. She's the vicar's daughter and she is decent, not like the old dogs you get around Bangall.'

'Come on then, take me over and introduce me to her.'

'This is Bert, you know, the one I was I telling you about.'

'Hello, Bert, it's very nice to meet you,' she said.
'Well, it's very nice to meet you too, my dear.'
Beth walked back to the house. 'Would you like something to eat before your train leaves?'
'I wouldn't mind, if it's not too much trouble. I haven't had anything since yesterday.'
'Come on in and I'll get you some bread and cheese. By the way, Barny, Father came back when you were out, he said there was a nail sticking out of one of the seats in the church and asked if you wouldn't mind going up there and fixing it for him before the service starts.'
'Right, I'll go over there straight away and do that.'
Beth and Bert went into the house. 'I have never seen Barny move so fast, only for his parents,' said Bert. 'You have a nice place here.'
'Thank you and do you live far from Barny?'
'I move around a bit, Beth, I don't like staying in one place for too long, people catch up with you if you're in one place for too long. What do you think of Barny then?' he asked.
'I really like him, he is so kind and considerate, I can't imagine him fighting every weekend, he doesn't seem the type.'
'That's what makes him so good, but he's had a rough time lately though. What with his girlfriend Violet going off and arranging to get married to someone else.'
'Yes, I know, he told me, it sounds like he thought a lot of her the way he talks about her,' she said.
'Cor, you can say that again, he worshipped the ground she walked on. Do you know he would have done anything for her and she just goes and lets him down. I don't think he will ever get over her.'
'Here you are,' she said, as she put the food down on the table, 'if you want any more, just ask. He'll will get over it in time, or when he meets someone else.'
'Well, let's hope so,' Bert replied. 'He is such a nice bloke, but thetrouble is, people are afraid of him when they first meet him because of his size and the reputation of being a good street fighter, but as soon as they get to know him and find out what he is really like, they are all over him. Where he lives now, he hasn't been there long, although he knew a lot of the people who come from around there before, but they all like him. They are forever coming up to me and asking where he is and how

he is getting on; his is very well liked. He talks a lot about you, you know.'

'Does he really?' she answered.

'Yes, and I think he's taken quite a fancy to you.'

Just then Barny walked through the door. 'Whose taken a fancy to what?' he asked, looking at Bert.

'I was just saying to Beth, that old Barny always takes a fancy to a bit of bread and cheese.'

'Come on, hurry up or you'll miss your train,' Barny said.

'Beth, you haven't got a piece of cloth I can wrap this in, have you? I can eat it on the train then.'

'I will put a bit more in there for you,' she said.

Barny and Bert left for the station. 'Now, don't forget, Bert, whatever my mother wants, you buy it for her and I will see you the same time next week.'

'OK Barny. You know she's a really nice girl, that Beth, you wouldn't go far wrong with her,' he said.

'Go on,' Barny shouted, 'be on your way, before I give you a good slap round the head.'

The following week Barny spent most of his days doing odd jobs, but also spent a lot of time with Beth. She would take him shopping, meeting people and getting more work in and also to all the beauty spots around the village and, at night when her father had retired to his bed, both of them would stay up for hours just talking round the fire. Although their backgrounds were totally different and Beth's lifestyle was something that Barny had never seen before, they got on really well; in fact Beth was becoming very close to him. One day, while they were sitting down by the riverside, Barny asked Beth if she had ever felt strongly about a young man.

'Yes,' she replied, 'there was a soldier once. He came to me in a very bad way. It was touch and go for the first few weeks, but I nursed him day and night until he was on the mend. In the end we became very close and by the time he was ready to leave the infirmary, we were very much in love.'

'What happened to him?' Barny asked.

'He went back and fought for his country, but this time he never returned, he died on the battlefield. They never found his body so I never had the chance to say goodbye.'

'That must have been hard for you, Beth,' Barny said.

'Yes, but God was with me and gave me strength and I vowed never to fall in love again, unless I was completely sure we would spend the rest of our lives together.'

'Sometimes you just can't hold back the feelings you have for someone. Although you know it's wrong to feel that way it's very hard to say no, I'm not going to fall in love. But then it just happens and there's really not much you can do about it.'

'They are very wise words and I can see you have been through the same pain as myself. Do you still miss Violet?'

'Yes, more than anything,' he replied.

'That's it then, we will have to take your mind off her, come on, let's go.'

'Where are we going?' Barny asked, as he was being dragged to his feet by Beth.

'Have you ever been horse riding?'

'Yes, I used to drive the horse and cart all the time back home.'

'No, I don't mean on a cart,' she said laughing, 'I meant bareback.'

Barny stopped in his tracks. 'Well, I don't know about that. I've never been on a horse without a cart before and how big are the horses and where do we get them from?'

'Don't worry,' she said, 'I'll teach you how to ride. Do you remember Mr Bains, whom I introduced you to in the village shop yesterday?'

'Yes, he was the one who was riding that big shire.'

'That's right, but he has other horses and he lets me go riding any time I want.' Beth spent the rest of that day trying to teach Barny to ride, but she realised it was going to take more than a few hours to get Barny riding bareback.

On the Saturday Beth was very quiet and Barny asked if he had done anything to upset her.

'No, of course not. I suppose you're going to the fights tonight?'

'Yes, I have to, it's the only way I can support my mother and father.'

'But you're getting more and more work in all the time,' she said.

'I know and I really appreciate that, but that's still not enough yet, I need to put some money away in case anything happens to me. I need to know that my parents will be taken care of if I'm not there to look after them.'

'Nothing's going to happen to you,' she said. 'Not if you give up fighting, and if something did happen to you, surely your parents could survive?'

'Do you know my worst nightmare? It's thinking of my parents having to go to the workhouse if I am not around to support them. I could never let that happen.'

'Are those places that bad? I thought they were there to help the poor and to look after them.'

'They are, but they are bad places. If my parents were sent there, my mother would be expected to pick oakum all day and my father would be breaking stones or chopping wood for them to sell. Even though he has a bad back he would still be made to do his fair share of work, and the food ... I know of one man who was in there, he was an old soldier, in the Manchester regiment I think that's what he said, anyway, he went out to the front, like any other man, and when he returned, he tried for weeks to find a job, but he couldn't find any regular work so, without any money coming in and no roof over his head, he ended up in the workhouse. After he had been there for a day or two, he was put to work breaking up ten hundredweight of stone a day. He worked his way through six hundredweight and then decided he had done enough and stopped working. When the master came over and asked what was wrong, he said he would not do any more stone breaking unless he was given more than bread and cold water for his dinner.

'The master asked him what he would like and the man replied, "Something hot, like gruel, skilly or tea, but I am not working any more until I have something better to eat and drink." The master did no more, he took him off to the police courts and the poor man was given seven days' hard labour. Now that man had fought for his country and, through no fault of his own, he was now doing seven days' hard labour.

'It's also full of sick people, just waiting in there to die. I remember once I had to deliver sacks of coal there and while I was waiting for the master to come and sign the ticket, I was having a chat with the porter in the gate house and he was telling me what food the inmates were supposed to have and I will never forget what he said. It consisted of, for breakfast: six ounces of bread and one and half pints of gruel and then, for dinner, they had one and half pints of ox head soup and six ounces of bread and if you had done a good day's work, you would get six ounces of cooked meat and 16 ounces of cooked vegetables. Then for supper it was six ounces of bread and you had the choice of two ounces of cheese or one ounce of butter. He said that if you were troublesome during the day you would only get some dry bread and cold water.'

'I always thought the workhouse was there to help the poor and needy and to give them some refuge, but it doesn't sound a very nice place to be in. You just don't know, do you,' she said.

'It's not only the food and the work that cause the problems,' Barny said. 'It's the other inmates as well. As I was talking to the porter, two constables were marching a man away from the workhouse. The porter said that his name was Edward Tulley and he had caused some trouble about an hour before I had arrived. He said that the man was in the dining hall, waiting for his dinner to be served, and all he was doing was having a laugh and a joke with the other inmates, but as he was messing about when the master walked in and saw what was going on, he immediately ordered Tulley out of the hall and to go without any dinner. Of course, Tulley wasn't having any of that. That was the main meal of the day and he wasn't going to miss it. He answered back to the master and explained to him that he had already missed his breakfast, due to the fact that there was a death in the bed next to his and they made him stay behind and help clear the mess up.

'When he wouldn't leave the hall, the master went up to him and tried to pull him off the bench. The porter said that when the master had done this to him, Tulley became really violent and threw himself on the ground he then got up and kicked the master. After this had happened, the assistant master came into the hall and ran over to help the master. He tried to grab Tulley's arm and as he did so, Tulley seized the assistant master's wrist and bit his finger. The master and the assistant then both jumped on Tulley and held him down until a constable was called for. The porter said that the man suffered from epileptic fits, but when the workhouse medical superintendent came down to help the master, he said that a good deal of these so-called fits were assumed and at the time of the trouble, the man was responsible for his actions.

'Can you imagine if my poor old mum was sitting nearby when all this was going on, she wouldn't know which way to turn. The porter said that this sort of thing happens every day. She would be frightened out of her life in there. That's why I would do anything I can to stop her going into that place.'

'But why have you got it into your head that you won't be around to look after your parents?' she asked.

'The police around where I live have really got it in for me and are just waiting for the chance to put me away,' he replied.

'Yes, but they can't send you to prison without a good reason,' she said.

'They can, you know, they will soon make something up about you. One of them, a Detective Sharp, has already told me that he is on my case and he has got me in line for a long stretch in prison. That's why I would like to rent Mr Welch's cottage and then I can bring my parents up here, where I can look after them and get away from all that trouble and away from that Detective Sharp.'

'Well, I do like having you around, Barny, there is no doubt about that, and I will do my best to get you that cottage. I'm just always so worried about you fighting, that's all. If the people of the village knew you were a bare-knuckle fighter, they wouldn't have much to do with you and they certainly wouldn't call on you to do odd jobs around their homes. Anyway, what time do you have to be at that old barn?' she asked.

'Not for another hour.'

'How would you feel about coming to church with me then, if I can't stop you from going to the fights, then we can both pray that God will stand by you and keep you safe.'

'Yes, of course I will,' he replied.

Barny left Beth at the church and made his way to the barn. He had three fights, which again he won with no injuries, and again the two men were in the front row, watching Barny's every move. After he had picked up his winnings the two men approached him and one grabbed his arm. 'I want a word with you,' he said.

'Let go of my arm,' Barny replied.

'Do you know who we are?' the man asked.

'I don't care who you are, if you don't let go of my arm, they will be carrying both of you out of here, the same as they did with my last three opponents.'

The man realeased his grip. 'If anyone else had said that to us, they would be dead now,' the second man replied.

'Look, just tell me what you want and I can get on my way.'

'We would like to take you on as one of our fighters. We have watched you fight over the last few weeks and you're good and we want you to come and fight for us.'

'What else would I have to do, apart from the fighting?' Barny asked.

'We will take you all over the country, and you'd be expected to fight every night and some fights you will have to lose, but we will let you know which ones to win and which ones to lose.'

'Go on, be on your way,' Barny said, 'I'm not interested. I have never thrown a fight in my life and I'm not going to start now, not for you and not for no one.'

'We will let you think about it until next week, but just remember this, we always get our own way and if you don't fight for us, you won't fight at all. Don't forget, we will see you next week and think hard about what we have said.'

As they left, the guvnor walked up to Barny. 'What did they want you for?' he asked.

'Nothing much, they just wanted me to go and fight for them,' Barny replied.

'Are you going to?' the guvnor asked.

'No, there's no way I would fight for them.'

'Good,' the guvnor said, 'those two are always up to no good, but be careful, they don't like being turned down. I think it might be a good idea if you left the fighting for a few weeks and kept away from them two.'

'Well, I thank you for your advice, guvnor,' Barny said, 'but no one tells me what to do and I will be back up here next week and the week after, you mark my words.'

The guvnor patted Barny on the shoulder. 'Just watch your back, son,' he said and then walked away.

Barny made his way back to the vicarage and found Beth and her father sitting round the fire talking. Beth looked up as Barny walked through the door. 'Are you all right?' she asked.

'Yes, I'm fine,' he replied.

'Well, come in, my son, and sit down,' her father said. 'Beth's been telling me you would like to rent the cottage from Mr Welch for your parents to come and live up here. That's very good of you, Barny, thinking of your parents, but do you think they would want to move away from their friends and family to a strange place?'

'Well, with respect, Father, you don't know what it's like round where we live At least I know that they will be safe living near the village.'

'Oh, but I do know. My brother is the vicar in St Saviour's Church, not far from where your parents live, but I know that some people get so used to their surroundings that it becomes very hard for them to change. What I'm trying to say, Barny, is – do you think it might be a good idea to find out if your parents want to move away from home, before making all the arrangements?'

'No, I don't think so,' Barny replied, 'I know what's best for my parents.'

Beth moved closer and took hold of Barny's hand. 'Why don't you go home and talk to your parents and then perhaps bring them back up here with you and let them see the cottage for themselves?'

'I can't do that, Beth, I cannot go home,' Barny said.

'OK we'll do it your way,' the vicar said, 'and then we'll see what happens.'

The next morning Barny was up early and out chopping firewood; he was counting the minutes until Bert arrived with news of his mother. Barny took a rest to wipe the sweat away from his face and as he looked up, he saw Beth standing there in the doorway. 'I've made you some breakfast, Barny,' she said. 'Do you know you were in a world of your own then, miles away? What were you thinking about, if you don't mind me asking?'

'I was just thinking about my mother and hoping that she is feeling a bit better this week.'

'We will just have to wait and see. Come on, leave that now and come and have your breakfast before it gets cold.' As they walked into the house, Beth asked Barny if he would mind if she went with him to meet Bert.

'Yes, of course you can,' he replied. So after breakfast they took a slow walk to the old barn. Barny took Beth inside to have a look. It was the first time that Beth had seen the inside a barn where they held the bare-knuckle fighting and she wasn't very impressed. She had a quick look round, but from the doorway she could see the pools of dried blood on the ground in the circle and also the blood-stained walls. This was enough, she wanted to come straight back out. Although she was used to all the blood and guts that comes with the carnage of war, she believed that this sort of violence was totally unacceptable. 'I will be so glad when you give up this fighting game, it's so uncivilised,' she said.

At the Precipice of Poverty

As Barny shut the door to the barn, he could see a figure coming across the field. 'I don't believe it. This is the first time I have ever known Bert to be on time. I hope he hasn't got bad news.'

Beth took hold of his arm and told him not to worry. 'How is my mother, Bert?' Barny shouted.

'I have got some bad news for you, Barny,' he replied. 'Your mother is still very poorly, she hasn't improved at all in the last week, in fact she has been slowly going downhill and she got so bad yesterday, that they took her to the infirmary. I really think you had better come home, she keeps asking for you all the time.'

Beth held his hand tighter. 'Barny, you will have to leave straight away, you must go back home and be by your mother's side at this awful time'.

'I know,' he said as he started to walk up and down. He turned and walked back to Beth. 'I hope you don't mind, but will you do me a big favour, would you mind walking back to the vicarage on your own? I need to talk to Bert and sort some things out.'

'No, not at all, but remember, if there is anything you need just ask, you know where I am.'

As she walked away, Bert turned to Barny. 'She's a good one, you won't go far wrong with her, Barny. She has the looks, the brains and she don't answer back not like all the women I know; you should get in there, my son.'

'I've got no time for that now, my poor old mum's the only woman on my mind now. We have got to start making plans,' he said.

'Plans for what?' Bert asked.

'There is nothing for it, I'm not staying away from my mother's bedside any longer. I've got to get back home and see my mother without getting nicked. They are not stupid, they will know I'll be coming back to see her, so they'll be keeping an eye out for me. So I've got to be one step in front of them.'

'Barny, this may be a silly question, but why will the coppers back home be looking for you? Have you been up to something and not told me about it?'

Barny turned to Bert and grabbed him by the collar. 'Are you stupid or what? Don't you remember that before I left last week, I killed Charlie Ede. That's the reason why I am staying up here.'

'When did you do that, Barny? You told me you had sorted him out, but you never said you had killed him.'

'I done him the day I left to come up here, in the coal yard, don't you remember, Bert? That's when I told you I was leaving to come up here. What's the matter with you, Bert, don't you remember anything?' he shouted to him.

'There's nothing the matter with me, old boy, but I think you have taken one too many blows to your head.'

'What are you talking about, you fool?' Barny replied.

'I'm sorry to disappoint you, but Ede's very much alive.'

'What do you mean? He's not dead? Fred told me I had killed him, he felt his neck and told me he was dead and that's why I had to rush off so quickly.'

'No, you have got it all wrong, you never killed him. I went straight round to the coal yard just after you left. I must admit, he looked dead, but when they got him to the infirmary they found him alive and kicking. Mind you, they had to amputate his hand the next day because an infection was setting in, but his hand wouldn't have been any good without fingers anyway. They said that he would have a permanent limp, due to the stab wounds in his thigh, but apart from that he's fine and he never told the coppers it was you.'

'How do you know all of this?' Barny asked.

'I had to go and visit him, to give him my best wishes.'

'My, you have got so much front. How could you go and see him in his sick bed after all you have done to him, behind his back.'

'Well, I knew he couldn't do anything to me, he can't even hold a chopper now, let alone take my fingers off.'

'I don't believe I'm hearing this,' he said. 'Do you mean to say I've been up here all this time, away from my mother while she has been ill and all for nothing? Why didn't you tell me last time you were up here?'

'Well, you never asked, I thought you were up here because of Violet, not because you thought old Ede had snuffed it. I'm sorry, Barny, I never meant to keep you away from your poor old mum.'

'It's all right, mate, at least I will be able to see the old girl now, without the fear of being collared. What time does the train go back?'

'I'm not sure, but I think it's in about two hours.'

'Right, we will go back to the vicarage and let Beth and her father know that we are going back home today. Come on, you fool, follow me.'

When they arrived back at the vicarage, Beth and her father were sitting around the table, talking. Beth looked up at Barny. 'Are you going back home today?'

'Yes, we hope to be leaving on the next train back to London.'

'Good,' she said. 'I have been having a word with my father and when your mother is well enough to leave the infirmary, she is going to need some good nursing at home, so I thought, if it's all right with you, I would like to come back and look after her until she is better, what do you think?'

'You can't do that,' Barny replied, 'I told you before, it's not a very nice place where we live, I couldn't let you go there. It wouldn't be right.'

Beth's father then interrupted. 'She has been in a lot worse places then that, I can assure you. We have spent five years in Africa.'

'What were you doing there?' asked Bert.

'Spreading God's word,' Beth replied. 'Sometimes we had it very hard, in the jungle, so I am sure I will be able to cope with Wilford Road.'

'It's not just that, where will you stay?' Barny asked. 'We only have three rooms.'

'We have thought of that. I will stay at my uncle's, do you remember, I told you, he is the vicar at St Saviour's church, not far from where you live. He has always wanted me to go and visit him, any time I was down that way. So that's settled,' Beth said, as she looked Barny in the eyes.

'It is really good of you and I really appreciate it, thank you, Beth,' he said.

'Right, I will do you two something to eat and then I'll go and pack a few things in a bag.'

Bert walked out to the scullery with her. 'I don't suppose it would be possible to have some of that bread that you gave me last time I was here?' he asked. 'I have never tasted bread like that before, it was beautiful.'

'It's home-baked,' Beth replied, 'and I'm sure I can find some more to take on the train with you.'

Chapter 7

In the Infirmary

Beth said her goodbyes to her father, and Barny thanked him for all the help he had given him and said that he would see him in about a week's time, all being well, and then they went on their way, in the direction of the train station.

Back home, Violet was missing Barny more than ever. She felt she had to be near him, but that was not possible, so she did the next best thing and spent all her spare time at the bedside of his sick mother.

Every so often his mother would wake up and see Violet sitting at her bedside. 'You shouldn't be here,' she would say, 'you will be married soon and you have another life now. You shouldn't be spending all of your time sitting next to an old woman.'

'You're Barny's mother, I care about you,' she replied. 'I want to be here with you and I feel close to Barny when I am near you.'

'Yes, that's all very well,' his mother replied, 'but you have made your choice, you have chosen another man, another life, and you must let go of Barny, not just for his sake, but for your sake as well.'

'But I have tried so hard to forget him,' she said. 'I just can't. There is not a day goes by when I don't think about him and I know it is all my fault that he has gone. He would be sitting here now if it wasn't for me, and now we don't know when he will coming back. I'll may never see him again.'

'Well, you have only got yourself to blame, my love. You know he thought the world of you and he would have done anything for you, but you have thrown all that away now. You know he's trying to start a new life, in another part of the country.'

'Do you think he will come back to see you here?' she asked.

'Yes, I think he will, when he gets the opportunity. That wouldn't be the reason why you're in here so often is it, that you might accidentally bump in to him?' his mother asked.

'Anyway, how are you feeling now, Mrs Sturt?' Violet said, changing the subject.

'Yes, I'm a lot better than I was, but I'm still getting a lot of pain in my chest; still, mustn't grumble. The doctor said I'm over the worst of it now and it's just going to take a bit of time to get back on my feet, but I will be a lot better once I'm allowed home. Just being in this place makes me feel ill. What's been happening down Wilford, since I've been away?' she asked.

'Oh, you wouldn't believe it,' Violet replied, 'the goings on down that road. Do you remember George Duncan – he comes from Forster Road, you know, he's been living with that Eliza Goodwood.'

'Yes, I know who you mean, she's the one who stands on street corners, waiting for men friends.'

'That's the one,' Violet replied. 'Well, I don't know if you heard, but it was about three weeks ago. I think you might have been laid up in bed. Anyway, there was a big quarrel over Eliza, between Duncan and Eliza's two brothers, George and Hugh. It started out in the road, outside Duncan's rooms, and in the heat of the argument, Hugh Goodwood ran into the house and came out with a knife and a poker. He gave the poker to his brother and they both started going into Duncan and, according to Mrs Bains, who lives next door, Duncan said to the Goodwoods, "I will fight either of you two, but in the proper English way, with our fists not with weapons." But the two brothers were having none of that, they just laid into him. Duncan managed to get away and with the brothers chasing him, he took refuge in an outhouse and locked the door. But it wasn't long before the brothers broke the door down and dragged Duncan out.'

'That Duncan must be a strong lad,' Barny's mother said, 'going through all of that and he's still fighting them off.'

'Yes, and he did manage to get away from them again, but before he did, George hit him across the head with the poker. Mrs Bains said that Duncan stood there, swaying about a bit after he had been hit with the poker, and then ran off, to his rooms at 35 Forster Road. The two brothers also ran to the house and saw Duncan looking out of an upstairs window. They shouted up to Duncan, "Open the door or we will come up and break it in," but Duncan remained inside. They did no more, but rushed up the stairs and burst the door in. Duncan, on hearing them coming, broke through a partitioning of a cupboard and escaped into an adjoining room.'

'Imagine that,' Barny's mother said. 'If you were sitting there, minding your own business, having a cup of tea and all of a sudden a man came through the wall, it would frighten the life out of you.'

'Are you all right, Mrs Sturt?' Violet asked. 'If you're tired I can tell you the rest tomorrow.'

'No, you go on, I'm all right, I've slept enough this last couple of weeks and I'm just getting into this. What happened next?'

'The next night, Duncan was walking down Princess Road when he met the two brothers. He challenged George Goodwood to fight him, and he accepted. Duncan took off his coat, and they started to fight, that's when I was walking by, there was a large crowd by that time. So I stopped to see what was going on and someone from the crowd shouted, "Look what he has in his hand." I was trying to look over the people's shoulders to see what the man was going on about and to find out what Goodwood had in his hand, when Duncan shouted, "That's not fair, Goodwood has got a knuckle duster." Just then two men from the crowd grabbed Goodwood, and took the knuckle duster away from him. The fight carried on and it was then that Hugh Goodwood came out from the crowd and stabbed Duncan on the head with the knife and Duncan fell to the ground.

'I ran up to him, but when I saw his injuries, it made me feel sick. The cut on his head was so deep that you could see the white bone of his skull, the blood was pouring out. By this time a constable had arrived and was blowing his whistle for assistance. I could see the brothers slowly walking towards Wilford Road. The copper shouted for them to stop, but they started to run, but to their misfortune two more coppers came round the corner and bumped into them. They put the cuffs on them and brought them back to the crowd. No one from the crowd would tell the first constable what had happened, until this little old woman walked up and said, "He did it, that man there, he was the one." Everyone was shocked that someone had pointed the finger at the brothers. They all looked at the old lady as she stood there shaking.'

'She had some guts,' Barny's mother said, 'did she not realise what she was doing or what she was letting herself in for?'

'I don't know,' Violet said. 'I don't think she came from around our way, she thought she was doing the right thing.'

'What happened next?'

'Well, three more constables came running down the road and one of them took the old lady away, I think for her own safety, and then they took Duncan off to the infirmary on a barrow and then they started to ask the two brothers what they had done to Duncan. Hugh Goodwood said, "Yes, all right, I gave him a good hiding and I stabbed him, he deserved it."

'They're a rough lot those Goodwoods,' Mrs Sturt said. 'I know their mother; you don't look at her the wrong way or you will end up with a black eye.'

'Yes, I know,' Violet said, 'if it wasn't for that old woman they would have got away with it again. I started talking to one of the constables as he was writing something down and he was saying that Hugh Goodwood had been brought up and spent his whole life among a terrible gang of thieves and receivers and on his last conviction, for housebreaking, the court gave him one last chance and instead of sending him to prison, they sent him to borstal in the hope that he would go straight. But the constable said that as soon as he left the borstal, he returned straight to his family and associated with the same old gang.'

'What do you expect?' Mrs Sturt said. 'You can't change someone like that, it's in their blood, they will never lead an honest life. Did they get put away in the end?'

'Yes,' Violet replied, 'they both got two months hard labour, but that's not the end of the story, it gets worse. After the court case, Duncan and Eliza were walking back home and when they turned the corner of Forster Road, they met Eliza's other brother and her father, who were standing there waiting for them. Duncan left Eliza talking to them and quickly went indoors. The Goodwoods followed and Eliza went upstairs to Duncan's room while her brother and father waited at the bottom of the stairs. When she went into the room, there was Duncan, his brother and the landlady Mrs Gould. Duncan walked over to Eliza and told her that he had had enough of her family and he didn't want to see her any more.'

'Well, you can't blame him,' said Mrs Sturt, 'all that trouble he's been through with her brothers, no wonder he wanted to call it off. What happened when he told her that?'

'She did no more,' said Violet, 'she went across the room to the table and picked up a knife and drew it across his chin, but only making a slight wound. Duncan looked at his brother and said, "Go for a constable now," which he did. They reckon Mrs Gould, the landlady, tried to get Eliza to put the knife down, but as she was talking to her, Eliza leant across the table again and drew the knife down the right side of his face, saying, "There, you can take that." It wasn't all her fault though, so it came out in court. Duncan led her a dog's life; he made her go on the streets to get money for him and his mother.'

'You're joking,' Mrs Sturt said, 'do you mean it was all his fault that she was out on the streets.'

'Yes,' replied Violet, 'he used to take her to all the public houses and to Tooting Bec common and other places for that purpose. Eliza told the coppers who came to the house that Duncan said that he was going to sharpen his knife to chop her brother's head off. She also said that he had fractured her ribs because she did not bring enough money in from the streets and she had to sell her boots and baby's shawl to buy food for him and his mother. On the way out of the house Eliza called to her brother and father and said, "They have got the knife and are taking me off to the station." Her brother turned to his father and said, "Old man, you stop Duncan and I'll do the copper," but as they were moving closer, two more constables came down the road and they never had the chance to get near to Duncan.'

'What happened in court?' Mrs Sturt asked.

'Eliza got off,' replied Violet. 'It sounds as if the court felt sorry for her, she has been in prison quite a few times in the past and what with the way she was treated by Duncan. They told her to sever her connections with Duncan and if she came before the court again, she would find herself in serious trouble.'

'So she never had any punishment at all,' Mrs Sturt said.

'She did in a way,' Violet said, 'they gave her one day's imprisonment, which would mean that she would be released at the rising of the court.'

'So she never had no punishment,' said Mrs Sturt.
'Not really, but she had been through a lot.'
'You do miss things, being laid up in here,' Mrs Sturt said.
'You will laugh at this,' Violet said, as she changed positions on the bed. 'You know Elisabeth Maisey, the laundress from Whitehorse Road, the big fat woman?'
'Yes, I've seen her walking up and down the road with her kids, never says hello, not very friendly. What's she up to now?'
'Last Friday night it was, yes, I'm sure that was the day. She was as drunk as a skunk in Whitehorse Road, and she had her baby with her, the one aged eleven months. Anyway as she was walking down the road, she must have felt a bit tired and she came across a mail cart outside one of the shops and, as she walked passed it, she plonked her baby in it and started pushing it along the road. They say she got as far as Boulogne Road and started to fall over. She must have had more drink in her because by the time she was half way down Boulogne Road she couldn't stand up. A woman, passing by, had to hold her up until a constable arrived. He asked her if she had been drinking and she replied, "No, I've only had a little, perhaps a glass or two of beer, but not much," and when asked why she took the mail cart she replied, "What mail cart? I put my baby on a tram as we were going to Thornton Heath to do a bit of shopping. I never saw no mail cart."
'Do you mean to say she mistook the mail cart for a tram?' Mrs Sturt asked. 'Anything could have happened to that poor little baby. What did the courts say?'
'She was discharged with a caution and they told her she ought not to take anything intoxicating again, especially with the baby in her arms, but you can bet your life she was drinking as soon as she left the courts. She is always drunk,' Violet said. 'I feel sorry for the kids and her husband.'
As Violet turned to look at Mrs Sturt, she saw a big smile on her face and her eyes were focused on the door of the ward. Violet looked round and there, standing in the doorway, was Barny. Violet's heart skipped a beat as Barny walked over to the bed. 'How are you, Mum?' he said, as he wrapped his arms around her and gave her a kiss on the cheek.
'It's so good to see you, Barny,' she said. 'I knew you wouldn't stay away while I was in here.'

In the Infirmary

'Yes, I came back as soon as I could, Mum. Sorry I wasn't here when you were took ill, but I will make it up to you now.'

Violet got off the bed and took a step back. She couldn't help noticing the pretty dark-haired young girl who was standing in the doorway looking over.

'Are you going to stay with me now, son?' his mother asked.

'For as long as I can, Mum, I've so much to tell you. I have been sorting everything out for us and you won't believe this. I have even brought you your own nurse so you can leave this place and be nursed at home. She will stay with you until you're back on your feet.' He looked across at Beth. 'Come over and meet my mother,' he said.

As Beth walked across the ward towards Mrs Sturt's bed, Violet's face dropped and she gave Beth the dirtiest of looks. They walked to the end of the bed and she started to feel in the way.

'This is Beth, Mum, she's the one I've been telling you about.'

'Hello, Mrs Sturt, Barny's told me such a lot about you and your husband.'

'Hello, my love. My, don't you talk nicely,' Barny's mum said. 'You're so neat and tidy, with such a lovely face. You don't get much of that around here I'm afraid, except Violet there of course, and what brings you down to these parts?'

'Well, I don't know if Barny has told you or not, but I'm a qualified nurse and I've come down to look after you until you're back on your feet.'

'Really,' she said, 'they told me I can go home if I had someone to look after me. Well, this is good news.'

As Mrs Sturt and Beth were talking and making plans, Barny looked across at Violet. Their eyes met and they just stood there staring at each other. 'Are you all right?' Barny asked.

'Yes, I'm fine,' she replied.

'I never expected to see you here,' he said.

'I've been coming every day since your mother was admitted, just to keep her company.'

'Thanks for doing that. By the way, do you know where my father is?'

'He's got himself a job now at Gillett and Johnson. I think he started there about two weeks ago.'

'Is that right, Mum?' Barny asked, interrupting Beth.

'What's that, love?'

'Father, starting work.'

'Yes, and he's doing really well; mind you he's only sweeping up and helping to make up the crates when they need doing, but he's enjoying it.'

Barny rubbed his head. 'But I told him I would look after both of you, there is no need for him to go out to work.'

'Yes, but you know what he's like,' his mother replied, 'he needs to get out and needs to keep himself busy. It's done him the world of good, he looks a lot better since he's been there.'

'I better be going now,' Violet said, as she picked up her bag from the bed.

'OK, my love, thanks for coming in and make sure you come and see me when I get home.'

Violet said her goodbyes and made her way to the door. Beth poked her elbow in Barny's side. 'You need to go and speak to Violet, you know, what we talked about earlier, the wedding and that.'

'Oh right, I'll go and catch up with her, I see you in a minute.' He ran out and caught Violet up in the corridor. 'Violet, I need to talk to you.'

'Well, I didn't think you would want to know me any more, now that you have your fancy woman,' she replied.

'It is my so-called fancy woman Beth, who has asked me to come and talk to you,' he said.

'Oh yes and what does she want you to talk to me about?'

'Well, Beth is the daughter of a vicar,' he said.

'I did wonder what those things were that was sticking out of her back. Of course, I should have known, it was her wings.'

'There is no need to be sarcastic,' Barny said. 'What I was going to tell you was that she knows what is right from wrong and she thinks you are making a big mistake getting married for the sake of your parents. It will only cause pain in the end.'

'What do you think?' Violet asked.

'You know what I think. You have told me what your plans are and there is not much I can do about it,' he replied.

'So, in other words, you don't care what I do,' she said.

Barny looked her in the eyes. 'I don't care,' he replied. 'When you told me on that day what you were going to do, it broke my heart and the next few days I went through hell and back. If it wasn't for Beth and her father, I wouldn't be here now.'

'What is she, some kind of saint, giving advice to someone she doesn't even know? And it looks like she has certainly charmed her way into your mother's heart.'

'Look, she was just a bit worried about you when I told her about the wedding, that's all. I told her all about what had happened between us and she feels you are getting married for all the wrong reasons and you should think twice about it,' he said.

'The bloody interfering bitch, who does she think she is, trying to tell me what to do with my life? If it wasn't for your mother being with her now, I would go back in there and smack her in her interfering face.'

'Look, just go home, Violet. I don't care any more, do whatever you want to, go and get married, ruin your life, see if we care,' he said.

'Oh, so it's we now, is it?' Violet replied. 'I knew you were more than just good friends, and I thought I was the one you loved.'

'Yes, that's right and I thought you loved me once,' he replied. She turned round to him and slapped him around the face and then ran down the corridor. Barny just stood there with tears in his eyes, not from the slap on his face, but to hear Violet's voice in anger. What can I do, he thought to himself, I do love her and I want her more than anything else in the world, but....

Just then Bert walked up to him. 'What's wrong with Violet, she has just run past me crying her eyes out.'

'Forget about it,' Barny said. 'What are you doing here anyway?'

'I've just come back to let you know that I have taken Beth's bags to St Saviour's and just thought I would pop back to see how your mother was.'

'Bert, you know how she feels about you and that Fanny woman you were seeing,' said Barny.

'Yea, but that's all over now, she'll be all right, she likes me,' Bert replied. His face soon changed when they walked into the ward and he saw Mrs Sturt's face, as she looked over to him. 'Hello, Mrs Sturt, and how are you feeling?' he asked.

'Hello, Bert, I'm all right and how is Fanny?' she replied.

'I don't see her any more, Mrs Sturt.'

'Why is that. You know her husband's laid up in here. I thought that would be an ideal opportunity for you to go round and see her.'

'Leave him alone, Mum,' Barny said.

'Well, I'm only speaking my mind. Anyway, thanks for coming to see me, Bert, and I'm glad you're not seeing that man's wife any more, the poor soul. Did you hear what happened to him, Barny?, she asked.

'No, I didn't, Mum.'

'Well, what the nurse has been telling me, he took a fall down at the coal yard, just as a train was going past and, as he fell, his hand went underneath the wheels of the train and it took all of his fingers off.'

Bert looked at Barny across the bed, as if to say, if only she knew what really happened to Charlie Ede's fingers.

After he had made sure Mrs Sturt was comfortable in her bed, with Beth looking after her, Barny and Bert made their way to Gillett and Johnson to meet his father. Gillett and Johnson was a large bell foundry and clock works, with a world-wide reputation for its bells. As they walked through the gates of the foundry, they heard a voice from the gate house. 'Hello, Barny, what are you up to?'

Barny looked round, it was his old pal Chas. 'How are you doing, you old rascal?' Chas asked.

'I'm all right, mate,' Barny replied. 'I never knew you worked in here.'

'Yea, I've been working here for about a year now, just keeping an eye on things and making sure no one nicks any of the iron. Do you know I wondered if that was your father who started here last week,' he said.

'Yes, I only found out myself today, that's why we're here now, I thought we would come and meet the old boy,' Barny replied.

'Well, you can go into the factory. I'll just see this horse and cart out and I'll be with you. If anyone says anything to you, just tell them I let you in.'

They left Chas trying to sort the horse and cart out while they opened the door to the factory and when they looked in, they could see Mr Sturt in the middle of the floor, leaning against his broom, just about to blow his nose. As they were standing there looking at Mr Sturt, two young lads, both aged about 24, walked over to him and then with no warning kicked his broom away, making him overbalance and fall to the ground. 'Come on, Sturty,' they heard one of the lads shout. 'You're not supposed to stand there and blow your trumpet all day. Get on with your sweeping, old man.'

Mr Sturt tried to get himself up and, as he did, one of the lads took his cap and threw it across the foundry floor.

In the Infirmary

'Come on, Barny, let's go and kick the life out of them,' Bert said. Just then Chas walked in behind them. 'I'm sorry about that, Barny, those two are right gits. That's all they do all day, go round taking the mick and picking on all the other workers. They tell everyone that they are really hard and there is no one harder than them where they come from.'

'Where do they come from?' Barny asked.

'Coulsdon, I think they said, I don't take a lot of notice of them. They say everyone's scared of them where they come from and I think it has rubbed off on the workers in here, even the foreman won't say anything to them. They get away with murder in here. I've been told that they have been picking on your father a lot since he's started working here, but this is the first time I have seen it happen.'

'What are we going to do?' Bert asked. 'We can't let them get away with it.'

'Go in there, Barny, and give them a good kicking, they are long overdue,' said Chas.

'No, my father wouldn't thank me for doing that, it will knock his pride if we go in there and sort them out in front of everyone. He will never admit that he needs help and he will never ask for it, he's a proud man. Is there still a loading yard around the back?'

'Yes, it's where the horses and carts come in off Union Road to be loaded.'

'Is there anyone round there now?'

'No, just a cart waiting to be loaded with a bell that is already on the hoist above it.'

'Right,' Barny said, 'give us a few minutes and then go down and tell them two that there's a young lady who wants to talk to them and she is waiting in the loading bay for them.'

'OK, Barny, I'll make sure no one else comes out there, so you can do what you like to them.'

Barny and Bert walked round to the back yard and waited anxiously until the door from the factory opened and the two men walked out, looking around them, expecting a young lady to greet them, but they were in for a shock. Barny jumped out from behind a stack of iron and grabbed them both by the hair, forcing them to the ground. Bert then ran up with a rope and started to tie their hands and feet together and

At the Precipice of Poverty

then put a rope around both of them. Once they were both bound tightly together, they lifted them on to the empty cart, which was waiting to be loaded with a two-ton bell, hanging five feet above the cart on a hoist. They pushed them directly under the bell and tied them to the cart and then Barny shouted to Bert, 'Pull the chain.' He jumped off the cart and grabbed the chain that made the bell go up and down. When his feet touched the ground he let the chain go. The bell had dropped about twelve inches.

This never frightened the young lads, they just carried on calling Barny all the names under the sun and telling him what they were going to do to him when they were free.

'Pull it again, Bert,' Barny shouted and Bert pulled the chain with all his might; the bell moved down another eight inches. The lads both realised now what was happening. The colour started to drain from their faces, burn marks appeared on their arms and necks from the ropes as they tried to move away from under the bell to avoid certain painful death.

'Another pull, Bert, and make it a hard one,' he shouted again. This time Bert climbed back on to the cart. He kicked the two lads in the legs and then jumped again at the chain, bringing it down with untold force, but he wasn't quick enough to let go of the chain this time and it threw him to the ground, breaking his thumb.

'I'm going to kill them two, Barny,' he shouted, 'you see if I don't.'

When the chain had finished going round the bell, stopped it; one side of it was now touching the two lads across the hips, the rest of their bodies had disappeared inside the bell.

'One more pull should do it,' Barny shouted. 'That should be enough to crush them and then we will leave them to die slowly under the weight of the bell.'

'No don't, please don't pull it down any more,' the two lads cried hysterically. 'What have we done to you? Why are you doing this to us? We don't know you, why are you putting us through this? If you want money we have a few pennies in our pockets, you can have that, but please don't bring the bell down any further.'

Barny walked over and looked under the big bell. 'You're ten seconds away from being maimed or worse,' he said. 'Now, how does it feel to be picked on by someone for no reason? It's not very nice is it?'

In the Infirmary

'We haven't been picking on you, so what argument have you got with us?' one of the boys asked.

'Do you know that old man in the foundry?' Barny said, as he grabbed one of the lad's legs and twisted it round. 'You know, the one that sweeps the floors, the one you just knocked over and threw his cap across the floor? Well, he's my father.'

'We never knew that,' the boys cried, 'we won't touch him any more if you let us go, we promise. We will make it up to him, please just get us off the cart.'

'Right,' Barny said, 'if you want to save yourselves then there is only one way you can do it. I want you to go back into the foundry, and get my father's cap down from the top of the crane where you threw it and give it back to him and then say sorry to him.'

'Yes, all right, we will do anything, just get that bell away from us.'

'OK, Bert,' Barny shouted, 'take the bell back up, I think they've learnt their lesson now.'

As the bell went up and the boys, faces appeared from under it, they looked at Barny, both still sobbing like two small children.

'Are you sure you want us to stop?' Barny asked.

'Yes, just please get us off,' they shouted.

When the bell was high enough, Barny dragged them off the cart and leIf I hear that you have been picking on anyone on that foundry floor, especially my father, myself and my good friend Bert will come back and I promise you we will break both your legs. Do you understand what I am saying?'

'Yes, yes,' they replied.

'Untie them, Bert.'

'Hold on a minute, Barny,' Bert shouted as he kneeled down by the side of the two lads. 'Tell me, where do you two hard boys come from? Are there no other men where you live?'

'Yes, of course there are,' one of the boys replied.

'Then how come we have been told that you two lemons are really hard around where you come from?'

'We never said that, we just look hard.'

'Oh, I'm sorry, I didn't realise, we should have been really afraid of these two, Barny,' he said. 'Right, now when I untie you, it would make me the happiest man alive if you both get up and start having a go at me, because you know what you two have done, you made me break my thumb and I would just love to put you both in the infirmary for that. But my friend Barny is in a good mood today and he has decided to let you off without a beating, so get up slowly, say sorry to me and Barny and then walk back in there and get Mr Sturt's cap down. Then say sorry to him and tell him it won't happen again and remember, we only live round the corner from here and the next time we hear you have been picking on someone, you won't be so lucky.'

Bert untied them and they got up and said sorry. 'Now be on your way,' he said, as he hit them both round the heads.

'Come on, Bert,' Barny said, 'let's go and meet my old man.' They walked round to the front of the foundry just as Mr Sturt came out of the doors.

'Oh, I might have known you two would have something to do with it,' he said, as he walked up to them.

'To do with what?' Barny asked.

'Those two boys in there, both were like devils this morning, now they look like two little lost lambs. I wondered who had spoken to them – it was you two weren't it? Well, you didn't have to, I could have sorted them out in my own time, I don't need you fighting my battles, Barny Sturt, I've told you before.'

'No, of course you don't,' Barny replied. 'Look, let's just go home and stop arguing shall we?'

'Well, as long as you know, I can stand up for myself.'

As they left the foundry Barny shouted over to Chas and put his thumb up to him and then the two lads walked out. Normally they would be shouting and pushing people about, but now they just walked out with their heads bowed. Barny's father said that he had to go to Whitehorse Road to pick up some mutton for their tea tonight and as they turned into Whitehorse Road, Barny was in front with his father talking and Bert was behind.

All of a sudden Barny felt Bert pull at his arm. 'Here, come and have a look at this.'

Barny looked behind him and to his surprise he saw a horse and cart come tearing down Whitehorse Road, going from one side of the road to the other and being chased by a constable on a bicycle, and every time the constable caught up with the cart, the driver would pull the horse to one side, forcing the constable to mount the pavement. Barny and Bert just stood there rolling up with laughter. They laughed so much that they were nearly falling over, even Mr Sturt had a little chuckle to himself. As the cart went past them, the constable was level with the three of them. He was pedalling like mad with his whistle in his mouth, blowing as hard as he could. He looked over at the three of them laughing at him and as he passed he pointed, as if to say, don't you dare laugh at me. A little bit further down, the cart drew across the road, forcing the constable back on to the path and into the wall of a shop and then as the cart turned back the other way, it also mounted the pavement and came to a halt hitting another front wall. The constable quickly picked himself up, still blowing on his whistle, ran over to the cart and pulled the driver down.

Barny, his father and Bert all walked over. Barny and Bert still couldn't stop themselves from laughing. The driver of the cart was as drunk as a lord, he couldn't even stand up. There was also another man on the cart and the driver said that the other man had the reins, but the officer soon put him straight. He called across to Barny and said, 'You have had your laugh now, son, come and give me a hand to tie the horse up and make it safe and then hold on to this man.'

Barny shouted back to him, 'Do it yourself, copper,' but Barny's father was there and he didn't like Barny using that attitude.

'Get over there, Barny, now,' he said, 'and help him out.'

Barny went straight across to the constable and asked him what he wanted him to do.

'Tie the horse to that gas lamp and then take hold of this man until help comes.'

Barny stood there with the man, holding him up against the shop door, while Bert took hold of the horse and kept it quiet.

The man who was driving the horse was trying to tell Barny that he was not the one holding the reins, but the other man was and he had not had a drink all day. Barny called across to the constable, 'Did you hear what this man is saying?

'Yes, I heard, but you know who was holding the reins, you saw him.'

'I never saw anything, I wasn't even looking that way,' Barny said.

'I saw him,' Barny's dad shouted, as he walked across the road, 'he was the one who was holding the reins.'

'Dad, just be quiet,' Barny said, 'you'll get the man locked up.'

'He was doing wrong, Barny,' his father replied, 'he could have killed someone, don't you realise that. He has to be punished.'

'All right, Dad, you know best.' Barny agreed with the constable that the man was the one holding the reins, against his better judgement.

After about half an hour a constable and Detective Sharp, an old enemy of Barny's, came walking up. The detective immediately took hold of Barny's arm and said, 'At last, Sturt, I've got you for something.'

'It's not me, you fool,' Barny replied pushing the detective away.

The first constable came up. 'He's right, it's not him, sir, it is him on the ground.'

The detective looked at Barny. 'I can wait,' he said.

Barny looked back at him and replied. 'You'll push me too far one day and you'll be sorry.'

'That will be the day I am waiting for, just give me one good reason to put you away for good,' he said.

As the police took the prisoners away, Bert came and stood next to Barny. 'That copper's got it in for you,' he said. 'I wouldn't cross him too much if I was you, Barny. You know how they can make things up. He'll have you inside straight away, you know he's just waiting for the chance.'

'That will never happen,' Barny replied, 'they will have to kill me first before they lock me away.'

'I don't think that will bother him too much.'

'What do you mean?' Barny asked.

'Well, I've heard that if he is out to get someone, he will do anything and he always gets them in the end, whether it's life in prison or dead in some alley, but he always removes them from the streets. You just need to be careful, Barny, where he's concerned.'

Just then Barny's father came over. 'Are we going to pick up that mutton and go home or what?' he asked.

'Yes. Anything to stop you moaning,' Barny replied.

'Well, I will be off now, Barny, I'll have a few things to do,' Bert said. 'I'll pop round and see you tomorrow.'

'OK, Bert, I'll see you later.'

When Barny and his father arrived home, the strong smell of stew was coming from the scullery. 'Who's out there cooking, is it Doris?' his father asked.

'No, that's Beth. Oh, I never had the time to tell you did I? She has come back with me to help look after Mother until she's on her feet again.'

In the Infirmary

'No one tells me anything around here do they?'

They walked into the bedroom and Mrs Sturt was sitting up in bed. 'That girl, Beth, is wonderful,' she said, 'nothing's too much trouble for her.'

'You look a lot better,' her husband said.

'I feel a lot better now that I'm back home.'

'Well, that girl might be wonderful, but where is she going to sleep?' Barny's father asked. 'There is no room here.'

'Don't worry, Dad, it's all sorted. The vicar at St Saviour's Church is a relation of hers and she is going to stay there, unless Mum needs her here of course,' Barny replied.

'What does Violet think about that?' his father asked. 'You know she has still got a soft spot for you, Barny.'

'It has nothing to do with her. She has made her choice and she can live with it.'

Just then Beth walked in with a tray. 'Here you are, Mrs Sturt. Now you must eat all of this,' she said. 'Hello, you must be Barny's dad. Pleased to meet you.'

'Hello, love, thanks for all your help with the wife and that, I really appreciate it.'

'That's OK,' she said, 'I have put your dinners on the table in the scullery, if you want to go through now and get them before they get cold. I'll stay with Mrs Sturt.'

After dinner they sat round Mrs Sturt's bed and Beth was telling them all about village life and her days in Africa, helping the people out there. 'Now what do you want me to do, Mrs Sturt?' Beth asked, 'I can stop here and sleep in the chair in the scullery or I can go and stay at St Saviour's and come back first thing in the morning. Now it's up to you, whatever you think is best.'

'No, my love, you go, I'll be all right, Mr Sturt's here with me now. Barny, get Beth's shawl and then you can walk her home.'

'I was going to walk her home anyway, Mum,' he replied.

On the way back to St Saviour's Church, Barny thanked Beth for all she had done, helping his mother.

'I don't want thanking,' she replied, 'I am happy to help out. By the way, did you speak to Violet?'

'Yes, I did, but she was not too pleased about what you said.'

At the Precipice of Poverty

'No, I never thought she would be, but you must keep trying, Barny, you must try and get through to her that she is making a big mistake. Perhaps it would be better if I spoke to her.'

'No, I don't think that would be a good idea. Leave it to me, I will have another word with her when I see her again.'

The next day, Beth came round bright and early and Barny opened the door to her. 'What are you doing?' he asked, 'I was just leaving to come and meet you. I told you not to walk round here on your own.'

'Don't worry, Barny, I'm all right. Anyway, how is your mother feeling today?'

'She seems all right, but you know she doesn't complain much, so I don't really know how she feels. My father's not at work today,' he said, 'he will look after my mother so you won't be needed and I thought I could show you around the town, if that's all right with you, that is.'

'Yes, that would be nice,' she replied. 'I will make sure your mother's comfortable and prepare some food for her and then we can think about going out.'

Once Beth had made sure Mrs Sturt was comfortable, she left with Barny. As they were about to walk out of the front door, Doris from upstairs was just walking in. 'Hello, Barny, I haven't seen you around for some time. Did they put you away for a little while?' she said.

'No, I joined the navy and I've been all around the world.'

'You lying little sod,' Doris replied, 'I know where you have been, your mother told me.'

'Well, why ask then?'

'Because I knew you would come out with some old cock and bull story, and who is this young lady?' she asked.

'Mind your own bloody business,' Barny replied. 'It's nothing to do with you, who she is.'

Beth quickly interrupted. 'Hello, I'm Beth. I'm looking after Mrs Sturt until she is back on her feet again.'

'Oh yes, that's good of you, and where are you going with this scallywag,' she asked. 'If you're supposed to be looking after that poor woman, what are you doing leaving her?'

'We are just going into town to get married,' Barny replied.

In the Infirmary

Doris looked at Barny with the dirtiest of looks. 'Your tongue will drop out one of these days, you see if it doesn't,' she said. 'Don't spend too much time with him, love. You look a nice girl, but you won't stay that way for long, not if you are going out with him.'

'Go on,' Barny said, 'get up them stairs before I tell all the neighbours that you've got holes in your drawers.'

'I have not,' she replied.

'You have. I've seen them on the washing line.'

'You wait, you little sod, I'm telling your mother about you,' she said, slamming the door in Barny's face and storming up the stairs.

'What was all that about?' Beth asked.

'She lives upstairs. That's what the real people are like around here. You have to give them as much as they give you.'

'Have you ever tried getting on with her?' Beth asked.

'No, that would be a nightmare. I feel quite happy after I've had a few words with old Doris.'

That was Beth's first encounter with a Wilford Road resident and she never dreamt that her next one would only be a few minutes away. At the same time as they left the house, Violet was just closing her front door across the road and she always looked across at Barny's house, in the hope that she would catch a glimpse of him, but she wasn't too happy with what she saw. At that moment, Barny was still laughing at Doris and Beth had both her arms around his neck, jokingly trying to stop him laughing at an old woman's misfortune. What Violet saw was a young couple having fun together, without a care in the world, unlike her situation.

She walked across the road to meet them. Barny looked up and stopped laughing. His face dropped. He knew Violet couldn't hold back her words even if she wanted to, she always said what was going through her mind. He took Beth's hand. 'Beth, this is Violet,' he said.

Beth looked up. 'Hello, I'm pleased to meet you,' she said.

'Are you,' Violet replied, 'and why would you be pleased to meet me?'

'Well, Barny's told me a lot about you.'

'Has he. Well, he's got no bloody right to tell you anything about my life.'

'Now hold on, Violet, Beth's only trying to be friendly.'

Violet looked round at Barny. 'That's it, take her side, you soon changed your bloody tune.'

'I'm not taking anyone's side,' Barny said. 'Beth was just concerned that you were making a big mistake.'

Violet started to raise her voice. 'The last thing I want is a toffee-nosed, stuck-up, posh-talking bitch telling me what to do with my life. She should keep her nose out of my business and you should keep your mouth shut. I bet you have had a right old laugh talking about me. Do you tell her everything, Barny Sturt?'

'You've got it all wrong,' said Beth, 'we would never laugh at you.'

'I told you what I think of you so I think it's best if you keep that mouth shut or you're going to feel the back of my hand,' Violet said, as she pushed Beth's shoulder.

'Right, that's enough,' Barny said, as he stood between them. 'On your way, Violet. Beth don't deserve all this, she hasn't done anything against you. She was just concerned, that's the sort of person she is; she cares. That's something none of us are used to around here.'

'I thought you were close to me, Barny, but all you're doing is sticking up for lady muck there.'

'I hope we still are close,' Barny said, 'but I won't let you talk to Beth like that, it's not right.'

Violet turned and ran across the road and back to her house, sobbing her heart out. 'You know she still loves you, Barny,' Beth said.

'I don't think so,' Barny replied. 'If she did, then why did she walk out on me and why is she marrying that sergeant bloke?'

'It seems to me that she is a very confused girl. What she is doing is not what she wants.'

Just then they heard a raised voice coming from across the road.

'Barny Sturt, I want a word with you.' They looked across the road and saw Violet's father storming towards them. 'Why can't you leave my daughter alone?' he shouted. 'Why do you keep upsetting her all the time? I thought we had seen the last of you when you left, but you keep coming back, trying to ruin things for her.' He walked up to Barny and pressed his finger against Barny's face. 'Now, I'm telling you for the last time, keep out of her life. She is going to marry a man who is going to make her very happy and she is going to have more than you could ever hope to offer her.'

Barny stepped back. 'Mr Blake, I respect you because you're Violet's father, but please take your finger out of my face,' he said.

'You don't frighten me, you scum, I've heard about what you get up to and it's about time someone with guts taught you a lesson you won't forget.'

'Please just go back to your house, Mr Blake, I don't want to fight with you,' Barny said.

Beth quickly got between them. 'Look,' she said, 'I'm his new girlfriend, he doesn't want anything to do with Violet any more. She is in the past. He has me now so let's stop all of this before someone gets hurt.'

'If that's the truth, then there is no point in giving him a beating, as long as he keeps away from my Violet.'

'Yes, I'm am sure he will now,' said Beth.

'You want to be careful, young lady, you seem like you have breeding. You're too good for him,' he said. Barny stood there biting his tongue. It took all of his will power to hold back his temper.

He wouldn't normally let anyone talk to him like that, especially in front of a crowd, which had gathered when Mr Blake started to shout. As Violet's father was going back to his house, he turned and said to Barny, 'I wouldn't be around here when Violet's sergeant gets home on leave. I shall tell him what you have been up to and you'll be in for a good beating.'

Barny shook his head and laughed, 'Who does he thinks he is?'

'You don't know what Violet has said to him, he is only protecting his daughter. Come on, let's go and forget about all of this.'

Beth remarked that she had never seen such a crowd gather in such a short time. 'Did they just stop to see the argument?'

'Yea, you don't normally get an argument around here without a fight and that's what they were waiting for. I have known them to stand out in the pouring rain and freezing cold to see some poor soul get his head kicked in; it's the only enjoyment some of them get around here.'

'You certainly weren't joking when you said it was rough where you came from. No wonder you want your parents to move away,' she said.

As they walked along Wilford Road, Barny said that he was a bit worried about Violet, he had never seen her so angry. 'She is jealous of me, that's why,' Beth said.

'If she doesn't want me any more, what has she got to be jealous about?' Barny asked.

'Well, perhaps if she can't have you, she doesn't want anyone else to be with you,' Beth replied. 'By the way, I hope you didn't mind me saying that I was your new girlfriend, it was the only thing I could think of at the time. I thought he was going to hit you.'

'No, I don't mind at all, at least it has got him off my back.'

'What are you going to do when that, what did he call him, yes, the sergeant, what are you going to do when he comes home? He's bound to go looking for you if he's been told a pack of lies.'

'Believe me, I will look forward to that, everyone's been telling me what an arrogant pig he is,' Barny said.

For the next four days, Beth spent half her time looking after Mrs Sturt and the rest of her time she spent with Barny. They became quite close. She came to like him a lot and the feelings were mutual.

Chapter 8

The Final Fight

On the Saturday morning, Barny had to catch the train back up to that little village deep in the heart of the Nottinghamshire countryside. He said his goodbyes to his mother and father and then Beth walked him to the station. When they arrived outside the station entrance, Beth asked him what platform the train left from. 'I'm not sure,' said Barny.

'But you have caught the train to Nottingham many times before,' she said, 'don't you remember?'

'No, I have never caught this train before. I have always hidden on the coal train and this is the first time I have been able to pay the fare,' he replied.

'The things you get up to, I don't know,' she said.

When they finally found the right platform they sat down on the bench together. 'The train don't pull in for fifteen minutes, Beth. You don't have to wait with me, you can go home if you want,' he said.

'No, I want to stay with you,' she replied. 'There is something I would like to ask you.'

'Oh yes, you have that serious look on your face. Am I going to like this?'

'I'm not sure, but I am going to talk to you about it anyway whether you like it or not. I feel that you really ought to think about giving up the fighting, for your parents' sake.'

'But I am doing it for them.'

'Yes, I know, but have you ever thought how it would affect them if something bad happened to you? I think it would just about finish your mother off.'

'Do you know something, Beth, you are so different from Violet. She was always egging me on to go up there and win the money, so we could go out and have a good time.'

'Well, she must have had her reasons, but I am sure it wasn't just for the money. Now, don't change the subject. Will you promise me that you will think about it this coming weekend?'

'Yes, I promise. Now are you sure you're going to be all right looking after my mother until I come back?'

'Yes, of course. Here comes your train. Now take care and give my love to my father and tell him I will see him soon.'

As Barny boarded the train he stopped and turned to Beth. 'One more thing, before I go, please don't go near Violet,' he said.

Beth laughed. 'What are you laughing at?' he asked.

'Is it me you're worried about or Violet?'

'It's you, of course,' he said, as he rubbed his hand gently on her face.

Beth put both her arms around him and kissed him on the forehead, but then their eyes met and then their lips and it was only the guard's whistle to say that the train was pulling out that stopped them kissing for any longer.

As Barny pulled away they looked into each other's eyes – no words were said. Barny winked and squeezed her hand tightly and left.

Beth sat back down on the bench. How did that happen? she wondered. I know he loves Violet and I can't fall in love with him, it would be wrong. She closed her eyes and sat there thinking about him. She knew it was too late, he was more than a just good friend to her now and she wanted him more than ever. No one had ever kissed her like that before and she had never felt like this about anyone else. After a short while she left the station and took a walk around the shops before she made her way back home, but Barny was all she could think about. After a short time of looking in a few shops and buying some flowers for Mrs Sturt, she jumped on a tram and headed for home. As she approached Wilford Road, Violet was just leaving the butcher's shop. They both stopped and looked at each other and then Beth carried on walking.

The Final Fight

'Where is lover boy this morning?' Violet shouted over to her. Beth stopped and looked back at her. 'I beg your pardon?' she said. Violet then walked up to her. 'Your innocent looks and posh words don't work with me. I know what your little game is, bitch,' Violet said. 'I know you're not down here just to look after some old woman, you're trying to get your claws into my Barny, isn't that right?'

'That's not true at all,' said Beth, 'you have it all wrong again. I only came down here to look after Mrs Sturt until she is back on her feet again and even if I did fancy Barny it has nothing to do with you any more. You left him, remember?'

Violet's eyes filled with anger and all she wanted to do was to smack Beth in the face. 'I suppose you know everyone's talking about you. Oh, what a pretty face she has and what a kind, helpful young lady she is. That's the sort of thing they are saying about you and it makes me sick. You come down here and everyone falls at your feet and goes out of their way to do everything they can for you, including Barny, but you can't pull the wool over my eyes. I know that you're a scheming little bitch and people won't be saying how pretty you are when I'm finished with you.'

'Do you know what, Violet,' Beth said, 'I feel so sorry for you. You have so much hatred inside you. Barny tells me you are a really nice person deep down, but why do you always have to put this act on all of the time? If you love Barny then go back to him, I'm sure he will have you back if you ask him. You know you can't marry someone for what they can just give you. It's not fair on you and it's not fair on your future husband.'

'Listen to you going on again,' Violet replied, 'telling me what to do with my life. Do you know, everyone around here, we all keep out of other people's business and don't interfere. You have left me no choice now. I am going to teach you a lesson that you won't forget and then perhaps you will pack your bags and sod off back to where you came from.'

Violet put her bags down and was just about to lay into Beth when a hand grabbed her from behind. 'Hold on, Violet, what do you think you're doing?' a voice said. It was Bert, who was just passing and could see what was going on.

'Keep out of this, Bert, it has nothing to do with you.'

'I don't think Barny would see it that way,' he said.

By this time a crowd was gathering and Violet always performed better in front of a crowd. 'I'm warning you, Bert, you had better let me sort that bitch out now or else I am going to sort you out.'

'I can't let you do that, Violet. Come on, Beth, I'll walk you back,' he said. He let go of Violet's arm and suddenly without any warning she swung her arm round to place a blow on Bert's nose, but she stumbled and just caught him in the mouth with a glancing blow. Bert felt the blood dripping down his chin from the split lip. 'Take my advice, Violet, don't ever do that again or I will give you one back and I won't miss, I promise you that.'

Violet was now fuming. She was dancing around shouting. 'Come on then, try it then, don't think I'm afraid of you just because you're a man.'

Beth pulled at her arm. 'Come on, calm down, you're only showing yourself up,' she said.

Just then Violet's father came walking out of Wilford Road. 'What's going on here?' he shouted. 'And you, boy, what are you doing to my daughter?'

Violet ran up to her father. 'They wouldn't let me walk past them. They said now that I'm getting married and bettering myself, I don't belong around here any more.'

'Come here, my love,' her father said. 'You don't belong around here, you're too good and the sooner you leave this place the better.' He then picked up her bags and took her home.

'I really don't believe that just happened,' Beth said. 'How does she get away with it? She has caused all of this trouble and then walks away looking all innocent.'

'That's Violet all over; she's always up to those sorts of tricks, but if I were you, Beth I'd keep well away from her, she can fight like any man when she's in the mood. I'm just going down to see how Mrs Sturt is, are you coming?'

'Yes,' she replied, 'and by the way, thanks for your help. I don't know what I would done if you hadn't come along when you did.' They walked down Wilford Road, looking across at Violet's house and wondering what stories she was coming out with.

By this time Barny had arrived at his destination and was just getting off the train. As he walked through the village towards the vicarage, people were stopping to say hello. He hadn't known these people very

The Final Fight

long, but they were all going out of their way to be friendly to him. When he arrived at the vicarage, he found that the door was locked so he made his way to the church where he found the vicar on his hands and knees, wiping up puddles of water. 'What's happened here, Father?' Barny asked.

'Hello, Barny, nice to see you again. Someone has been up on the roof during the night and taken the lead off from the main soak away in the middle of the roof and the rain has been coming straight through all night. It has taken me over an hour to clear this mess up and it looks like we are in for another downpour. Enough of my troubles. How is Beth and how is your mother? I hope she is a lot better since Beth has been looking after her?'

'Yes, my mother's getting better all the time and Beth, well, she is such a wonderful girl, so caring, and she has helped my mother so much over the last week. I really don't think she would have got better so quickly if it wasn't for Beth's help. She sends her love to you.'

Barny then picked up some rags and helped to mop up some of the water. 'I don't suppose you know who took the lead, do you Father?' Barny asked.

'Well, I don't know who took it, but I certainly know where it will end up.'

'You do?' replied Barny.

'Yes, there is a small village about ten miles going north and there's a tavern called the Highwayman in the village and every crook, cut-throat and murderer gathers there, and I would put money on it that that's where my lead is. I should imagine on the back of some cart waiting to be sold.'

'Would you mind if I went and had a look to see if it is there?' Barny asked.

'No, I couldn't let you do that, it would be far too dangerous. You don't know what it is like there, Barny.'

'Well, I thought I might be able to talk to the person responsible and perhaps persuade them to give it back. You never know, it might work.' Barny knew what he would do to the people responsible and it wouldn't be to persuade them to give back the lead, but he couldn't let the vicar know that. Barny continued. 'I don't know what else we can do; to replace it would cost a fortune and you do need it as soon as possible, to stop the rain coming in.'

'Yes, you're right, it would be the only way we could repair the roof in the next day or so, otherwise we would have to shut the church down. Are you sure you don't mind?' the vicar asked.

'No, not at all, but it will take me some time to get there.'

'That's no problem,' said the vicar, 'Bill Gibbs takes a load of hay there for the blacksmith's on a Saturday afternoon, we should just catch him if we leave now.' They left for Meadow Farm and, as they were crossing a field near the farm, they could see Bill just coming up the lane on his horse and cart. They shouted out to him and explained why Barny needed to go with him and, when he knew it involved the church, he was only too pleased to help out. It took just over an hour and half before they drove into the village. Bill pointed out the Highwayman tavern and told Barny to be on his guard. 'They don't like strangers going in there. And if you want a lift back, I shall be leaving in about an hour's time. Wait for me by the blacksmith's.'

'Thanks, Bill,' Barny replied, 'but I think I should be OK for a ride back, if everything goes according to plan.'

Barny crossed the road and looked through the glass of the front door of the public house. He couldn't believe it, he felt as if he was back in Wilford Road – the same goings on, the same sort of people. He opened the door and, as he walked in, he could feel the eyes of everyone in there looking at him. He made his way to the bar and the landlord looked him up and down. 'What do you want?' he asked.

'Just a drink,' Barny replied.

'Haven't seen you around these parts before. Where do you come from?' he asked.

'I've come up from London,' Barny replied.

'If I was you, I wouldn't stay in here for too long, they don't like strangers round these parts.'

'I'm after some lead for a job I'm doing,' Barny said, 'and was told I might get some good second-hand stuff from someone in here. Would you know anyone who can help me?'

'I might do, but it will cost you.'

'That's all right, I'm getting paid well for the job.'

'Wait here and I'll send someone to fetch the man who might be able to help you out.'

The Final Fight

Barny waited for half an hour until the landlord nodded at him and looked at two men sitting in the corner. He nodded again at Barny as if to say, they are the ones.

Barny walked over to their table. 'I hear you two might be able to get some stuff for me,' he said, as he sat next to one of the men.

'Is it lead you're after?' one of the men asked.

'Yes, that's right.'

'We might be able to help you out, but it will cost you and it doesn't come cheap,' the other one said. 'We've got the lead if you have the money. What do you need it for?'

'I'm doing a church roof in the next village down. The lead disappeared overnight, but what I think happened was that the roof was leaking and the vicar asked someone to come in and fix it and they removed the old lead and didn't bother coming back to replace it. So the rain's pouring in and the vicar needs it to be done before tomorrow's service.'

'Why would he call someone from London to come all the way up here, just to fix his roof?' one of them asked.

'Well, his brother is the vicar of a church near where I live and I've carried out some work on his roof, so he recommended me because I've found a new way of putting lead down, instead of just laying it, I melt it first so it sticks to the roof and no one can take it back off.'

The two men sat there, listening to every word, and good job they did because Barny did not have a clue what he was talking about. He had made it all up to get them to trust him and it worked.

'OK, we will sell you some, it's outside on the cart,' one of them said. They told Barny the price and he agreed. The two men couldn't believe their luck, they had stolen the lead off the roof the evening before and now they were selling it back to the same church. They laughed when Barny agreed the price. 'Now, how will you get it back to the village?' they asked.

'Well, I was hoping you would drop it off for me,' Barny replied.

'We can, of course, but it will cost you.'

'That's OK, the vicar's paying.'

The two men got up from the table. 'Come on, let's get going, we don't want to be out all day.'

On the journey back to the church, Barny sat in the back of the cart listening to the two men laughing. They were thinking to themselves that they had got a right result, but little did they know that Barny had planned his every move.

When they finally arrived at the church, Barny asked them if they would help him to unload the lead into the church. 'It will cost you,' they both said at the same time. When they had finished unloading the cart they turned to Barny and asked him for their money. Barny replied that he would have to go to the vicarage and pick up the money from the vicar. He told them that it was only down the lane and wouldn't take long to get there. So the two men climbed back on to the driver's seat and Barny got up into the back of the cart and as they started to move off, Barny picked up a length of rope that he had seen earlier tucked under the driver's seat. The young man who was driving the cart had some trouble turning the horse around in the confined space of the churchyard. They started shouting and swearing at the poor old horse, but when they had completed the turn and pulled out into the lane they sat back on the seat and it was then that Barny made his move. He quietly wrapped the rope around both his hands and then suddenly jumped up and threw the rope over both their heads and around their necks and then pulled it tight until both their faces were turning blue and they were gasping for breath. He then pulled them over to the back of the cart and while they were still trying to get their breath back, Barny tied their hands together and waited for them to come round.

'What's going on?' one of them shouted.

'You thought I was a fool,' Barny said. 'You really thought I never knew that it was you two who took the lead from our church roof. Only the lowest of the low would steal from a church. You have committed a sin and you must be punished.'

'What are you going to do with us?' they asked.

'Well, if you promise never to return to this church again, then I won't touch you, but if you do return I will promise you, may God be my witness, I will kill you both.'

'You don't have to worry about that, we won't come back here.'

'That's good enough for me,' Barny said, as he pulled them out of the cart and they hit the ground with a thud.

'Now get up,' he shouted.

'You said you wouldn't hurt us,' one of them cried.

The Final Fight

'Just stand still and I won't touch you,' Barny said as he began to tie them to the back of the cart and then walked to a bush at the side of the lane and broke off a thin branch. He walked back over to the cart.

The two men were now shouting. 'Please don't whip us, please don't.'

Barny stood by the men and laughed, he then walked up to the horse and raised his arm and hit the horse across the back with the branch and at the same time shouted out. The horse reared up and galloped off with the two men being pulled behind. Barny watched them as they went off down the lane and, as they were just going out of sight, he saw both of them fall to the ground to be dragged round a bend.

Barny pulled the door of the church shut and left for the vicarage. The vicar couldn't believe it when Barny told him that he had returned with the lead and it hadn't cost the church a farthing. 'How did you do it?' he asked.

'Well, I just spoke to them nicely and asked them if they wouldn't mind returning the lead and they agreed.'

'That's wonderful,' the vicar said. 'Do you think you will be able to repair the roof? All the villagers are worried that the church would have to be shut down, but if you could repair it for us, we would all be most grateful.'

'Yes, I should think I will be able to repair it. I will make a start first thing in the morning and try and get it ready for the morning service.'

Barny had a bite to eat and then left the vicarage and made his way to the barn where the fight was to take place, but before he could shut the front door, he heard the vicar shout out to him. 'Barny, could I have a quick word with you.'

Barny turned. 'Of course, what is it?' he asked.

'I did mean to tell you when you first arrived, but with all that rain water on the church floor, I completely forgot. I had a word with Mr Welch the other day and asked him about you renting his cottage and he said if you wouldn't mind repairing the fire damage to the kitchen and paying a month's rent in advance, then you are most welcome to move in as soon as you like. He's also going to leave all the furniture and carpets, so you don't have to bring anything with you.'

'That's good news, Father, I can't wait to tell my parents.'

Barny then made his way to the barn, but he arrived too early, so he sat down at the side of the barn and waited for the guvnor to turn up.

At the Precipice of Poverty

He sat there for about ten minutes before he fell asleep. He was awoken by someone kicking at his leg. He looked up and saw the two men in suits who had spoken to him before. 'I hope you have come to tell us what we want to hear,' one of them said.

Barny got to his feet. 'What might that be?' he answered.

'That you're going to fight for us. We told you what would happen if you don't.'

Barny wasn't afraid of the two men, but as he was about to walk away from them, four other men walked up from the bushes and surrounded him. Barny knew he couldn't take the six of them on and if he did he wouldn't be able to take on his opponents, and he needed all the money he could get now for Mr Welch's cottage. So he had no choice: he had to agree to throw the fights.

'That's better,' one of them said, 'we knew you would come round to our way of thinking. Now listen carefully; you can win the first two fights, but we want you to take a fall in the third fight and don't forget, don't make it too obvious, do you understand?'

'What if I don't do it?' Barny asked.

'If you don't, then after the fights you will have to come out of the barn at some time and we'll be waiting for you and will make sure you don't ever fight again.' Barny knew he had to go along with them at least until he could think of some way to get out of it.

After the first fight, which Barny won with ease, he took a seat until his next opponent came in. He looked at the two men, who were sitting in their usual place at the front of the circle. He knew that if he threw the third he would lose all his money, because the guvnor automatically put his winnings on to the next fight. His second opponent came in and the fight was quickly over without a mark on Barny's face. He would have to think of something now, before it was too late.

His third opponent came in and Barny looked him in the eyes; he knew it wouldn't take much to knock him down. As he walked round the circle with his opponent he looked over at the two men and they stared back at him, nodding their heads. The fight began, Barny took a few blows to the face, but never returned the punches, it was now or never, he thought. Again he looked over at the two men – they were both smiling as the blood ran down Barny's face. If he took a fall he would avoid being maimed or even killed, he had heard that the two men had a reputation for that, but he would also lose the cottage

The Final Fight

because he would lose the money for the month's rent. He then decided, and his pride got the better of him. He had never let anyone tell him what to do in the past, apart from his parents, that is, and he wasn't going to start now. As he was still working out what to do, his opponent placed another hard blow to the side of his head that dazed him enough to allow his opponent to place a right hook up and under his chin. This one knocked Barny off his feet. The crowd screamed and his opponent started to dance around the circle with his arms raised in the air. Barny knew he had to do something quickly. There was now the chance that he might lose the fight without meaning to. The two men were now standing up and shouting out to Barny, 'Stay down, stay down.' With all the noise and confusion Barny slowly came to his feet; his opponent was still dancing around and still had his hands in the air with his back towards Barny, not knowing that the giant man that he was fighting was now back on his feet and, as the man moved round towards him, Barny placed an almighty blow on his opponent's chin, knocking him completely out and making him fall on to the people in the front seats.

Barny looked round quickly at the two men. They had sat back down in their seats and had begun arguing amongst themselves. He had never seen anyone look so angry. One of them called out to one of their henchmen, who walked over to them carrying a large piece of lead piping. At the same time two men were over by Barny's opponent, trying to bring him round. They had a large metal pail, filled with water, which they quickly threw over the man's head, but this still did not bring him round, so in the end they had to carry him out of the barn.

Barny noticed the metal bucket that they had left behind, which was just by the two men, who were now shouting and swearing. He knew he had to make his move and quickly. If he had surprise on his side he might stand a better chance of getting out. He slowly walked over to the two men, as if to talk to them, but when he was close enough he made a grab for the handle of the metal bucket, picked it up and swung it around his head with all of his might and then pushed it into the men's faces. The sound of the bucket hitting against the heads of the two men echoed around the barn. Barny had hit them with so much force that the people sitting as far as five feet away on their right-hand side were splattered with blood that flew out of the men's mouths on impact with the bucket.

The henchman, who was standing next to the two men, just stood there with his mouth open. He had dropped the lead piping and had frozen to the spot not knowing what to do. Barny took this opportunity while the man was standing still; he swung the bucket up in the air and brought it down right on top of the henchman's head, knocking him out cold. Barny knew it wasn't over yet, there were three others somewhere; he had seen them outside before the fight and he knew it wouldn't be long before they would come inside to find out what all the commotion was. He couldn't take a chance of running into them, so with the bucket still in his hand he moved round inside the circle and this was when he saw an oil lamp, hanging from one of the beams in the corner of the barn. He quickly threw the bucket over at the lamp. It smashed and the oil caught fire underneath it. Barny knew that there were enough men in the barn to put the fire out so there was no danger of anyone getting hurt. With the confusion of the two men getting their heads split open and now the fire, Barny had a chance to make his move. He ran to the far door, where the guvnor was standing and asked him for his winnings.

The guvnor took the money from his pouch and as he was giving it to Barny, he said, 'You certainly don't do things by half, son, mind you, those two deserve everything you gave them.' Barny thanked him and ran out of the barn and back to the vicarage.

When he opened the front door the vicar had retired to his bed, but the fire was still roaring, so Barny sat in front of it and started to think about his parents, Violet and Beth. Why is everyone I love so far away, he thought, and when I move up here, will I be able to cope without seeing Violet at all? Although Beth will be here, if she still wants to be with me. There were so many things going round in Barny's head, in the end he just lay back in the chair, closed his eyes and fell asleep.

The next day Barny left the vicarage before the vicar had even opened his eyes. He began work on the church roof and had carried all the lead up to the roof and was replacing it when the vicar turned up with some bread and cheese. 'Barny,' the vicar shouted, 'you left this morning without any breakfast. Here, I have brought you something to eat now.'

'Thank you,' Barny replied as he banged the last bit of lead down.

'Will you be finished in time to join in with the Sunday service?' the vicar asked.

The Final Fight

'I should think so, Father. At least your roof's watertight now.'

The vicar left Barny and went down to welcome his flock into the church. Barny followed him down a short while later; the roof was now finished, but so was the service and the people were just leaving as Barny walked to the church doors to join the vicar. He couldn't make out why all the people were smiling as they walked past him. He asked the vicar if he knew.

'Well, my son, this church means a lot to the people around this way and if we hadn't been able to get the church roof repaired then we would have had no choice but to shut the church down. We would have carried on the services in the church hall, but it wouldn't have been the same, so they are very grateful to you, so grateful in fact that they asked me how they could repay you in some way, I told them that you were moving in to Mr Welch's cottage and you would welcome any work they could offer. I told them what you did, of course, so the way they were talking, you can expect quite a bit of work to come in.'

'Thank you, Father, that's very kind of you. This is like a dream coming true,' Barny said.

The vicar's words came true the following week. Barny had so much work coming in, he didn't even get the chance to start work on the cottage, although he had paid the month's rent to Mr Welch, so officially he was now the new tenant.

The following Saturday, Barny was sitting in front of the fire again thinking about his parents and the life they were going to leave behind. Although life was really hard in Wilford Road Barny would miss it in a strange way; he had become used to all the arguments and fights. Would living up here be too quiet for him and would he be able to settle down? But then he thought of his parents going for long walks through the lanes on a summer's evening, that was something they had never done before, and then there was Beth. She would be close by and he was just beginning to realise just how much he was missing her since he had been away. Slowly but surely his feelings were growing stronger for Beth and weaker for Violet. His love for Violet would never die, she was his first love and there would always be a special place in his heart for her, even though in a few weeks she would be married and he probably wouldn't be able to talk to her again.

He knew he would have to leave soon for the night's fights, but these would be his last. He had saved up quite a bit of money now, which the vicar was keeping safe for him in the vaults of the church, and with all the extra work that was coming in, he could make sure his parents would have a safe and comfortable life in their new home. He started to worry about the fights, not because of his opponents, but it was only a week ago that he beat the two men in suits up, and he just had a funny feeling that something might happen tonight. I will have to take special care and keep my eyes open, he thought.

Before he left the cottage, he stoked the fire up for the vicar, who was still in the church, and then he left for the fight. He made sure he arrived at the barn a good hour before the fights began and waited in the bushes to see who was turning up. There was fifteen minutes to go and he hadn't seen anyone out of the ordinary, so he walked up to the door and looked in. Everything seemed OK. The guvnor was there in his usual place and seats where the two men in suits always sat were taken by a couple of old boys. Barny walked in, his eyes looking everywhere. The guvnor looked up. 'I didn't expect to see you in here tonight, son,' he said.

'This is my last night,' Barny replied.

'Well, be careful and as soon as the fights are over, I would make your way home if I was you, don't hang around.'

Barny walked into the circle for his first fight. His opponent caught him in the eye with a lucky blow, but it was soon over; all it took was one punch that hit the right place on the man's chin and he was down. Barny had to wait half an hour for his next opponent so he waited at the back of the barn, out of sight, but kept a close eye on who came in. The guvnor waved him in and he began his second fight of the night. This opponent was one of the mouthy ones. He called Barny all the names under the sun to try and make him lose his temper and his concentration, but Barny was having none of it; he just listened and smiled. It was the other man who began to lose his temper. He started to jump about and shout out, 'Come on, you prat, come and get me,' but Barny kept his distance. 'Come on, you cockney fool, where is your mother tonight, out whoring?'

Barny had to bite his tongue, he knew that if he let the man get to him, then he would lose the advantage, but he couldn't take much more of the man's foul mouth. Luckily for Barny the man lost it first; he had wound himself up so much trying to get Barny to lose his temper that he suddenly took a run at Barny with his guard down. It was then

The Final Fight

easy for Barny, he just placed a punch on the man's nose, which broke it and splattered it across his face. The man was on his back shouting 'No more. I have had enough.' But Barny grabbed him by the hair and lifted his head off the ground. 'What did you say about my mother?' Barny asked.

'I didn't mean it,' the man shouted.

The guvnor walked over. 'That's enough, son, you've beaten him, now let him go, there is no need to go any further.'

Barny thought for a second and then threw the man's head down.

'Come on, get up, go and get some fresh air,' the guvnor said. 'I will give you a shout when you're next on.'

'All right,' Barny replied, and then made his way outside and sat down round the side of the barn. He was only there a little while before he noticed a man walking up and down. He approached Barny and asked him if he knew where he would have to go to get himself a fight. Barny was just about to tell him when the man threw some sand or salt into Barny's face. Barny turned his head away, rubbing his eyes, which only made them hurt more. He then felt a hand on each arm and one holding his head. He was dragged into the bushes and placed face down on the ground with two of the men sitting on his back.

'What do you want of me?' Barny asked.

'We've been hired by someone to kill you,' one of them replied.

'You had better make a good job of it,' Barny said, 'because if you leave one ounce of life left in me I will come and find each one of you and I swear on my mother's life that I will make sure that none of you will ever walk or see again. I will crush every bone in your legs and then dig your eyes out with a knife.' Barny kept his cool; he knew if he could put the fear of Christ into them he might get away with his life and it was working.

One of the men shouted to the other. 'Go on, do it, finish him off.'

'No, I can't, you do it,' he shouted back.

'Well, one of you wants to bloody well do it,' the third man shouted.

What they were told to do was to beat Barny over the head with a thick branch and then drag him into the trees to die, but when it came down to it none of them had the guts, being frightened by what Barny had threatened to do to them. The one holding the branch couldn't force himself to bring the branch down on Barny's head and none of the others wanted to take the branch from him.

'Come on, we have got to do something,' one of them shouted. 'If we let him go now he will definitely do away with us.'

'Give me the branch and come and sit on him,' one said. He took the branch from the man and picked up a rock and placed it under Barny's left hand. 'Hold his arm tight.' He then stood up and brought the thick branch down again and again on Barny's hand.

Barny screamed with the pain and the man carried on until all the bones in his hand were broken. He then threw the branch down and shouted to the others to let him go and run. Barny was left on the ground rolling around in pain, still not being able to see.

The guvnor then walked out of the barn looking for Barny. He stood by the door and could hear Barny groaning. He then looked round the side of the barn and saw him moving on the ground. He helped him to his feet. 'I need to wash my eyes out,' Barny said. The guvnor went and fetched a jug of water and splashed some in Barny's eyes, trying to wash the sand out.

'Your hand's in a bit of a state, Barny,' the guvnor said.

'I know, but I've got to go on with the fight, it is my last one and I don't want to lose all the money I have already won.'

'Well, I will have to see what I can do with it,' the guvnor said. He went away and came back with some strips of sheeting and bound Barny's hand up tightly. 'That should do. At least you won't do any more damage to it, if that's possible.'

Barny's eyes were beginning to clear and the guvnor said, 'We had better go in now.'

Barny looked at his opponent, who had now been waiting some time for Barny to turn up. He was a tall man, not very broad, but thickset. Barny knew the man had a body that could move fast with hidden strength – this could be one of the hardest fights he had ever had.

Barny started to move around his opponent with his bad arm hanging limp at his side. He managed to get the first punch in, a straight jab to the chin. With one arm at his side he couldn't get much strength behind it, but it still knocked his opponent off his feet. Barny stood back, the pain from his hand was unbearable. His opponent got up and was looking at Barny's bandaged hand, he raised his fists and moved towards Barny and without any warning he jumped up and kicked at Barny's hand. A scream of pain filled the barn. Barny held his injured hand and looked down at it and just as his head lowered, his

The Final Fight

opponent brought left hook round and hit Barny square on the chin. Barny went down and hit the floor with a bang. His opponent wasn't going to miss out on a chance like this. He grabbed hold of Barny's head and placed four blows down on his face, he then tried to pull Barny to his feet. He put his arm under Barny's arms and punched him five or six times in the stomach. Barny was finished, but his opponent kept going, placing punch after punch on to Barny's body. The guvnor ran up to the man and told him to stop, but the man turned and placed a punch on the guvnor's nose, knocking him out cold. So there they were, Barny one side and the guvnor the other side, both knocked out and the man dancing around treading on both of them.

The next thing Barny knew when he opened his eyes, it was fairly dark and he could hear the flow of water. He closed his eyes again until he felt the splashing of cold water on his face. The shock of the water made him jump and as he moved, he felt pain from every part of his body. He opened his eyes again, his vision still blurred, but he could hear someone calling his name. 'Barny, Barny, wake up.' He could see the outline of someone kneeling over him, but still couldn't make out who it was. He felt more cold water go on his face and he lifted his hand up to rub his eyes and looked again at the figure. 'Bert, is that you?' he asked in a soft, weak voice.

'Of course it's me, you old sod, what have you been up to?' Bert replied.

'Don't ask, anyway what are you doing up here?'

'It's a good job I turned up when I did or else you would still have that animal jumping all over you. I had a job and half trying to get you out of that barn.'

'You still haven't told me what you are doing up here?' Barny asked.

'Don't worry about that now. Can you sit up? Here give me your arm.'

'Ah, not that one,' Barny screamed.

'Cor mate, you are in a bad way. I've never seen you like this before. Come on, let's sit you up and try and sort you out.'

Barny grabbed his arm as he pulled him up. 'It's not my mother?' he asked. 'That's not the reason why you're up here is it?'

'No, she's fine. In fact she looks a lot better than you do. I will tell you later why I am up here, it's not important now. Now, let's try and get you up on your feet – you've been lying on that wet ground for over three hours.'

Bert lifted him to his feet. 'Now put your arm around my shoulder.' Barny groaned with the pain. 'We need to get you to a doctor. Where is the nearest one around here?'

'No, I don't need a doctor, just get me back to the vicarage,' Barny replied.

'What are you going to tell the vicar, that you fell off your bike?'

'No, it's all right. I got some lead back off two men today, they nicked it off the church roof. Just tell him you saw them beating me up down the lane and you stopped them.'

It took a long time to reach the vicarage. Bert opened the door as the vicar was just coming down the stairs. 'Oh my God,' he said, as he saw the state Barny was in. 'What's happened to him?' he asked.

'He will be all right, Father, if I can we get him on a chair.'

In God's name, what happened to him?'

'It was two men. I found them beating him up as I came walking down the lane and as they ran off they shouted something about some lead.'

'Oh my gosh,' the vicar said. 'It must have been those chaps who stole my lead off the church roof. I thought it was strange how Barny got it back so easily without any trouble. Oh dear, it is all my fault he has been beaten.'

'Father, he is getting very heavy. Can we put him in a chair?' Bert asked.

'No, take him straight up to his room,' replied the vicar.

Bert looked at the vicar. 'Do you mean to say he has his own room here?' Bert asked in disbelief.

'Yes, come on we will lay him on the bed and then I will try to attend to his wounds. I'll just get my bag.'

Bert struggled to get Barny up the stairs, but finally got him to his room and on the bed. Bert looked around. 'You crafty old sod, Barny Sturt, no wonder you keep coming back up here. It's not the fights, it's this room you keep coming back to. This room is bigger than the one I live in now and I share that with two other men.' Just then the door opened and the vicar came in with a medical bag.

'I didn't know you were a medical man, Father,' Bert said.

'No, I'm not, well not exactly, but I learnt a lot in Africa. I had to see to some horrible cases out there. No one else to do it you see, so I had no choice, but I saved a few lives I'm proud to say.'

'So I suppose that's where Beth gets it from,' Bert said.

The Final Fight

'Yes, but she is very good. I'm not as skilled as her. Now, let's see what we have here.'

'I think his hand is in the worst state,' Bert said.

The vicar took hold of Barny's injured hand. 'I think you're right. It feels like every bone has been broken.'

'He will be all right, though, won't he?' Bert asked.

'I'm not sure. I will strap it up tightly and he won't be able to use it for some months and he will need to go to the infirmary and get it seen to professionally. Oh dear, this finger's quite bad, the bone has come right through the skin. I will have to push it back in and strap it separately.'

'It will be all right, Father?' Bert asked again.

'Well, I don't really know, the more I look at it the worse it gets. His hand is in quite a bad way. In fact, he might have to have it off, if an infection sets in, but that will be down to the infirmary. I couldn't possibly do that. Bert, can you clean up his cuts around his face while I'm fixing his hand. The quicker we get him made comfortable the better it will be for him.' They spent over an hour cleaning him up and trying to repair his broken body.

Barny was still out of it when they had finished, but he looked a lot better now that the cuts had been cleaned and dressed. It was just his hand that the vicar was concerned about. 'Let's leave him now,' he said. 'I presume you could do with a strong drink after all that.'

'Yes, I won't say no to that,' Bert replied, 'but only to be sociable.'

'Yes, I think we deserve one.' As he poured the drinks out, he asked Bert where he was going to stay for the night.

'I haven't had time to find anywhere yet, but I will be all right.'

'No, you will stay here. We have a spare room and you're more than welcome to use it.'

'Well, thank you very much,' Bert replied. 'It will be the first room I have stayed in where I have not had to share with anyone else.'

'That's funny,' the vicar said, 'do you know, that's just what Barny said when I took him up to his room.'

'Well, we are not used to such luxuries as our own rooms; even if you are sent to prison you have to share. Yes, this will be a first for me. Can I go to my room now, Father, if you don't mind that is?'

The next morning Barny was up early and had made his way down the stairs and into the chair by the fireside. The vicar couldn't believe it when he came down and saw Barny sitting in the chair. 'What are you doing down here?'

'I feel a lot better now, Father, thank you, just a bit sore, that's all.'

'How is your hand?' the vicar asked.

'There is no pain, in fact, I can't feel anything at all,' Barny replied.

'Yes, well you had better get off to the infirmary as soon as you can. I'm not very happy about it.'

'Was it you who fixed me up last night?' Barny asked.

'I did my best. I felt a bit guilty seeing as it was because of my church roof that this happened to you, but I can't believe how much you have improved overnight. They must turn you out really tough back at Wilford Road.'

'No, not really, it's surprising what a good night's sleep can do for the body. Tell me, Father, was I dreaming last night or did my mate Bert turn up help me home?'

'You weren't dreaming, my son, and it was lucky for you that he did turn up. By the way he was talking, he got you away from those hooligans just in time' he replied.

'Surely he didn't go back home then?' Barny asked.

'No, not at all, he is upstairs enjoying a lie in I shouldn't wonder. He was a bit overcome with his room last night.'

'I think I will go and get him up if that's OK with you.'

'Yes, of course, I will put some breakfast on and have it ready for when you both come down.'

Barny crept upstairs and slowly opened the door. He saw Bert sitting back in a chair like the lord of the manor. 'What are you doing in here Bert,' Barny shouted.

'I feel like a king in my own room!' he replied. 'Anyway, what are you doing up and about? I thought you would still be half dead from the beating you received.'

'Well, you know you can't keep me down for long, Bert. Listen, I am really grateful that you came up last night. But what are you doing up here? I wasn't expecting you.'

'Here, Barny, what about this room? I can't believe that I have been in here all night on my own, if only Fanny could see me now. I've been walking round most of the night. I've never had such a big soft bed in such a lovely room.'

The Final Fight

Barny walked over to him. 'I thought you had stopped seeing Fanny. Now, come on, tell me why you're up here?'

'Do you know, I could really get used to this, living the good life, I think it really suits me, don't you?'

'Look,' Barny said. 'I know I owe you a lot for getting me back last night, but if you don't tell me what you have come up here for I'm going to throw you straight out of that window and we will see how you like your new room then.'

'Sorry, Barny, you know I get a bit carried away. There were two reasons for me coming to see you: one there's a police sergeant after me and I had to get away.'

'Why, what have you done now?' Barny asked.

'That don't really matter, now that I am up here and out of the way. I can tell you all about that later, but what's more important is that Violet wants to see you urgently.'

'What?' Barny shouted. 'Why does she want to see me now?'

'I don't know, she wouldn't say, she just said that it was really important that I find you and give you the message; she even paid for my train fare up here.'

'Do you think she has changed her mind about getting married?'

'I don't know, but she was having a right old go at Beth the other day. She was just about to hit her when I came along and stopped her. She told me to tell you that she would meet you at Fred's office in the coal yard at six o'clock today.'

'Fred won't be there,' Barny said, 'and I don't have a key any more.'

'No, she has sorted that out, she's already seen Fred and he has lent her a spare key,' he replied.

'You have got me thinking now, Bert. If she brings her sergeant friend with her and a few of his mates, I won't stand a chance in the state I'm in.'

'You know, I will always come with you,' Bert said.

'No,' Barny replied. 'If they are there, I will take them on, bad hand or no bad hand. Come on, we had better go down. There's some breakfast waiting for you.'

'I've never had it so good,' said Bert. 'Now I could really get used to this sort of life.'

'Well, don't get used to it too soon because you're coming back with me today. I can't leave you up here on your own with all the women, they wouldn't be safe.'

Barny told the vicar that he would be leaving in a few hours' time and thanked him for all that he had done.

'No, thank *you*,' he said. 'If it wasn't for you, the church would have been shut now, for I don't know how long. Now remember, get that hand looked at as soon as you get back.'

'I will, Father,' Barny replied.

'No, I mean it. If you don't see a doctor, it could become really nasty. Now before you go, let me make up some bread and cheese for you to take with you on the journey and as soon as I have done that I will have to be off, so have a safe journey. Would you like me to keep bringing the work in for you?'

'Yes, if you wouldn't mind. Hopefully I should be back within a few days.'

They finished their breakfasts and Barny left the table. 'We had better make a move in a minute,' he said to Bert as he took his coat off the chair. 'We've got another hour and half before the train leaves.'

'Yes, I know, but there is something I want to show you first before we leave.'

They left the vicarage and made their way down the lane. On the way they walked past the barn where the night before Barny nearly lost his life. 'I've no need to go in there any more,' he said. 'Last night was my last night. Here Bert, did you see the guvnor last night when you dragged me out?'

'I saw an old man on the floor who was lying next to you, but he was out cold and I was too busy trying to get you out to worry about him.'

'I wonder if he's all right. He was a good friend to me, I would have liked to have been there to help him when he needed it.'

'You were in no fit state to help anybody,' Bert said. They walked on for another half hour and as they turned the next bend, Barny stopped. 'What's the matter, Barn?' Bert asked. 'Are you feeling all right?'

'Yea, I'm OK. You see that cottage just over that hedge there?'

'Yea, just about, why is that?' asked Bert.

'That's my new home, well me and my parents.'

'You're having me on,' said Bert.

The Final Fight

'No, it's true. I've just got to do some work in the kitchen and it will be ready to move in.'

'How did you manage to get it, I mean the money and everything?' Barny explained about the fire and how he had been saving some of the money he had won at the fights and the money from all the work he had been doing since coming up here.

'Your life is certainly changing for the better. I hope it all works out for you, but make sure that Violet don't spoil it for you.'

'Listen Bert, I was going to ask you. You know we have been through a lot together and we do make a good team and I was wondering if you would like to join me, you know come and live up here with my family and help me out with the work?'

'Of course, I would, I would love to do that,' Bert replied.

'Don't you want to think about it first?' Barny asked.

'No, I've thought about it already and I would love to move up here with you, but where would I stay?'

'Don't worry about that, there's five bedrooms in that cottage.'

'Do you mean I will have my own room?' he asked.

'Yes, of course you will.'

'Then put me down for one, my son. I would love to move in with you and your parents. Tell me first, there is nothing that can go wrong, is there?' he asked. 'I don't want to get all my hopes up and then, well you know what I'm going on about. This will be the first real home I've ever had and I don't want to get all of my hopes up and then something goes wrong.'

'No, nothing can go wrong. I'm getting plenty of work in and my name's on the rent book now.'

'What about your mother, won't she mind?' Bert asked.

'As long as you don't bring that Fanny woman with you I don't think she'll mind. She's got quite a soft spot for you, Berts, believe it or not. Come on, we had better get to the station before we miss our train.'

On the train journey home Barny asked Bert what the other reason was for coming to see him. 'Do you really want to know?' Bert asked.

'There is nothing else to do, is there? You may as well bore me with your story.'

'Since you have been up here I have been walking out with a young girl. Her name's Rose and she's a lovely little thing.'

'She isn't married is she?' Barny asked.

'No, I have had enough of married women now. Anyway she is in service at one of the big houses on the hill, not far from the house where Violet works as a nanny, and I used to go up there and meet her when she had finished work and walk her home. One day she was late coming out so I got talking to one of the gardeners, who just happens to be Rose's brother, and he was telling me that he was told by the head gardener to order a load of leaf mould for the flower beds. Well, it just so happens that the Sunday before I took Rose for a tram ride up to Shirley Woods, you know, I thought I would treat her; you know what I am like, Barny, like to give a girl a good time and all that.'

'Stop waffling and carry on.' Barny said.

'Well, as we went past the grounds of the Shirley Park Estate, I just happened to look over the fence and I noticed that there was loads of leaf mould under all the rhododendrons. So, of course, when Rose's brother said he needed some, I thought, well I'm your man. I said to him leave it with me and I'll deliver it up here for you tomorrow. But I will have to have some of the money up front, you know, just for expenses and that and he agreed, the fool, only because Rose had put a good word in for me. Well, that evening I popped round to Thomas Tugwell's house, you know, him from 32 Wilford Road, and told him all about it.

'I thought of him because I knew he had a big coaster's barrow. When I had told him the plan he said, "Yea, I'm up for it." So we waited until about ten o'clock and then made our way to Strathmore Road, you know, where the old sack factory is. We jumped over the gates and nicked about two dozen sacks and then went back to Tom's house. I said to him that I would have to stay round his place for the night so we could get up at four in the morning, so no one would be around when we nicked the leaf mould. But his wife wasn't too happy about me staying the night, but there you go, you can't please everyone. During the evening, Tom said he was going round to the Fish to pick up a jug of ale, so I said I would go with him. I didn't want to stay in the room with his wife, not on my own, she's a right old dragon. Anyway, we came back with three jugs of ale and spent most of the night drinking them and when they were finished Tom and his wife went to bed and I slept on the floor in the kitchen.

The Final Fight

'When I woke up the next morning it was 5.30; we had both overslept. We then had to rush about to get ready and we pushed the barrow up to Shirley Park Estate. That took over an hour and half. We parked it by the fence, jumped over and started to load the sacks, but what we didn't know was that the bailiff of the estate was doing his rounds with one of the stable lads and he saw us jumping over the fence. He told the stable lad to take a horse and go and fetch a constable from the police station. Without knowing, we carried on loading the sacks. We must have loaded about ten sacks by this time and were unaware of what was happening until we heard a crash out on the road behind us. We looked round and saw two coppers, who had thrown their bicycles to the ground, were jumping over the fence and coming towards us. I shouted to Thomas to run for it, which he did, but he ran straight into the bailiff, who grabbed him around the head and threw him to the ground. One of the constables then got hold of him and put the cuffs on. Barny,' Bert shouted shaking his arm, 'are you a sleep?'

'No, no, I'm just resting my eyes. I'm still listening to you. What happened next?' asked Barny.

'I kept running through the trees and bushes with the other copper chasing me. We must have been running for two minutes when I heard a yell and, as I looked back, I saw the copper who was still running, but had tripped over something and was overbalancing and couldn't stop. The next thing I knew he landed straight in the middle of this bush. His arms, head and all the top half of him had disappeared and there were only his legs showing. Well, I stood there, Barny, and I couldn't stop laughing and while I was rolling up the copper was shouting at the top of his voice, "Get me out of here." Which made me laugh even more. Eventually, he dragged himself out, but he had scratches all down his face and hands and twigs and leaves in his hair. I was still standing there laughing and then he started to chase me again. We ran a bit further and then came to the end of the estate and there were these iron railings, which were about four foot high with spikes on top.

'So I jumped up and put one foot between the spikes and then over. I started to run again until I heard another yell. I stopped and looked round and you should have seen it, Barny, I just curled up with laughter again. I could see then that the copper was a sergeant and he had tried to jump over the railings the same as I had, but he had caught his trouser leg on one of the spikes and, as he fell down, his coat caught on another spike he was just hanging there. He couldn't move up or down. I slowly walked back to him and as he looked up at me he said, "Get me off here now." I bent down and looked him straight in the face and said, "You prat, you look like a stuffed pig hanging up there."

'So why didn't you just run off while you had the chance?' Barny said.

'I couldn't,' Bert replied, 'I knew he wasn't going anywhere and I couldn't resist having a go at him. I said to him, "Did you want me for something?" and he replied, "Get me off these railings, boy, or I'm going to put you away for a very long time." I started to laugh again. I said to him, "Look at me, sergeant, I'm shaking in my daisies. You know you really frighten me being stuck on them spikes." I then walked back a few steps and said, "Do you know what the biggest part of your body is from this angle?" He looked up at me, he was so full of anger that I thought his face was going to burst. "I'll give you a clue," I said, "it looks like a sack of potatoes hanging down." "You're going to pay for this," he said.

'"You still can't get it, can you? All right, I'll show you what part of your body I'm talking about," and then I gave him such a hard kick up the arse I thought he was going to jump off the railings. He screamed like a pig and then when I had finished laughing, I said, "I have got to be on my way now. I would love to stay and chat with you, but I have things to do. Now, don't you hang around here for too long, you'll get cold."

'As I walked away he was screaming and shouting and swearing at me. "You had better listen to me, boy. If it takes me the rest of my life, I will find you and, I promise you, I will put you away for a very long time. I mean it, I'll be after you every day until I get you. No one treats me like this and gets away with it."'

'So what happened to old Tom?' Barny asked.

'Well, I found out from his wife that he was already due to appear in court that day for embezzling £1 12s 3d from the Empire Theatre. That's where he used to work and she was telling me that a few nights ago the lady superintendent gave him eight dozen cakes, six dozen penny packets of chocolate and 150 programmes to sell in the theatre but, as soon as she gave them to him, he walked out of the back door and took them home for his wife and kids. The police were round his house the next day and took him off to the station.'

'So how come they let him out again?' Barny asked.

The Final Fight

'He appeared in court but, half way through, he collapsed and had to be carried out of the dock and then they thought he wasn't quite right in the head and he was sent home and ordered to come back on another day. She told me there was nothing wrong with him, he just collapsed because he knew that would stop the case and he would be sent home but now he will have to appear again for nicking the leaf mould.'

'I don't know why you took him with you, he doesn't sound all there to me,' Barny said. 'You ask for trouble you do, what with that copper you kicked. You know there is no way he is going to forget you now.'

'You can say that again,' Bert replied. 'When I left him on the railings I thought to myself, it's not worth going home now so I might as well jump on a train and go up the maker to buy some flowers. I still had the money for the leaf mould in my pocket so I bought some flowers, came back and picked me basket up and stopped in George Street to sell the flowers. I was doing quite well until I looked down towards the High Street and who should be walking up, yes, that bloody sergeant. As soon as he saw me he started to run. I had no choice then, I had to leave me flowers there and make a dash for it.

'He chased me down Park Street and along the High Street and I finally lost him in Surrey Street amongst all the people. I walked past the Dog and Bull and thought I'd pop in for a quick glass of ale. I was up at the bar with a couple of my mates when one of them said, "Who's he looking for?" I looked up and there he was looking over the top of the curtains through the window. I had to leave my ale on the bar and run out the back door. I didn't know which way to turn; he was getting like a hump on my back and every time I looked round he was there, coming after me. I thought the best place to hide would be at your house and I wanted to see how your mother was anyway. I thought that would be the last place he would go looking for me.'

'So I made my through all the alleys and back streets and finally arrived at Wilford Road without seeing him. I knew I was safe then. I spent about two hours talking to your poor old mum and then Beth did me a bit of tea. She is a good girl, that Beth. Then I waited until it was dark, said my goodbyes and made my way home and you will never guess who was there. I turned into my road and I couldn't believe it – he was standing outside my house leaning against a wall. I thought to myself, don't he ever go off-duty? He shouted and started to run towards me so I turned and ran up Princess Road and into Queens Road and then jumped over the cemetery railings. I looked round and he had stopped chasing me. I don't think he was going to take another chance of getting caught on the railings again. I walked up to the burial chapel and waited there for three hours. I knew he'd be gone by then. Here, Barny, have you ever been in there at night?'

'No, I can't say I have,' Barny replied.

'You don't want to, mate. Boy, was I frightened. I kept hearing noises and people groaning. You know, I've only got one pair of pants and I had to wash them out in the horse trough, that's how frightened I was. I was so glad when I walked out of that place. I made my way back down Princess Road and came across the house where the Kings used to live, before you drove them out. No one had moved into their rooms and they were still empty, so I went around to the back of the house and broke in through a window and that's where I spent the night. I don't know what them Kings used to get up to, but in every room there was blood up the walls. I was a bit scared of staying in there on my own, but needs must and I never left there until seven the next morning. I thought, before I do anything else I must go and see if my basket is still where I left it. But when I got there, the kids had been kicking it up and down the road so it was no good at all. I was right cheesed off and started to walk towards the station. I got as far as the bridge and who should I bump into? Yea, it was that arsehole of a sergeant. I couldn't turn and run because I had already noticed a constable walking down George Street so I had no option, I had to run at him. I ran into him and knocked him flying. His helmet went one way and his cape went the other, he ended up in a heap on the ground. I ran down the side of the station and then saw Fred walking into the coal yard. I ran past him so fast and just shouted, "You haven't seen me, Fred, you don't know where I am." I went round to the back of the coal yard and hid in one of the old trucks for an hour or so and then decided to get out. I looked over the top and who do you think was standing there? He nudged Barny on the arm.

'Don't tell me, Bert, let me guess I bet you it was that sergeant who fancies you.'

'No, you're wrong this time, Barny. It was Violet, she had come to see Fred. I jumped out of the truck and she came running over to me. "Where is Barny?" she asked. "He is up north, working," I told her.

The Final Fight

"I need to speak to him, I've got to speak to him," she said. "Can you find him and tell him I really need to see him." "Well, I would like to help you out, Violet," I said, "but I've spent my last penny this morning and I don't have the train fare to go there now." "I'll pay," she said. With that she gave me some money and told me to go straight away. So I jumped on the next train and I knew where you would be at that time on a Saturday night – in the barn – and the rest you know. Mind you, I was glad she did ask me to come and find you, at least I got away from that sergeant. He was driving me around the bend.' Bert turned to Barny.

'Oh that's charming,' he said. Barny had fallen asleep.

Chapter 9

Corrosive Poisoning

When the train pulled into the station, Bert shook Barny's shoulder. 'Wake up,' he said, 'we are here.'

Barny looked around him. 'Have I been asleep?'

'Yea, most of the time.'

'It's your fault, you must have bored me to sleep all the way home.'

As the train slowed down Bert pulled down the window and looked out.

'Watch you don't get your head knocked off,' Barny said. 'Mind you, it wouldn't make a lot of difference to you would it, Bert? Here, I can see Fred putting stones in the coal sacks, he doesn't care who sees him.'

The train stopped and they made their way out of the station.

'I'm going in to see Fred first before I make my way home,' Barny said.

'I might as well come with you,' Bert replied. 'I can't go home in case that sergeant is waiting for me.' They shouted out to Fred as they walked through the gates to the coal yard.

'How have you been doing, Darky?' Fred asked, when he saw them walking up to him. 'It looks like you have been in the wars. What have you been up to?'

'It's a long story, but I'm all right now,' Barny said.

Fred turned and asked Bert how Fanny was getting on.

'Why does everyone keep asking me about her? I don't see her any more and no one believes me.'

Corrosive Poisoning

'So what's been happening, Darky? Have you had enough of it up there and decided to come back home?' Fred asked as they walked over to his office.

'No, not at all. Bert came up last night and said that Violet wanted to see me so I've come down to find out what she wants. I suppose it's something about nothing.'

'No, I don't think it is this time,' replied Fred. 'I've heard that the parents of that sergeant chap, whom she was going to get married to, are in a bad way, money and healthwise. The last I heard was that the old man had lost all his money and suffered a heart attack, but I don't know how he is now. You don't hear much about those sorts of people, but I should think Violet's having second thoughts about the wedding, now that the money's gone.'

'No, she wasn't marrying him for his parents' money, Fred,' said Barny, 'she was just carrying out her parents' wishes.'

'Well, that's a good enough excuse as any. Anyway, Bert, I meant to ask you, what was that copper after you for yesterday?'

'Don't mention him to me, he was after me all day and it didn't matter where I went, I just couldn't get away from him.'

'He has been round here this morning as well, asking about you,' said Fred.

'You're having me on, surely he's not still after me, is he?'

'Four times he's been here asking about you, I don't know what you have done to him, Bert, but you have really upset him.'

'Right, he's done it now, I'm going to report him to the mayor,' Bert said.

'How can you do that after what you put him through?' said Barny.

'Well, he can't keep chasing me for the rest of my life can he? No, wait a minute, I won't be here very much longer and he won't be able follow me up north will he? I'll be free.'

Fred looked across at Barny. 'What's he going on about now?' he asked.

'He's going to be moving up north with me and my parents. I'm already renting a cottage up there and I have got enough work, so it won't be too much longer now.'

'I'm sorry to hear that, Barny,' said Fred. 'I will really miss you and your family.'

'Come on, Barny, let's go before that sergeant comes walking through the gates.'

Bert spoke too soon. The sergeant already had his head over the wall, looking for him. He shouted across to Bert to stay where he was, but Bert was off, like a rabbit down a hole. 'I will see you at your house, Barny,' he shouted as he disappeared over the railway lines.

Barny had a slow walk home with people stopping him and asking him how he was. It was over half an hour before he reached his front door. His mother's face lit up as Barny walked into her bedroom. 'Hello, son. What have you been up to? What's wrong with your hand and all them cuts on your face?'

'It's all right, Mum, it's nothing to worry about.'

'I've missed you so much, son.'

'I've missed you too, Mum. How do you feel now?'

'A lot better,' his mother replied. 'Your father and Beth are in the kitchen. Do you want to go through and see them?'

'No, I'd rather spend a bit of time with my old mum first.'

'Not so much of the old,' she replied, laughing.

'Mum, you are all right now, you would tell me if anything was wrong?'

'Of course I would, Barny. Beth has really looked after me, you know we owe her a lot. I wouldn't be as well I am if it wasn't for her. Do you know, she is very fond of you; she talks about you all the time.'

'Does she really? I wouldn't have thought I was her type.'

'A girl like that don't have types. She's a genuine person and you wouldn't go far wrong with her.'

'One day perhaps, one day.' Just then Beth walked in the bedroom, as Mrs Sturt had finished praising her.

'Hello, Barny, I never knew you were back,' she said as she walked up and kissed him on the head, but then she looked down and noticed his bandaged hand. 'Did my father tend to your injured hand?'

'Yes, it's not that bad really,' Barny replied, 'your father said it just needs strapping up for a few days.'

'Can I take a look?'

'Yea, you can later on, but not now,' he said.

'Go on, let me have a look now. You don't mind, Mrs Sturt, do you?'

'No, you go ahead, love. I know he's in good hands with you.'

'Come on, Barny, give me your hand.'

'OK, but in the kitchen, and then you can bathe it as well.'

They walked out of Mrs Sturt's bedroom and into the hall. Beth pulled him back and wrapped her arms around his neck and kissed him on the lips. 'I've missed you so much, Barny, more than I thought,' she said.

'Yes, and I've really missed you too, Beth.' They kissed and then Beth asked him why he didn't want her to look at his hand in the bedroom. 'I didn't want my mother to see it. Not yet, anyway, not until you've seen it. Your father said it's quite bad and I've haven't had any feeling in it since he strapped it up.'

'Come on,' she said, 'in the kitchen.' As they opened the door Barny's father looked up.

'You all right, son?' he asked.

'Yea, I'm not bad, Dad.' His father then looked down at his bandaged hand.

'I can see what you have been up to. Mark my words, you will get yourself killed one day and you know what that will do to your mother, it will break her heart.'

'That was my last fight.'

'Mr Sturt, would you mind going in and sitting with Mrs Sturt just while I change the bandage on Barny's hand?' Mr Sturt left the kitchen and Beth quickly undid the bandage. When she saw his hand she closed her eyes and took a deep breath. 'I think your hand is too far gone.'

'What do you mean?' Barny asked.

'How on earth did you do it? It's completely crushed. I don't know how you have managed to leave your bed, let alone walk aroud. We need to get you to the infirmary right away.'

'Now hold on, Beth,' Barny said. 'I can't go spending time in the infirmary, my mother would worry herself sick, I will have to wait until she is up and about.'

'No, I'm sorry, Barny, but I'm afraid you have no choice. Your hand is completely dead and it won't be long before gangrene sets in and you could lose your arm or, worse still, you could lose your life and I'm not going go let that happen to you. I have only just found you and I don't want to lose you, so please let me take you there now.'

'Can't you just patch it up for now, Beth? You're a nurse and it can't be that bad, I told you I can't even feel it. I know it looks bad and if it was painful then I could understand why I would have to go to the infirmary now.'

At the Precipice of Poverty

'Barny, listen, you don't understand. You can't feel any pain because there is no life left in your hand.'

'But it will get better, given time. Like all my other injuries; they have all healed up in the past without having to go to the infirmary.'

'This is different, look, wait a minute,' she said, as she opened up the cupboard and took one of Mrs Sturt's hat pins out. 'Now, put your hand on the table and turn your head away.'

Barny placed his hand on the table and Beth prodded the pin into his fingers and then in the palm of his hand. Barny never flinched, he couldn't feel the pin going in. 'Now, that proves it, Barny,' she said, 'I'm going to take you to the infirmary right away.'

'Look, please, Beth, just leave it for a few days and I promise I will go and have it seen to. I just want to give my mother enough time to get back on her feet. If she knows how bad my hand is she will only worry and that will put her straight back in the infirmary, so can we leave it just for a little while?'

'I don't really want to, Barny I can't force you to go, but I'm telling you the longer you leave it, the less chance they will have of saving your arm.'

'What do you mean? What's my hand got to do with my arm.'

'You still don't understand do you? Your hand is so badly damaged they will have to take it off. There is no doubt about that.'

Barny looked down at his hand. 'Tell me you're joking, Beth,' he said.

'It's not the end of the world,' she replied. 'I've seen many young soldiers lose their limbs and they still lead a normal life.'

'I need both my hands for work. If I can't work we will lose that cottage,' he said as the tears were building up in his eyes. 'This is all I have dreamt about for years – giving my parents a nice quiet life and somewhere decent to live.'

'You can still do that. You just get someone to give you a hand. Oh I'm so sorry, I didn't mean to say that. What I meant was you can get somebody to help you with the work.'

'What will happen if I don't let them cut my hand off?' Barny asked.

'You will die and you have too many people who love you to let that happen. You have got to go,' she said.

'I need to go for a walk. I need to think about this.'

'All right, I'll strap your hand back up before you go. Would you like me to come with you or would you rather be alone?'

'No thanks, Beth, I won't be long. Tell my mother I have just popped down to the shop.'

While Barny was out, Bert arrived and knocked on the bedroom door. 'Come in,' Beth shouted. Bert walked in.

'I'm knacked,' he said as he sat down on the end of the bed. 'How are you, Mrs Sturt? I must say you are looking a lot better than when I last saw you.'

'I'm fine, Bert, and what have you been running down the road for?' she asked.

'Oh, I've been trying to get away from …' He then realised it was Mrs Sturt whom he was talking to and he couldn't tell her that he had been running away from a police sergeant. He carried on, 'Well, it doesn't matter who, Mrs Sturt.'

'No, it doesn't, but I suppose it's that Fanny's husband again after you.'

'No, I don't do that sort of thing any more.'

'Why don't you leave the boy alone,' her husband said. 'It's his life and he can do what he wants with it.'

'So, what do you think about us all living together then, Mrs Sturt, I suppose you'll be like my mum in a way.'

'I beg your pardon?'

'Hasn't Barny told you yet? He said it might be all right if I moved in with you.'

'We haven't got the room, son, you know Barny has to sleep on the floor as it is.'

'No, not here, Mrs Sturt, in your new home. You know, the cottage Barny has got for you.'

Beth looked round at him. 'Do you mean the cottage near where I live?' she asked.

'Don't tell me he hasn't told you either. I've put my foot right in it now. I think I had better wait until he comes back and let him tell you the rest.'

'You bloody well won't,' Barny's father said, 'you tell us now.'

Bert explained everything about the cottage and the work that Barny had taken on and the church he had saved.

'I don't believe it,' Mrs Sturt said. 'He has arranged all of this, just for us.'

'Now, hold on a minute,' her husband said. 'It's a strange place up there and we don't know what it's like.'

'Don't you be so silly,' his wife said, 'Beth has told us all about it and it sounds beautiful.'

Beth then turned to Bert. 'Has he really got the cottage?'

'Yea, he's already paid the first month's rent.' He leant across and whispered in Beth's ear. 'He's still got to do the kitchen up first, you know, where that old girl snuffed it.'

'Bert, that's not a very nice thing to say about her,' she replied.

'So you're going to be my new lodger are you, Bert?' said Mrs Sturt, with a look of hesitation on her face. 'You know I won't have no carrying on under my roof; now you know that, don't you.'

'Of course, I wouldn't dare think of doing that,' he replied.

Just then Barny walked into the room. 'Come here, son,' his mother said, holding her arms up to him. Barny walked across and received a hug and a kiss. 'They have told me all about it,' she said.

Barny looked round at Beth thinking she had told his mother about his hand. 'Have you told her?'

'Bert's been telling your parents all about the cottage you're renting and all the work you have taken on,' she said, trying to change the subject.

'Sorry about that, Barny, I thought you had already told them, still they know now,' Bert said.

'What do you think about it, Dad?' Barny asked.

'Your mother's right, it does sound very nice the way Beth explained it, but we will have to wait and see,' he said.

Beth walked over to Barny. 'Will you come and help me make some tea?' As they left the room Barny's mother was asking Bert how Fanny's husband was; he did not know she was only winding him up.

In the kitchen Beth held Barny's hand and closed the door. 'Well,' she said, 'have you thought about it?'

'Yes, and you are right. I will have Bert with me so we should be able to manage, but I'm not going to have it off until my mother's on her feet again. The shock might kill her the way she has been over the last few weeks.'

Beth put her arms around his waist. 'Thank you, Barny,' she said. 'It won't be that bad and anyway you will always have me around to look after you.'

Corrosive Poisoning

'Look, Beth, I don't want to have any secrets from you so I want to tell you that the reason why I am back is that Bert brought a message up to me from Violet. She says she wants to see me.'

'What about?' asked Beth.

'I don't know, she wouldn't tell Bert what it was about, but it must be serious. Bert said she was very upset when he saw her, so I don't know what's happened.'

'Just promise me that you won't forget about your hand. You can't afford to get into a fight with anyone, not even for Violet's sake. So if she wants you to sort anyone out just tell her that she will have to get someone else to do it.'

'I will, I promise. I have thought hard and long about what's happened and I'm finished with fighting now for good.'

Barny left for the coal yard and as usual Violet was late. He waited thirty minutes for her and then she finally turned up. 'You haven't changed, Violet, always late,' he said.

'You never used to mind about that, I remember when you would have done anything for me.'

'Yes, and I would still help you if you needed it, but you have got to remember you walked out on me. You will never know how much you hurt me, Violet. I have never been through anything like that before. I was so bad that I even considered taking my own life.'

'I suppose Beth talked you out of it,' she said.

'No, she wasn't there at the time, but she has helped me, she has really helped me a lot.'

'Well, she would. Everyone knows she's perfect, your parents like her, everyone likes her, but I know she is just a scheming little posh bitch.'

'Don't talk about her like that. She hasn't done any harm to you,' he replied.

'She has really got to you, Barny, and she can't put a foot wrong in your eyes. Don't you have any feelings left for me?' she asked.

Just then two coal carts came into the yard. 'Have you got the key to Fred's office?' he asked, 'We will be better off talking in there, but I am not arguing with you, Violet. You can tell me what you have to say and then I'm off.'

'So that's what it has come down to is it?' Violet shouted. 'I tell you what's on my mind and then you just go and leave me here.'

The two carts stopped nearby and the drivers were looking over. 'Go on, son, give her a good slap. Don't let her talk to you like that,' one of the drivers shouted over.

'Bring her over here, I'll show her where a woman's place is, right underneath me,' the other one shouted, both trying hard to stop themselves from laughing.

Barny looked over. 'Go on, Barny,' Violet said, 'go and sort them out. You don't let them talk to me like that.'

'They are not from around here, they don't know who I am and I'm not going to beat them for no reason,' he said.

'My God, that-stuck up cow has really changed you. I can remember the time when you would have run over there and pulled them off their carts before they had stopped shouting and given them a damn good beating.'

'Well, we were together then, but you have chosen to marry someone else now so there is nothing between us. You never gave me any commitment at all and I've realised that now, since we have been apart.'

'Well, you never know, there may be some commitment between us in the future.'

'What do you mean?' he asked.

'I'm just saying things change and you never know what the future holds.'

'Violet, you're talking in riddles,' he said. 'I don't understand what you're trying to say to me.'

'Come with me into the carriage and we'll talk.' They walked into the carriage and sat on the same bench as before.

'Cor, it's cold in here, give me a cuddle,' she said.

'What are you up to, Violet? I really don't understand you sometimes, what's all this about?'

'Just cuddle me, Barny,' she said.

'No,' he replied. 'You can't go around from one bloke to the next. If I put my arms around you it wouldn't be fair on that sergeant bloke you're going to marry. How would you like it if someone done the same thing to you? Now just tell me what you want to say and I'll be off, I've got a lot of things on my mind at the moment and I haven't got time to mess about in here with you all day.'

'Don't bother,' she said, 'go on, be on your way, if you don't want to hear about the most important thing that is going to happen in your life then just go. It doesn't bother me any more.'

This was getting too much for Barny, he couldn't stand the thought of being hurt by Violet again so he walked over to the door. 'This is it, Violet, very soon I'm going to start a new life in a village up north with my parents and Beth and you won't see me any more. I thought we would part on better terms than this. You have what you want, you're marrying into money, now please just let me do what I want to do and be happy for me.'

'I don't think so,' she replied, 'when you hear what I have got to tell you, you won't be going anywhere, not without me anyway.'

'Do you know what, I feel really sorry for you,' he said as he walked out of the door.

Violet followed shouting out, 'Don't you dare walk out on me, Barny Sturt, I haven't finished with you yet.'

Barny kept on walking. The two men who were on their carts earlier were now standing by the carriage, laughing at Violet's antics.

'You come back here, Barny Sturt,' she shouted as she chased after him.

The two men laughed even more and one of them shouted out. 'Come back here, you old trollop, we'll sort you out.'

Violet stopped and walked back to the two men. 'What did you call me?'

'Trollop, that's the name your sort of women are called,' he said. 'Now, if you want a real man you had better follow me in there and I'll show you what it's all about.'

'You two can sod right off,' she said, 'and go back to the sewer where your mother lives.'

'Come on, trollop, don't be like that,' one of them said, as he pinched her bum.

Violet let out a scream and punched the man in the mouth, knocking him to the ground. Violet was known for having a loud voice and her scream carried across the coal yard and within the earshot of Barny. He turned round and saw one man on the ground and the other one struggling with Violet. He thought Violet was being attacked, but it was the other way around, the poor man was trying to get away from her. He rushed across the coal yard to help Violet, but, as he approached her she threw another punch and knocked the other man to the ground.

'I thought you were in trouble,' Barny said.

'So you do care,' she replied, 'or else you wouldn't have come running back to help me.' While they were arguing one of the men started to get up. Violet saw him and kicked him back down.

'I can see that you don't need me,' Barny said, and started to walk away.

Violet started shouting again. 'Barny, please come back I haven't told you what I have to say yet.'

'It's too late for that, Violet. I'm not coming back now. I don't care what you do any more.'

Violet shouted at him again. 'Barny, stop, Barny, please, I'm having your baby.'

Barny stopped and turned. 'You're what?' he said.

'That's what I have been trying to tell you, me and you, we are going to have a baby together.'

'Violet, please tell me you're messing about,' he said as he walked back.

'No, it's true I've been to the doctor's and he has confirmed it,' she said.

'How,' Barny asked, 'how do you know it's mine?'

'You bastard,' she shouted back. 'How dare you say it's not yours. I haven't been with anyone else except you.'

'Violet, you're well known for all the different men you have been with,' he said.

'Yes, just to go out with for a good time, that's all, but not to sleep with. You were the first and this baby is yours.'

'What about that sergeant, you have been seeing him for some time, you must have been with him.'

'No, I swear I haven't, not that I didn't want to, of course I did, but we just never had the opportunity.'

'Come on inside,' Barny said, 'we had better talk this through.' They sat down on the bench and she asked Barny again to put his arms around her. 'No, wait, I need to get my head around this first. Have you told anyone else?'

'No,' she replied, 'well, only my best friend, Mary, you know the one I told you about who has rooms in Wentworth Road. I had to tell somebody.'

'So your parents don't know?'

'No, but I'm hoping that, because they will be gaining a grandchild, they might change their minds about you and accept you.'

'Oh, Violet, what am I going to do with you?'

Corrosive Poisoning

'Well, for a start, you can help me bring up our child. I will never be able do it on my own and you want your child to have the best life possible, don't you?'

'Well, of course I do,' he replied.

'Then you will have to stay with me.'

'Yea, if that's what you want,' he replied.

They put their arms around each other and Violet went to kiss him, but he pulled away from her. 'What's wrong now?' she asked.

'I want to explain everything to Beth first before we get back together, it wouldn't be fair on her otherwise.'

'That's all right, I don't mind,' she said. 'As long as you tell her that you're finished with her for good and I want to be there when you do.'

'No. There's no way I'm going to do that, not with you standing there gloating. She is going to be hurt enough as it is without you enjoying it. What about the sergeant, how will he take it?'

'I don't know. He's home on leave next Thursday so I will have to tell him then.'

'What about the big wedding you were arranging?'

'Oh, that's already cancelled,' she said.

'What do you mean, I thought you hadn't told anyone?'

'No, I haven't. It was cancelled last Friday.'

'Why? I don't understand.'

'Well, it's a long story, but Percy's father has been lending a lot of money to his brother who has a farm in Kent. He has had a lot of problems over the last year and has only survived because Mr Bylett has been helping him out. Anyway Mr Bylett has had to have a lot of repairs carried out at his shops and after the builders had finished he did not have the money to pay them and was declared bankrupt, so all the money he had for the wedding has been taken from him to pay for some of his bills. He has even had to move to a smaller house. My father was furious, not so much because the wedding was cancelled, but to see a nice respectable man thrown out of his home without anything left.'

'I hope that's not the reason you want me back,' Barny said.

'No, of course not. I'm telling you, Barny, I just couldn't bring up a child on my own.' They carried on talking trying to sort out what they were going to do.

Meanwhile, back in Barny's mother's bedroom, Beth, Bert and Mr Sturt were all sitting on Mrs Sturt's bed talking. Beth was trying to find out as much as she could about Barny. 'What was he like as a child?' she asked.

'He was a lovely boy,' Mrs Sturt said, 'the same as he is now, always going around helping people and always getting into trouble.'

'That's right,' Bert said, 'I went all through school with him. He was always sticking up for the weak lads and that's why people liked him so much. He would do anything for anyone, nothing was too much trouble, and it's the same with the people around here. They all respect him and they know who to go to when they are in trouble. Do you remember poor little Doris Probert?'

'Yes, I do remember her, the poor little mare. She was only fourteen years of age and she lived not far from where we used to live and she thought the world of Barny. When she was younger she used to come and knock for Barny and ask me if he was allowed out to play. But Barny would never push her away, he would always talk to her and have time for her; he was also friendly with her parents. Anyway she was put into service in one of the big houses and one Saturday evening her mistress sent her on an errand to pick up some picture frames that were being repaired. When she arrived at the shop, the door was locked and a sign said "Back in half hour". So poor little Doris waited for the owner, whose name was Edward Seymore. That was the name wasn't it, Bert?'

'Yea, that's right, Mrs Sturt.'

'Tell Beth what happened next, Bert, it still upsets me,' she said.

Bert carried on. 'Well, little Doris asked the man Seymore if her mistress's frames were ready. He replied to Doris, "We will have to see. Come with me to the workshop." Which was out at the back of the shop. Doris said that when she was out at the back of the shop with the owner, he was showing her the frames and then put his arms around her waist and then kissed her and when she struggled to get away, he committed an assault on her. Doris said that he then told her that she mustn't tell anyone about what had happened and he gave her a threepenny piece and some postcards.'

'She must have been terrified,' said Beth, 'why would someone want to do anything like that?'

'He must have a screw loose,' replied Mrs Sturt, 'that's the only thing I can think of. No normal person would do a thing like that to a little child.'

'So what happened when she left the shop?' asked Beth.

'Well, she took the frames back to her mistress and then returned home; it was about nine o'clock and she had finished her work for the day. Anyway, when she got home her mother asked her where she had got the postcards from and she replied a man had given them to her.'

Mrs Sturt interrupted then: 'The poor little mite. Her mother thought what any other mother would think, that she had pinched them, so she started to shout at her. This made little Doris cry and then she told her mother what had happened in the back of the shop.'

'It wasn't the first time,' Mr Sturt said, 'she then admitted that it happened once before.'

'What did Barny say – I bet he went mad,' asked Beth.

'He didn't know at the time,' said Mrs Sturt. 'The first we knew of it was when the girl's father came and asked Barny if he would go and help him sort the man out. Barny hit the roof when he heard what had happened, he went straight out to the back yard and picked up a piece of lead piping, but when he came back in I told him to leave it to the police. I said it would do no good beating the man – it would be better if he was charged and sent to prison. After a time he agreed and said he would go and report it, but I knew what he would do as soon as he left the house – go straight to the shop, so I said I would report it and told his father to keep him in the house with the girl's father.'

'You did the right thing, A spell in prison on hard labour would soon cure the shopkeeper,' said Beth.

'That's what we thought, but to cut a long story short: the man went to court and Doris gave her story of what happened, but the man denied it and we think because he was on the council committee and a respected businessman, the court fined him 5s and 4s 6d.'

'That was nothing to a man like him,' Bert said, 'but he got his punishment in the end; that right, Mrs Sturt?'

'That certainly is, Bert,' she replied.

'After the court case her father came to our house and told us what had happened. Well, Barny went mad. I knew I wouldn't be able to stop him now.

'You know I can't stand violence, Beth, and it turns my tummy when Barny's fighting, but that afternoon I wanted to say to him go on, son, go and teach him that git that he can't go around abusing little girls and get away with it.'

'What happened then?' Beth asked.

'They left to go the shop and Barny returned after about half an hour and he wouldn't say a word. I did ask him what had happened and he just replied. "It's all right, Mum, there is nothing for you to worry about now, it's all been sorted."'

'So you never knew what happened to the man?' asked Beth.

'Not at the time, but a bit later on, old Nelly from down the road was returning from her sister's and, as she passed the man's shop, she saw being taken him away. She said his face was unrecognisable, where he was so badly beaten. No one can say he didn't deserve it, he won't be touching any little girls around here any more,' Bert said.

'No, that's right,' said Mr Sturt. 'After two weeks his shop was empty and up for sale and he had moved right away.'

'Didn't Barny ever mention to you what happened?' asked Beth.

'No, from that day to this, he has never said a word about it.'

'You get some right goings on around here, Beth. Mind you, I think I will miss it when we move. Here, do you remember Kate Penrith?' Mr Sturt asked his wife.

'I will never forget her,' she replied. 'What a carry on that was, I had to go to court and give evidence. Yes, it's true, I had to wear my best hat, all proper like.'

'What happened to her?' Beth asked.

'Well, here, Bert, go and make a nice cup of tea and I'll tell Beth all about it.'

'All right Mrs Sturt, shan't be long. Now, I do remember what happened to her, very nasty it was,' he said and left the room, leaving Beth anxiously waiting to hear all about Kate Penrith.

'Come on, what happened to her? You don't get anything like this happening where I live.'

'Well, Kate was in service; now how old would you say she was?' asking her husband.

'About twenty-two I should think, yea, that's right, I remember it being said in the court.'

'Yes, that's right, anyway I had met her in the butcher's shop. She was in there getting some rabbit for her mistress and she looked really upset, so I asked her what was wrong and she told me she had just lost her granny. I felt so sorry for her. I said to her, "Look, come back with me and have a rest before you go back to work, we only live round the corner." Anyway, she came with me, but I had to pop in to the cobbler's first and then we went home, she didn't seem too bad then.'

Mrs Sturt turned to her husband: 'Do you remember that day?' she asked. 'You were off work with your chest.'

'Yes, she did seem like a nice girl, I couldn't see any harm in her,' he said.

Mrs Sturt carried on. 'She stayed for about an hour and when she was ready to go, I said to her if at any time she was passing, to just pop in to see us. She told me she never had many friends around here and she would like to come and visit us if it was all right. Anyway she started to come round on her evening off and it went on for about two years.'

'What did Barny think of her?' Beth asked.

'He only saw her a few times, he was always out, but when he did come home when she was there the girl would go all quiet and look down at the floor. I think she was very shy.'

'Carry on, Mrs Sturt,' Beth said.

'Well, one night she knocked on our door and she was in a terrible state, crying and shaking. I said to her what on earth's the matter? I brought her into our room and sat her down and when she had stopped crying, she told me that her mistress had accused her of stealing a lace handkerchief. I remember her looking up at me with those big blue eyes. "I never took it, Mrs Sturt," she cried, "honestly, I wouldn't steal from anyone." "It's all right, love, I believe you," I said to her. After she had stopped crying, I settled her down and gave her a drink. She said she had nowhere to go now and she would be out on the street all night, so I told her she could stay with us until she got herself sorted out, but I said she would have to sleep on the floor. How long was she with us for?' she asked her husband.

'She stayed a fortnight,' he replied.

'Yes, that's right, about two weeks, and then she went and found service at Chuckfield. The next I heard from her was a telegram asking if I could meet her at the station that same evening, so I went up there and met her off the train. When she walked up to me she said, "I've come to see you, Mrs Sturt, but I have come in trouble." She had a baby in her arms and I asked her where she had got the baby from. She replied that it was hers. Well, you could have knocked me down with a feather, Beth. I couldn't believe she had gone away and then come back with a baby in her arms.'

'Did she tell you who the father was?' Beth asked.
'No, she said she never knew,' Mrs Sturt replied. 'So I took her home and she stayed the night, the baby was such a cute little thing.'
'How old was it?' Beth asked.
'I think about fifteen days. The next day Kate said she was going to the infirmary with the baby and I said to her that I would go with her, but she thanked me and said she would rather go on her own.'
'Strange, that,' Mr Sturt said, 'we never did find out why she went there.'
'Go and see if Bert's made the tea, love,' Mrs Sturt said to her husband.
As her husband left the room Beth moved closer to her. 'How long was she in the infirmary for?' she asked.
'The first day she sent a letter out with one of the porters; she asked if I could go and fetch her when she was well enough to leave and also bring some clothes for the baby. I remember taking her a cream woollen shawl. She also said in her letter that she was going to put the child out with a Mrs Thomas of Cherry Orchard Road.'
'What did she mean?' asked Beth.
'Well, there are some ladies around who look after young ladies babies, for a small fee, of course.'
'Oh I see, but how do the young ladies pay her if they have no work?' she asked.
'Well, that's the problem. Sometimes they bring the babies to them and don't return and the babies end up in the workhouse.'
'So when did you next hear from her again?' she asked.
'Four weeks later I received another letter and she said that she had seen a Mrs Ford of the Rescue and Preventive Association and a Sister Bullen, who had thought that they might be able to get her boy adopted by someone. I then met her the next day at the infirmary and took her home. The baby was lovely, such a dear little fellow. She had something to eat and then fed the baby; later on that day she told me she was going to take the baby to Mrs Thomas, in Cherry Orchard Road, and from there to a lady in South Croydon, who was going to adopt him.'
'How did Kate seem in herself?' Beth asked.
'Not too good at all. She was very upset and never stopped crying. I said to her, "Don't go, stop here until you're feeling a bit better," but she wouldn't hear of it. She left at about half past five. Later on that night, me and Mr Sturt were sitting down talking when there was a knock on the door and when Mr Sturt answered it, Kate was standing

there crying, without the baby. It must have been about twenty minutes to nine.

'Where is that Bert with that tea?' she asked. 'Has he gone down to the docks to get the tea off the clippers?' Just then the door opened and Mr Sturt walked in with the tea.

'Where is Bert?' Beth asked.

'He's out in the yard talking to that bloke next door. He never even started to make the tea, the lazy sod. He will have to pull his weight a bit more when he moves in with us.'

The door opened and Bert poked his head round. 'Your cups have disappeared,' he said.

'Disappeared?' she replied. 'The time it took you to get the tea ready, we all would have died from thirst.'

'Sorry, Mrs Sturt, I was talking to old Harry from next door, he was telling me that he was in court last week.'

'Oh yea, and what's he been up to?' Mr Sturt asked.

'No, it wasn't him, what happened was, he went up to Mr Randall's shop for a pint of milk and when he got it home he thought it never tasted right so he had a closer look and found it contained a lot of water, you can tell by the colour or something.'

'I wouldn't know the difference,' said Mrs Sturt.

'He did. He said he used to live on a farm and said he knows when some water has been added.'

'That's right,' said Beth, 'we get the milk straight off the farms at home and you can tell if water's been added.'

'What did he do then?' asked Mr Sturt.

'He went to the police station and they sent an inspector round to his shop. After the inspector had finished, he went round to old Harry's house and told him that a young lad who worked for Mr Randall had taken delivery of the early morning milk and had put a steam pipe into it to sterilise it. This was now an obsolete way of sterilising milk, but the boy was new and never knew this. He put the pipe in without sufficient pressure of steam, and this had caused the difference of 13 or 14 per cent. He then asked Harry if he still wanted him charged and Harry said yes. Anyway, they went to court and the shop owner Mr Randall said that he was adopting an entirely different system for sterilising his milk.'

'What happened to him?' asked Mr Sturt.

'He was fined 40s and 16s costs.'
'That was a lot for one pint of milk.'
'Yea, but they are getting really hot on people selling food now. George, in the greengrocers, said he can't wipe the mould off the tomatoes any more; he has to take them off the shelves.'

'I must say that was really interesting, but I really want to find out what happened to Kate,' said Beth.

'Oh yes, now be quiet, Bert, while I finish the story,' Mrs Sturt said, and carried on: 'When Kate came back without the baby, I said to her, "They have taken the baby then," and she replied, yes. She looked a bit upset so I made her bed up on the floor and she fell asleep. The next day when I walked into the kitchen, as I picked Kate's coat up off the floor and put it behind a chair, I noticed a stain on it. When she woke up, I asked her where the stain had come from and she replied, "It must have been something I spilt on it."'

'So where had she been?' asked Beth.

'The night before I had said to her, "You do look tired, it looks as though you have walked miles," and she replied, "Yes, I am tired, I have walked a long way today," and she also had the baby's shawl with her. The one I had taken into the infirmary for her. I thought then, that's strange, but then perhaps the woman who had taken the baby never wanted the shawl. Then I remembered that when I was picking her coat up the night before I also picked up the baby's shawl and noticed that it was very wet. Well, then I made her some tea and asked if it would be all right if I went to visit the little baby only I got quite attached to it when it was here. She turned to me and said abruptly that no, he was not in my charge any more and couldn't let me see him. "All right," I said, "don't worry, I was only asking." After a while she got her coat and went out and while she was out the police came. Well, I got the fright of my life: the first thing that came to my mind was Barny. I asked the constable what had happened to him.'

'Well, you would do, you'd think he'd had an accident or something like that,' Beth said.

'That's what I thought, but the constable looked at me a bit strange and asked me if I knew a Kate Penrith. I said, "Of course I do, what's happened to her?" "No, she's all right," the constable said, "it's her poor little baby. We found it last night at about midnight on a piece of waste ground; I'm afraid it was dead." I got the shock of my life. I had to go into the scullery and have a sit down.

'The constable followed me in and said that I would have to give evidence in court the next day. Well, I didn't get a wink of sleep that night and the next day I was so nervous. Barny's dad came with me though and helped me through it, but in the end I only had to say when Kate stayed with me and what she had written in her letters and how the baby looked when I last saw her.'

'So, how did the baby die?'

'Oh, it was terrible. The police officer who had come round to see me said that when the baby was found, he was still alive, but was suffering from corrosive poisoning. They took him to the infirmary, but he died the next day.'

Beth was wiping away the tears from her eyes. 'The poor little thing, he must have really suffered. Did they have any proof that he died of corrosive poisoning?'

'That is just what I asked,' Mrs Sturt replied. 'They carried out a search around where they found the baby and came across a baby's bottle, which contained spirit of salts. That's what they say the baby was given before he died, and about a mile away they found the baby's clothing, wrapped up in newspaper.'

'How did they know it was Kate's baby?' Beth asked.

'Well, after they had found the baby, they went round all the chemists in the area, knocking them up and getting them out of their beds and asking how many people had bought spirit of salts the day before and luckily there were only six altogether. Four were very old people and one was a young schoolgirl and the last one, who was unknown to the chemist, was the suspect. The chemist gave them a good description of the girl and, lo and behold, when Kate left our house that morning, she got to the top of the road and two constables recognised her and then took her away.'

'Did they find her guilty?' asked Beth.

'Firstly, the coroner asked if she would like to give any evidence and she said, "I reserve my defence," and then she made a loud noise and fell back in her chair; she had fainted. When they carried her from the court she was moaning and groaning. Anyway, the jury found that the dead child was the child of Kate's and returned a verdict of wilful murder.'

'How awful, there must have been something wrong with the young girl,' Beth said.

'I did like her at first,' replied Mrs Sturt, 'she seemed respectable and clean, but there was always something about her, you know, like the lights were on, but there was no one in, that sort of thing.'

'You can't tell these days, there are some evil people about,' said Mr Sturt, 'it's best to keep yourself to yourself. That's what I keep telling Barny, stay out of other people's business and let them sort their own troubles out, but does he listen. Does he heck as like. He'll get into something one day and he won't be able to get out of it.'

'Don't listen to him, love, my husband wouldn't speak to anyone if he had his way. Where is that son of mine anyway, he's been a long time. Bert, Bert,' she called out.

Poor old Bert had fallen asleep on the end of the bed only to be awoken by Mrs Sturt's big toe prodding at his nose. 'Do you know where Barny's gone?' she asked.

'No, I don't, Mrs Sturt,' he said, rubbing his eyes. 'Do you know, Beth?'

'No, I don't know where he is, he just said that he was going for a walk.'

'Beth, do you know,' Mrs Sturt said, 'when you have known someone for a very long time, you get to notice little things about them. Now, I have known Bert all his life and I have noticed that when he's not telling me the truth, his left eye twitches.'

Bert gave her a strange look and then got up and walked to her dressing table and looked in the mirror. 'There is nothing wrong with my eye.'

'Well, you're not lying now are you? Look at me, Bert,' she said. 'Now, tell me if you know where Barny is?'

Bert looked at Beth and then at Mr Sturt, he then looked round at Mrs Sturt. 'Sorry I forgot, I think he said he was going to the coal yard, he might be seeing Fred.'

'Your eye never twitched then, so you must be telling me the truth,' she said.

Back at the coal yard, Violet and Barny were still talking. 'So you are going to stand by me, Barny?' she asked.

'I need time to think about this, Violet.'

'You said you will stay with me for the baby's sake.'

'Yes, I know, but it doesn't just affect me, it's my parents, Beth and then there's Bert. We were all moving away, you know, starting a new life. Well, I suppose we can still move,' he said, 'you can come with us, Violet.'

'You're joking, I couldn't live out in the sticks, I would be bored stiff. No, Barny, we would have to find somewhere to live around Wilford Road. All of my friends are around there and people know you, they respect you round here.'

'OK, there's a lot to be sorted out anyways, we just have see what happens. So when are you going to tell the sergeant?' he asked.

'He is coming home on compassionate leave on Wednesday afternoon, only for the day. He will be going back on Thursday. His train gets in at three o'clock in the afternoon.'

'Why have they given him compassionate leave?' Barny asked.

'Because of his father's situation, you know, he used to be in the regiment. Well, they are sending Percy home to help his father sort things out,' she said.

'So he doesn't know about anything else, he just thinks the wedding's off and his father's lost everything.'

'God no, he doesn't know about the baby, I don't know what he will say when I tell him that, he'll probably kill me after everything else that has happened,' she said.

'If you're frightened, I will make sure I'm there when you tell him,' said Barny.

'No, I will be all right. I am going to tell him in front of my parents, get it all over and done with in one go,' she said. 'Though I don't know what they are going to say, they thought I would be happily married to Percy in a month's time, living in a nice house and all of that.'

'Look, I will have to be off now, Violet,' he said. 'If you need me to be with you when you tell him just call me.'

'Well, give me a kiss before you leave,' she said.

'No, I've told you I'm going to sort it out with Beth first, before we do any of that.'

'Suit yourself,' she said, 'but you are going to walk me back home.'

'No, not this time,' he said. 'I've got things to do and I'm not going straight home yet.'

They left the carriage and Violet went her way and Barny went his. He *was* going straight home, but had taken the long way round. He needed time to think, on his own. When he did finally arrive home, he could hear his mother laughing. He walked in and shut the front door and, as he turned, Doris was just coming down the stairs towards him. They both stopped and looked in each other's eyes. 'Barny,' she said.

'Doris,' he replied and he opened the bedroom door. Doris tried to follow him, but Barny closed the door quickly before she got the chance to walk in.

'Who was that in the hall with you?' his mother asked.

'No one, Mum,' he said.

'Bert, will you go and have a look and see who it was?' she said.

Bert opened the door and Doris was still standing there, with a look of anger on her face.

'I'm sorry, Doris,' Barny said, laughing 'I didn't see you out there.'

Doris looked over at Mrs Sturt, 'I can tell you're getting better, I heard you laughing upstairs.'

'Yes, I do feel a lot better thanks to Beth. Where are you off to tonight?'

'I just received a message from my ex-husband. He wants to talk to me again. I don't know what about, he never makes any sense. I've got to meet him up the Fish.'

'Do you think that's wise, Doris?' Mrs Sturt said. 'You know how badly he beat you the last time you met.'

'Yes, I do remember, and he did it the time before that as well, but I can take care of myself,' she said.

'Doris, don't be silly, take Barny with you.'

'No, I will be all right. I'll pop in to see you when I get back,' she said, 'just to let you know that I am all right.' She then said her goodbyes and left the house on her way to the Fisherman's Arms.

'Barny, go with her,' his mother said. 'Her ex-husband is a bastard – he is so violent and she always comes back with a black eye or worse after she has seen him.'

'Mrs Sturt, did I hear you say a naughty word then?' said Bert.

'Shut up, you,' she said. 'Go on, son, run after her.'

'Do I have to? You know we can't stand each other.'

'Yes, you do, now, go on.'

Barny left the house and just as he was shutting the front door, he could see Doris turning into Windmill Road. He ran after her, shouting her name.

When he finally caught up with her she asked him what he wanted.

'My mother said that I had to come and look out for you.'

'I don't need looking after,' she said. 'You go back home to your mother. I can take care of myself.'

'Well, if you're sure, but don't forget to tell my mother that I did offer to help you.'

Barny returned home and Doris carried on to the Fisherman's Arms.

'She didn't want my help,' Barny said as he sat on the bed.

Bert looked over at him. 'Was there anyone else out there?'

'Yes, there is always plenty of people out in the road.'

'No, you know, was there anyone we both know standing out there?'

'Yes, of course there was, we know all of them. What's wrong with you, Bert?'

'Did you see someone who's good at running, you know in a blue suit?' he asked.

'Oh, you mean that sergeant who's been looking for you.'

'Oh bloody hell, Barny, you've told your mother now,' he said.

'What have you been up to now?' she asked.

'No, it's nothing, Mrs Sturt, I was just in the wrong place at the wrong time.'

'Go on, tell me or else you won't be moving in with us,' she said.

'All right, it was the other morning, I went out for an early morning stroll up by the Shirley Park Estate and as I was walking past the grounds I looked over the fence and someone was putting leaf mould into sacks. I shouted to him, "Oy stop that," and just then, out of nowhere, came two of the biggest coppers you have ever seen. One jumped on me and the other jumped on the man with the sacks. I managed to get away, but one of them chased me and has been following me ever since. Isn't that right, Barny?'

'Well, if Bert says so,' he replied.

'Bert, is that your left eye I see twitching before me?' Mrs Sturt asked.

'No, it's the truth honestly, he's really has been chasing me everywhere I go; tell them, Barny.'

'Well, it don't matter about that now. What did Fred want you for, Barny?' his mother asked.

'Fred, I haven't seen Fred,' he replied.

'Oh, I thought it was Fred you were seeing at the coal yard,' said Bert, looking at Mrs Sturt with his head bowed down. This is more trouble I'm in, he thought. I'll never be able to move in with them at this rate.

'No, it was Violet, Mum, she wanted to see me,' he said.

'What for?'

'Well, it's a long story. What happened was, that sergeant's father, the one with all the money, well, he hasn't got the money for the wedding any more and it has now been cancelled. He has lost everything – his house, the shops, the lot,' he said.

'So the wedding's off, is it?' asked Beth.

'It looks that way,' replied Barny. 'Everything they had arranged had to be cancelled.'

'That's a shame,' said his father. They all looked over at him.

'I didn't think you were that interested in the wedding,' his wife said.

'No, not the wedding,' he replied. 'The fact that Mr Bylett has lost everything, he was a good man.'

'How do you know?' asked Barny.

'Well, I used to be in his regiment; he was an officer and I was only a sapper, but he treated us well, I give him that. He was the only officer who thought about our lives before he sent us over the top. If there was any way he could save a life he would, not like some of the other officers. He was a good man. It's a shame it's ended like this for him.'

Barny sat on his mother's bed looking around him. There was Beth, the nicest girl he had ever met, she was so kind and considerate and he had fallen deeply in love with her. He knew it would break both their hearts if he had to let her go back home without him. Then there was Bert. He had a good heart, but he kept it well hidden. He had never had any real family life, his parents threw him out when he was only twelve and he had been in and out of trouble all his life. He was really looking forward to starting a new life with a new family. It would be the first real family he had. He deserved the chance to make something of his life and he wouldn't get the opportunity if he stayed round Wilford Road. It would be only a matter of time before he ended up in prison. His father, who had never been settled since he had to give up work: the fresh clean air of the countryside wouldn't do his bad chest any harm and he would be able to have his life back again, going out with his son and Bert, helping with the work and teaching his trade; he would be helping to bring in the money and be made to feel useful again.

Then there was his mother, the most precious person in the world to him. He would do anything for her, he would do his utmost to make her every wish come true. She meant more to him than life itself and he knew that she really wanted to move to that little village in the middle of nowhere. She had spoken of nothing else all day. Beth had told her all about it and she was really looking forward to seeing it for herself. She had lived a very hard life and this was Barny's chance to change all that and to make her really happy.

If he did leave Wilford Road and Violet, would he ever see his unborn child? Would Violet be able to bring the child up on her own or would she abandon it, like so many other young mothers of her age? What was he to do, stay with Violet and make sure his child had all the love and happiness he could give and turn his back on his family and friends? Or turn his back on Violet and his child and start a new and better life with Beth, Bert and his parents? It was a decision he had to make and it did not help not knowing for sure if the child was really his, and there was no way of knowing.

Chapter 10

The Final Journey

Barny's father looked over at his wife. 'I think I might turn in now, love,' he said, yawning.

'That's a good idea. You do look tired, you go to bed,' said Bert.

'Well I would Bert, if you weren't sitting on my bed.'

'Oh, I'm sorry,' said Bert. 'Do you know, I feel a bit tired myself as it goes. Yes, I think I'll turn in, too. Goodnight everyone.'

As Bert left the room, Beth looked round at Barny. 'Would you mind walking me home?'

'No, of course not, I'll go and get your shawl.'

Beth wished Mr and Mrs Sturt goodnight and then they left the house. As they walked half way down Wilford Road, Barny noticed that Doris had just turned the corner into Wilford Road. 'Hold on a minute, Beth,' he said. 'I just want to have a quick word with Doris.' As she walked up to them Barny could see she had marks all around her face.

'Are you all right, Doris?' he asked.

'Yes, I'm fine, just a bit sore, but nothing that won't be gone in a couple of days. Why, were you worried about me?'

'I suppose your ex-husband done this to you, did he?' Barny asked.

'Yes, just because I couldn't give him any money to buy ale. I thought he might have changed by now, but he's still the same.'

'And is he still up the Fish?' Barny asked.

'I don't know and I don't care, and don't think you're going up there to sort him out, Barny Sturt, he's not worth it.'

The Final Journey

'You can't let him get away with hitting you like that. He needs to be taught a lesson. He needs someone to beat him like he has beaten you, he would know what it feels like then.'

'Now, you keep well out of it,' she said, 'it's between me and him and there's no need for you to get involved. Now both of you be on your way.'

'Well, if that's what you want,' Barny replied. 'If you hurry you will just catch my mother before she goes to sleep,' he said.

'Yes, I think I will just pop in and see her, I could do with a chat and a cup of tea.'

Barny started to walk away from Doris with Beth holding tightly on to his arm. 'My father's not going to be too pleased,' he said. 'He will now have to stay up and listen to Doris going on about her old man.'

Beth looked at him and laughed. 'Here, how come you told me before that you can't stand the sight of that woman and yet you were prepared to go up to that public house and fight her husband for her?'

Barny looked round. 'I can't stand it when a woman gets beaten by a man, whether he's drunk or not. There is just no excuse and if anyone touched you, I would kill them with no doubt in my mind at all.'

'Yes, I can understand that and I know that you're right, but no one knows what goes on between a man and a woman and sometimes the man could be pushed over the edge. You know, the last resort, nothing left but to take his anger out physically on the woman, that may be his only option.'

'A man always has another option, Beth, walking away; that should be his last resort.'

'OK, smarty pants, you win, I know you're right. It was a shame about Violet's wedding, I feel quite sorry for her,' she said.

'Yes, still, if it wasn't meant to be.'

'So what did she really want to see you about, Barny?' Beth asked.

'I was going to talk to you about that. Now this is going to come as a bit of a shock to you, Beth, it did to me.'

'Go on then, I'm listening.'

'Well, she wanted to see me to let me know that she is having my baby.'

'You're joking! And what did you say to that?'

'Well, as I said, I was so shocked that the first thing that I asked her was if it was mine or not and she assured me it was, in no uncertain terms. I can't understand it, Beth, it was only the once the first day I met her and it was my first time.'

'That was the worst thing you could have said to her, Barny. I bet that made her feel really cheap.'

'Yes, I know,' he said, 'but I didn't know what to say. That was the last thing I expected her to come out with.'

'So do you know what you are going to do now?' she asked.

'No, well I know what I should do, but I wanted to talk it through with you first, Beth. I love you more than anything now and I don't want to lose you.'

'Yes, but you loved Violet when I first met you,' she said.

'Yes, I know, but she has changed so much. She's not the same person I first met and I can't give my love to a girl that has turned like she has.'

'Well, you know I love you, Barny, and I want to spend the rest of my life with you, but if you go away with me you may never see your unborn child,' she said.

'That's all I've been thinking about, but I can't let you walk out of my life and never see you again.' He stopped and put his arms around her. 'Beth, I need to ask you something and whatever you say, it won't change the way I feel about you.'

'What is it? Tell me,' she said.

'I want to go away with you like we planned, but how would you feel if we both came back when the baby was born and, if Violet didn't want it, then we would take it back with us. I know it's a lot to ask and I won't blame you if you say no, but I just had to ask you.'

Beth kissed him on the forehead. 'Of course I wouldn't mind,' she said. 'I was so worried I was going to lose you, I don't care what I have to do as long as we can be together.'

They carried on walking. 'I feel so much better now,' Barny said.

'So do I,' replied Beth. 'Are you going to see Violet tomorrow?' she asked.

'No, she wanted me to, but I said I was too busy. I told her I would see her on Wednesday evening at eight o'clock, outside the cemetery gates. She is telling her parents and the sergeant about the baby at six that evening.'

'What are you doing tomorrow then?' she asked.

'Well, I thought perhaps you and me could spend the next two days together. We could take a tram ride into the country and then stop off at the tea rooms.'

'That would be really nice,' she said, 'but do you know what I would really like? I would love to go and see London. I've never been there before.'

'Well, that's sorted then,' he said, 'I will take you all round London and show you the sights. I didn't think, when I said we'd go for a ride in the country. Of course, you live in the country all the time and you must get sick of it, sorry.'

The next two days were the happiest Barny had ever spent. As they came back to Wilford Road, on Tuesday night, he said, 'One more week living around here and we will be gone. I can't wait.'

'Your parents are really looking forward to it as well,' said Beth.

'I know, they can't wait. I'm glad I've made this decision, Beth, we will be so happy together even if we have Bert with us.'

'He's not so bad,' Beth replied, 'he would do anything for you, Barny. I think he would even lay down his life if you wanted him to, he thinks that much of you.'

'I know, he's not a bad bloke really. Mind you, I have got him out of so many spots in the past, trouble just seems to follow him around. I just hope he leaves them all behind when we move.'

On Wednesday they stayed in. Barny sat with his mother for most of the day and Beth cleaned the rooms from top to bottom. 'I don't know why you are doing that,' said Barny, 'we'll be moving out soon.'

'You know I would never leave these rooms dirty,' his mother said. 'If Beth wasn't here, I would be up doing the work myself.'

'Where's Bert?' Barny asked.

'He is in the back yard I think. Do you know he hasn't been outside the front door since you both came back last Sunday. Is he in bad trouble?' she asked.

'No, he just wound this sergeant up the wrong way that's all, and he is frightened that if he gets arrested he won't be out in time to come with us.'

'Do you know, in one way, I shall miss living around here, especially the people; they might be rough, but they are genuine. You know where you stand with them and they will always help you out if you needed them. Fred came round yesterday, he was nearly in tears, a tough old boot like him. He's going to miss us a lot. We have known him for so many years. I said he could come up and visit us, I hope that was all right.'

'Yes, of course it was,' Barny replied.

Mrs Sturt continued, 'I've had a lot of people come in over the last few days, just to see how I was getting on. They all said they are going to miss having you around; they would have to get someone else to sort their problems out.' They had tea and Barny helped Beth to wash the plates up.

'I'll have to be going soon,' he said.

'OK,' she replied. 'You know, Violet won't like it when you tell her you're still moving away. You had better expect a few tears,' she said.

'Yes, I know, but I have made my mind up now and she will just have to get used to it.'

They gave each other a hug and a kiss and Barny went to get his coat. He popped his head around the bedroom door. 'I won't be long, Mum,' he said. 'I just have a few things to sort out.'

'OK, love, you take care, come over and give me a kiss before you go.'

'He is a grown man now, not a baby,' her husband said.

'Be quiet, you don't understand,' she said to him. 'He's a good boy. I just like to show him how much I love him, that's all.'

'You go ahead, Mrs Sturt. I wish I had someone who cared for me that much,' said Bert.

'You can shut up and all,' her husband said.

'Sorry,' replied Bert, knowing that he couldn't put a foot wrong in case they changed their minds about taking him with them when they moved away.

It was coming up to a quarter to eight when Barny left his house. He made his way to the cemetery gates to meet Violet. When he turned the corner of Princess Road, he could see Violet was already there. That's unusual, he thought to himself, this is the first time she has ever had to wait for me to arrive. As he walked closer to her, he noticed her face. He could see that her eyes were swollen and her lip was cut.

'Violet, what's happened?' he asked, as he lifted her face up to the gas lamp. 'Who has done this to you? Come on, tell me what happened.'

Violet looked at him and started to cry. 'Oh Barny, please hold me,' she said.

He put his arms around her. 'Was it that sergeant bloke, did he do this to you?'

The Final Journey

'Yes,' she replied, 'he was the one who beat me. I met him from the station and we went for a walk before going back home. I was going to tell him then, but he never stopped going on about his father, how bad it was that the wedding had to be cancelled and that we wouldn't have a nice house to move into when we did finally get married. I couldn't believe what he was saying – his father had lost everything he had worked for and he was seriously ill and all he kept going on about was the things his father wouldn't be able to buy him. So I just kept quiet and said we had better go home now. When we got to the front door he pulled at my arm. "Your father, he still wants us to get married, don't he?" he asked. "Yes," I replied, "now come on, come inside, we need to talk."

'When my father saw him he gave him his usual welcome with open arms and told him how sorry his was to hear of his father's plight and then they both sat around the table talking. My mother went into her bedroom and I was left sitting there on my own. So I got up and said to my father, "I have something to tell you both," but he just turned and said, "Not now, Violet, we are busy, you will have to wait until later to talk to us." I looked at both of them sitting there, and I couldn't take any more of it, Barny, I went into my mother's bedroom and asked her to come out and sit at the table. We both went into the other room and I sat next to my father and told him that I needed to speak to him now, not later. "What's the meaning of this?" he shouted. "I told you we were busy. Now go to your room, both of you."

'That was it, Barny, I just lost my temper then and I shouted back at him to listen to what I had got to say. My father's face dropped, he had never heard me shout like that before, especially not to him. He sat back in his chair and folded his arms. "What's so important that makes you behave like a spoilt brat who can't get her own way?" he asked. "Look," I said, "something else has happened which affects all of us." "Well, come on, don't just sit there, spit it out, girl," my father said.

' "I will, if you just give me a chance," I replied, I was getting so angry now. At first I was lost for words – angry as well as being frightened. Then I didn't know where to begin and in the end I just took a deep breath and said, "I'm having a baby."

'My father looked round at me in total disgust.

'"You're what?" he shouted. "I am having a baby, Dad." He then went absolutely mad; he started shouting at me and swearing and calling me all the names under the sun. It was terrible, Barny. My mother was crying and Percy was just sitting there looking down at the floor, not saying a word. My father left the table and threw the chair across the room; he then turned on me and slapped me around the face. He then looked down at the sergeant. "I'm ashamed of you, boy," he said, "I thought you were a decent lad, you coming from the regiment, but obviously I was wrong."

'I started to cry, because I knew what was coming next. Percy raised his head and looked over at me. "How could you do this to me, Violet, how could you do it?" My father then started to have a go at Percy. "Don't you go putting all the blame on her, it's just as much your fault as well as hers," he shouted.

'Percy looked up at him. "Mr Blake," he said. "It's not my fault, because it's not my baby."

"What?" my father screamed. "If it's not yours then whose the bloody hell is it? Oh no, don't tell me," he said, "it's that bloody Sturt's baby."

'He walked across the room to my bedroom and went in and after a few minutes he came back out with all my clothes and threw them at me. "What are you doing?" I asked him. "Get out of my house," he shouted. "I never want to see you again." I begged him not to throw me out, but he grabbed me by the hair and pulled me to the door. "Now get out and never come back in my house again." I walked out of the front door and just sat on the doorstep crying, not knowing what to do.

'Then the front door opened and Percy walked out. "I am so sorry," I said to him, "I really didn't mean to hurt you." He stood in front of me and bent down, grabbed my arms and pulled me up and around to the side of the house and pushed me hard against the wall. "Tell me why you did it, Violet? Why did you humiliate me like that in front of your parents?" he asked.

"I don't know why, it just happened."

'With that he raised his hand and hit me across the face two or three times, I can't remember, but the last punch knocked me to the ground. As I looked up at him, he brought another blow down to the top of my head and then turned me over and kicked me in the guts. I screamed out in pain and he then ran off.'

'Is the baby still all right?' Barny asked.

The Final Journey

'I don't know, the kick caused me so much pain, Barny, I didn't know which way to turn.'

'Where will you go now?' he asked.

She looked him in the eyes. 'Well, I thought I could ...' but before she could finish, Barny interrupted her. 'You know there is no room at our house.'

'No, well, that Beth's there isn't she? I suppose she is more important than me and your baby,' she said. 'Anyway, it doesn't matter, my friend Mary has rooms down Wentworth Road and she always said that I could stay with her if I had nowhere else to go, so it looks like I will have to stay there if you don't want me at your house.'

Barny watched her walk away and then he ran all the way to his house. As he opened the front door he could hear Bert singing in the scullery. He knew his father and Beth would be in the bedroom with his mother, so he walked straight through to Bert.

'Hello, Barny, you're back early.'

'Listen, I need you to come out with me, Bert,' he said.

'Why, Barny, is something wrong?' he asked.

'Yes, you know what that sergeant looks like, who's been seeing Violet, don't you? Well, I want you to come with me and look for him and then point him out to me.'

'Barny, if I go out there you know I will get chased all over town and I don't want to take the chance of getting caught, not now we are this close to moving away.'

'Yes, I know, and I am really sorry, Bert, but I can't worry about that now, it's important that I find that sergeant tonight before he goes back.'

'All right, I will get my coat and help you find him, but I must keep my head down.' Bert walked out of the front door first and Barny followed but, as he shut the door, he caught the sleeve of his jacket on a nail sticking out of the wall. He cursed.

'If my mother catches her arm on this, I'll kill that bloody landlord,' he said as he tried to free the sleeve of his jacket. Bert was already out in the road looking up and down when suddenly he shouted back at Barny.

'Quick,' he shouted, 'he's up there standing on the corner.'

Barny looked up. 'He's where?'

'Up on the corner, the sergeant, I can just about see him.'

With that Barny pulled away from the nail, ripping the sleeve of his jacket, and then he started to run as fast as he could towards the corner of Wilford Road. Bert put his hand out to stop him and shouted, 'Barny wait, don't go, hold on.' Barny was so worked up he didn't even hear what Bert was shouting, he just pushed past him knocking him down and then ran off up the road.

The sergeant was standing on the corner looking along Windmill Road with his hands in his pockets, but he noticed out of the corner of his eye that someone was running towards him and when he looked round he could tell by the look on Barny's face that he was coming for him. But before he could take his hands out of his pockets Barny was on him. He gave him one almighty punch in the face, which knocked him backwards and on to the ground. Barny knelt down on the sergeant's chest and was just about to place another blow on to the sergeant's face when he felt someone on his back trying to pull him off. It was Bert. 'Barny,' he shouted. 'You don't understand, come on, you have got to stop.' Barny only had one good hand and Bert managed to pull him off and, as they were both struggling on the ground, the sergeant was getting to his feet. Barny saw this and stood up with Bert on his shoulders, he then pushed him off and Bert hit the ground with a thud. The sergeant was just about to get to his feet when Barny went running over to him and kicked him in the face. 'That's one for my unborn child, you bastard,' he shouted. The sergeant's body left the ground with the force of Barny's kick and then fell backwards and, as he did so, the side of his head cracked open as it hit the kerb stone.

Barny jumped on him again but, as all this was happening, Detective Sharp and two constables were just walking into Windmill Road from Forster Road. Detective Sharp could see it was Barny on top of the other man. 'Quick,' he shouted to the two constables, 'grab hold of him.' They ran up to Barny and pulled him off, but it would take more than the three of them to hold him down. He kicked out at one of the constables and hit him in the face, he then fell backwards and was knocked out cold. The other constable immediately started to blow his whistle for assistance. It was lucky for them, but not so lucky for Barny. Three more constables were just walking out of Union Road and heard the constable's cry for help. When they saw what was happening, they rushed over the road and then grabbed hold of Barny and now, with five of them on top of him, holding him down, they were able to get the cuffs on him.

'Barny was now helpless, he was cuffed and had one of the constables sitting across his legs and another one across his chest. While all of this was going on and with Barny now under control, Detective Sharp went over to the sergeant whom Barny had begun the fight with. He hadn't moved since Barny's last blow and was lying in a pool of blood. Detective Sharp put his fingers against the sergeant's neck and then looked up at Barny. 'You've done it this time, Sturt, good and proper,' he shouted across to him. 'You've gone and killed a copper. You will hang for this, my boy, and it's long overdue.'

'Don't mess me about, you pig, that's no copper,' Barny shouted back. 'It's a sergeant from the army.'

Just then Bert was just getting to his feet; he looked around him and knew what had happened straight away. Barny looked across at him and shouted out, 'Tell him, Bert, tell him that's not a copper, it's that sergeant who Violet was seeing.'

Bert walked over to him. 'Barny, you fool,' he said. 'Why didn't you just listen to me before you ran off? 'I was trying to tell you.'

'Tell me what?' Barny asked.

Bert started to cry. 'I was trying to tell you that he is not the sergeant you were looking for; he is the one who has been chasing me around for weeks.'

'Do you mean he's a copper? What was he doing around here without a uniform on?'

'I told you he has been after me day and night, even when he has been off duty; that's why he was in plain clothes.'

Barny lowered his head and shook it from side to side. Bert tried to tell Sharp that it was all a big mistake and it wasn't Barny's fault, but Sharp wasn't having any of that, he had waited for years to get Barny and now he had him. While all this was going on, a crowd was gathering all around them and it was getting more hostile by the minute. Detective Sharp told his men to march the prisoner to the station. As they lifted him off the ground a stone came from the crowd and hit one of the constables on the head. 'Draw your truncheons, lads,' the detective shouted and they pushed their way through the crowd bringing their truncheons down on the heads of some of the men.

Bert was still standing there as they took Barny away; he couldn't take in what had just happened. A man came up to him and asked if he was all right. Bert looked at him. 'It's a mistake,' he said, 'just a bloody mistake.' He slowly walked back down Wilford Road, not knowing how he was going to tell Mrs Sturt what had happened. Shall I not tell her? he thought. I'll wait until the morning and then go and find out if Barny's all right. He walked into the bedroom. They were all standing by the front window looking out.

'What's happening up the top of the road?' they asked, as he walked into the room, but he just went over to the bed and sat down and put his head in his hands.

'What's wrong, Bert?' Mrs Sturt asked, but Bert just sat there in silence. Beth walked over to him.

'Bert, what's wrong? Is it Barny?'

He looked up at her with tears rolling down his cheeks. 'It wasn't his fault, Beth, he didn't know who it was.'

'What are you talking about, Bert? What's happened to him?'

'He's gone and killed a copper,' Bert said shakily.

Mrs Sturt fainted when she heard what Bert had said. As they lifted her onto the bed, Beth said, 'We can't just sit here and do nothing I'm going down to see if I can see him.'

'No,' Mr Sturt said, 'you stop here and take care of my wife and Bert and myself will go down there.' They left the house, leaving Mrs Sturt and Beth to comfort each other, both wondering how all this happened, both hoping that this was a nightmare and that they would wake up from it soon.

Four hours later they heard the front door open. 'Is that them out there, Beth?' Mrs Sturt asked.

They walked into the bedroom, not saying a word.

'Well, what's happened?' asked Mrs Sturt.

'Nothing,' replied her husband, 'they wouldn't tell us a thing; all they said was that he was in custody and we should go home, they wouldn't even let me see him.' Mr Sturt sat on the bed, holding his wife's hand. 'What are we going to do, love?' he said.

They stayed awake all night, just sitting in silence and wondering what Barny was doing. At four o'clock there was a knock on the bedroom door. 'I'll get it,' Bert said and as he opened the door, Barny's uncle Billy was standing there. He looked across at his brother. 'I have some bad news for you,' he said.

The Final Journey

Mrs Sturt told him to come in and sit on the bed and say what he had to say. 'I came straight round here,' he said, 'as soon as I saw him I left and ran all the way here.'

'Who did you see,' Beth asked, 'and where have you come from?'

'He works in the infirmary, Beth,' said Mr Sturt.

'Who did you see, Billy,' she asked. 'Was it Barny?'

'No,' Mrs Sturt cried, 'please don't say it was Barny in there. He is safe down at the police station, it can't be him.'

Beth put her arms around her and wiped the tears away.

'I am so sorry,' Billy said, 'I'm afraid it is Barny. They brought him in about half an hour ago. He was surrounded by coppers and they wouldn't let anyone get near him.'

'What injuries did he have?' Beth asked.

'Well, he had a bandaged hand and one small cut on his forehead that was bleeding. He had some other cuts on his face, but they looked old ones.'

'No, he already had them before he left tonight,' said Beth.

'Well, I couldn't see much, but I did speak to one of the nurses and she said he was in a coma.'

'But how?' cried Mrs Sturt. 'He was with the police. Surely he would have been safe in their hands? How could he come to any harm with them?'

Beth got up. 'We will have to go and see him,' she said and, as she turned, she saw Bert sitting in the corner, crying. 'Come on, Bert, we don't know how he is yet, not until we see him.'

'I know, Beth, but it was my fault. If I hadn't shouted to him he would still be here taking the mick out of me and slapping me round the head like he always did.'

'Don't blame yourself, Bert. Come on, get up, we are going to see him now.'

Mrs Sturt shouted over to Beth. 'Help me get dressed, love.'

'You're too ill to go anywhere and it's really cold out there tonight.'

'Now please, don't argue with me. My son's lying in the infirmary and I've got to go to him. Billy, you and Bert go and wait outside until I'm dressed.'

When Mrs Sturt was ready to go, they all left for the infirmary. When they arrived Beth went up to a doctor who was standing just inside the door. 'We have come to see Barny Sturt.'

He looked at Barny's mother and she was still crying. 'Follow me and I will take you to him.' On the way Beth asked him what was wrong with Barny.

'We are not sure, but we know he has some sort of head injury and he has a very badly injured hand, but that seems to have been done some time ago.'

'What about his head injury? How bad is it?'

'Well, we can't do any more for him, it's down to him and God, but I don't hold out much hope for him. He hasn't regained consciousness since he was brought in. It's one of those cases where you just have to wait and see what happens.'

'Did they tell you how he received the injuries?' she asked.

'I've heard some of the constables talking, it seems he fell down some concrete stairs leading down to the cells, but I don't know the whole story, you will have to ask the police.'

The doctor opened the door to Barny's room. Beth walked in first and she saw Barny lying there in the bed. She stopped and froze to the spot; she then put her hand over her mouth to try and stop herself from crying. She had seen the look on Barny's face, the look she had seen many times before, on wounded soldiers in the field infirmary and she remembered that none of them had pulled through.

Mr and Mrs Sturt squeezed past Beth and went to the side of Barny's bed. Bert stopped at the end of the bed holding on to the iron rails, crying uncontrollably.

Mrs Sturt picked up Barny's hand. She spoke to him, but not all the words came out, she was too choked up; the cheeks of her face were shining from the tears that had been falling down them. She squeezed his hand tightly. 'Barny,' she said, in between her sobbing breaths. 'It's me, son, your old mum, now I want you to wake up.' She stopped to wipe the tears from her eyes that were stopping her from seeing her son. 'I want you to wake up, son. I want to take you home now, but you must wake up first. Barny, please look up at me.'

There was no response from Barny. He just lay there in silence and deathly still. She lifted his hand up a little and placed her other hand under his arm. She began to raise her voice. 'Barny, now do as your mother tells you, we are going home. Beth has cooked your favourite tea, but you must wake up, come on, son.' She started to shake his arm. Beth looked over and could see that Mrs Sturt was becoming hysterical.

She quickly wiped the tears from her own eyes, pulled herself together, walked over to Mrs Sturt and put her arms around her.

'Come,' she said, 'walk over by the window and breathe in some fresh air, it will make you feel better.' She looked up at Mr Sturt who was just standing there staring at his son with a blank look on his face. Beth nudged his shoulder twice before he turned round and helped her to lift Mrs Sturt off the bed, but before they could get her up, Bert tapped her on her shoulder. 'Don't worry,' he said, 'leave it to me, he will wake up for me.'

They walked Mrs Sturt over to the window and Bert sat on the bed next to his best friend. Barny had never seen Bert cry before and Bert was trying hard to hold back the tears, but it was fight he was losing. 'Barny, now get up, this your old pal Bert,' he said in a shaky voice. 'Now come on, mate, you've got to pull yourself together.' He bent forward and put his head next to Barny's and started to whisper in his ear. 'Look, I can't let your mother hear me, so I'll have to be quiet, but you have put more blokes in here than I care to remember and you can't just lie here all day, you will lose your reputation out there and where will you be then?'

There was still no response from Barny. Bert got up and the tears started to fall again. 'Come on, you're the only true friend I have ever had, you can't leave me now, not now. You have never broken a promise to me in all the time we have been together and you promised to take me with you when you moved up north. Please Barny, don't let this be the promise you break.' He started to raise his voice a bit. 'You're a bloody fighter, remember, you haven't lost a fight yet and I'm not going to let you lost this one; now come on, get up.' He waited a short while, wiping the tears away with the sleeve of his jacket and then laid his head on Barny's chest. 'Barny, come on, you can't lie here all night, please get up.'

Beth walked over and lifted Bert's head up. 'Come on, Bert, it will be all right, just give him some time,' she said. As Bert stood up, Beth put her arms around him. 'Barny, look,' he cried out. 'Me and Beth, we're starting to walk out together.' He looked down at his old pal and there was still no movement. He turned and looked at Beth.

'I know he's really bad this time. This time yesterday he would have picked me up and thrown me out of the window if I said I was walking out with you.' He then broke down in Beth's arms and cried his eyes out.

'Come on, Bert, you need to be strong,' she said. 'Barny wouldn't thank you if you let his parents down, now would he? They need you and they need you now.'

'Bert got up and, as he walked away from his best mate's bedside, he noticed the constable standing at the doorway. He had been there all the time, but Bert was too upset to notice him before. He walked up to him and grabbed his jacket.

'Get out of here,' he shouted.

'I can't do that, son,' the constable replied, 'I've got my orders.'

Bert pulled him from the door. 'I don't care what orders you have, if you don't leave this room right now, I will take you outside and throw you down the stairs.'

'All right, son, calm down,' the constable said, 'I will wait outside.'

Bert slammed the door behind him and walked over to Mr and Mrs Sturt and put his arms around them both.

Beth stood by the side of Barny's bed, just staring down at him. She lifted his hand up and sat down by the side of him. She held his hand gently and pressed it tightly against her chest. She slipped her other hand slowly under Barny's head and gently raised it off the pillow slightly. She leaned over and kissed his lips. 'Barny,' she whispered, 'I love you so much, please don't leave me now we have so much to look forward to together.' The tears were rolling down her cheeks and falling on the Barny's face. 'You have so many people who love you, please don't let them down, we need you more than ever now, please don't leave me, Barny.'

She put her head down next to his, crying into his pillow, when all of a sudden she felt Barny's hand tighten around hers. She lifted her head quickly. Barny's eyes were half open; she kissed him again and then called Mrs Sturt over. She moved to one side. 'Quick, take his hand,' she said to Mrs Sturt.

Mrs Sturt held Barny's hand. 'Thank God, thank God.'

Beth stood behind her with her hands on her shoulders. Barny opened his eyes slowly. His first sight was of the two people he loved the most in his life, his mother and Beth. He tried to smile, but the pain in his head was too much for him, he could only screw his face up. He tried to speak, but there were no words. Beth walked to the other side of the bed and again gently raised his head off the pillow.

'Mum,' he groaned, but then started coughing.

The Final Journey

Beth got her handkerchief and wiped the blood from his mouth. He tried again to speak. 'Mum, I love you and I am so sorry.' He started to choke and Beth raised his head a bit higher. 'Mum, please take care of my child.' It then took all of his strength to turn his head round to Beth – he looked her in the eyes and the tears were dropping from his face. 'Beth, I love . . . ' He then started to choke more violently, took a deep breath, closed his eyes and quietly passed away.

Beth had been so strong, ever since Billy had walked into their bedroom with the bad news. she had been the backbone of the other three, but she could no longer hold her feelings back. She rested her head on Barny's body and broke down. Mrs Sturt had seen the reaction on Beth's face and fainted in her husband's arms. Bert had fallen to his knees, sobbing like a lost child and holding on to the end of the bed.

Just then the door opened. It was Fred from the coal yard and as he walked in he couldn't believe what he was seeing; he didn't have to ask how Barny was, he knew. He walked over to Mr Sturt and squeezed his shoulder.

The doctor then came in and gave Mrs Sturt some smelling salts. She eventually came round, but never spoke at all, just sat there shaking.

'I think you had better take her home now,' the doctor said to Fred. The doctor then walked round to Beth and asked her if she was all right. She never answered. He asked her if she could help the elderly lady. Beth looked up; she knew she was needed. She kissed Barny for the last time and walked round the bed to help Mrs Sturt, but then she saw Bert on the floor. She held his arm and helped him up.

'Where are you going, Beth?' he asked.

'We have to go home now, there is no more we can do for Barny now.' She got one side of Mrs Sturt and Fred the other side and they helped her out of the room. Beth looked behind her and saw Mr Sturt kiss his son on the face. She then remembered, Barny had once told her that his father had never ever kissed him; it was not the sort of thing a father would do where they came from. Mr Sturt left his son and walked up to Beth. There was only Bert left by Barny's side.

A little way down the corridor Beth noticed that Bert still wasn't with them. She went back into the room and found him sitting on the bed with Barny in his arms, talking to him as if he was still alive. She put her arm around him. 'Come on, he's at peace now, he's safe in God's hands.'

'I can't leave him, not on his own, not with all of them coppers around,' he said.

'They can't hurt him any more,' she replied as she held his hand and pulled him away. She walked him to the door, but he wouldn't take his eyes off Barny. 'Say goodbye to him, Bert,' she said. He stood there for a short while, rubbed his eyes and walked out of the room with Beth.

They walked over to the stairs, Beth still holding his hand and, as they started to walk down, Detective Sharp was on his way up with three officers. He stopped. 'I'm sorry about Barny,' he said, 'but it was only a matter of time before he got collared and tonight he pushed his luck a bit too far.'

With that Bert pushed Beth away and punched the detective in the face, knocking him down the stairs. The three officers jumped on him and cuffed him.

Beth stood there crying. 'Bert, why did you have to do that?' she said, as they dragged him away. She met up with the others at the main entrance. Fred asked where Bert was. 'He left by the back door,' she said. She caught Fred and Mrs Sturt up, but couldn't tell them that Bert had been arrested. As they walked out through the gates of the infirmary, Mr Sturt asked Fred how he knew that they were in the infirmary.

'Old Bill Bates was hit with a bottle in the Four in Hand tonight and he took himself off to the infirmary and he saw them bring Barny in. He came straight back out and told us.'

'Are you all right, Mrs Sturt?' asked Beth. She never answered. She had been quiet like that since they left Barny's bedside. As they turned into Wilford Road, people were standing outside their houses, waiting for news of Barny. As they walked past them the people could tell by their faces that Barny had gone. The men took their caps off and the women bowed their heads.

There was only one family who never came out – the Blakes. The news never travelled as far as Wentworth Road so Violet was unaware that the father of her unborn child had died.

It was just getting light when they reached their front door. Doris was outside waiting. She put her arms around Mrs Sturt and said how sorry she was to hear of Barny's death, but Mrs Sturt remained silent. Fred took Mr Sturt through to the scullery and Beth put his wife to bed.

The next morning Mrs Sturt still hadn't spoken to anyone and Beth was trying to get her to talk or to cry or do anything just to try and help

The Final Journey

her start grieving. Beth knew she couldn't let it build up inside her. Mr Sturt and Fred were still in the scullery, when Billy walked in. 'How is your wife?' he asked his brother.

'She has been in the bedroom since we got back last night and hasn't spoken a word to anyone. Thanks for coming round last night and telling us about Barny.'

'That was the least I could do,' his brother replied. 'I have another message for you now, from one of the doctors. He said apparently Barny had a bad injury to his left hand and it had been done for some days. The trouble they have is that gangrene has started to set in and they need to get him in the ground as soon as possible.'

'Oh Christ,' Mr Sturt said, 'we wanted to have him laid out in the bedroom for a few days before he was buried; his mum won't like that.'

'Do you know, I thought I could recognise that smell in his room, but I thought it was coming from another part of the infirmary. I didn't think it was Barny. Do you remember it from the battlefields. The stench was all around us then. I will never forget that smell.'

'How soon do they want us to have the funeral?' asked Fred.

'The doctor said no later than a few days; tomorrow's Thursday, so I suppose it will have to be Friday,' Billy replied.

'Well, that don't leave us much time; it only gives us two days, but don't worry about that, I will sort it all out for you,' said Fred.

Mr Sturt looked up at him. 'We've hardly got any money, so we can't afford a big funeral.'

'Don't you worry about that, I'm paying for it. He was a good boy and he helped me out many times in the past and I'm going to make sure he has the best funeral money can buy; it's the least I can do for him.'

'Well, if you're sure; it would help me and the wife out.'

'Yea, you just leave it to me, I'll get it all arranged for Friday.'

Back in the bedroom, Beth was still trying to get Mrs Sturt to talk or cry, but with no success. 'I'll go and make us a nice cup of tea.' She shut the bedroom door behind her and walked into the scullery.

'How is she?' asked Mr Sturt.

'I'm really worried about her,' said Beth. 'She needs to get it out of her system, but she just won't give in.' Beth leant against the sink and burst into tears. 'I'm going to miss him so much,'

Mr Sturt put his arms around her. 'Come on,' he said, 'it's been a long night, why don't I ask Doris if you can have a few hours sleep in her bed.'

At the Precipice of Poverty

'No, I can't do that, I can't leave Mrs Sturt now. I'm sorry, I'll be all right,' she said, as she wiped the tears away. She made the tea and took it back in the bedroom. As she opened the door, she saw Mrs Sturt standing by the dresser looking at a photo of Barny.

'What are you doing?' Beth asked. 'You should be in bed.'

Mrs Sturt just stood there looking at his photo and then she started to cry. 'Go on, Mrs Sturt, that's it, let it all come out,' said Beth. She stopped crying as soon as she had started and turned to Beth. 'What did Barny mean,' she asked, 'in the infirmary when he, you know, before he left us? He asked me to look after his child, what did he mean by that?'

'He was going to become a father.'

'Is it yours, Beth?' she asked, all excited.

'Come on, let me help you back into bed.'

'No, I want to know now, please tell me if you're having Barny's child.'

'No, it's not me, but how I wish it was now. It's Violet.'

Mrs Sturt smiled. 'So I haven't lost Barny now, his son will now take his place. Where is Violet? I want to see her.'

'I don't know,' said Beth, 'I haven't seen her. I don't even know if she's been told about Barny yet.'

Mrs Sturt made her way to the kitchen. 'Where is Violet?'

The three men looked up in amazement. 'Are you all right, love?' her husband asked.

'Don't worry about that now,' she said. 'I need to speak to Violet. Where is she?'

'What's wrong with her? Why does she want to see Violet?' Billy asked.

'Violet is carrying Barny's baby, we will have to go and find her.'

There were no volunteers to find Violet and tell her of Barny's death. 'I will go,' said Beth. 'I'll try across the road at her home first. Her parents must know where she is.'

She took her shawl from behind the door and went across to Violet's parents' house and knocked on the door, which Violet's father opened. 'Yes, what can I do for you?'

'Could I speak to Violet, please?'

'No, she doesn't live here any more.' He stepped inside and went to shut the door, but Beth held it open.

'Look, what do you want? I've told you, you will not find her here,' he shouted.

'Well, can you tell me where I can find her?' asked Beth.

The Final Journey

'Have you come from across the road, from the Sturts' house?'

'Yes, I have, as a matter of fact.'

'Well, you can go back over there and tell that pig Barny that she doesn't live here any more and she won't be back.'

'Mr Blake, you are a very rude man. Barny Sturt died early this morning and we need to find Violet.'

'Oh, I wondered why all the animals were gathering outside their hovels. Well, that's the best news I've had for a long time. At least Violet can't marry him now he's being put in his hole.'

Beth stepped forward and slapped him round the face. 'Barny was worth ten of you, at least he had manners,' she said, as she walked away. She crossed back over the road and, as she opened the door, Fred was just walking out.

'You all right, love?' he asked.

'No, not really, Violet doesn't live across with her father any more. I don't know where to look next.'

'Try the old girl who lives upstairs, she knows everything of what goes on around here.'

So Beth climbed the stairs and knocked on the door.

'Hello, love,' Doris said. 'How are you feeling now?'

'Yes, not too bad,' replied Beth. 'I was wondering, do you know where Violet Blake is living now?'

'It's funny you should ask that, I saw her last night in the Fish, just before my husband, well you know what he did. Yes, I asked her how her mother was and she said she didn't live there any more. She told me she was living with a friend at Wentworth Road.'

'Is that very far away?' Beth asked.

'No, my love, it's only about thirty minutes' walk, that's all. What do you want her for?'

'Well, she doesn't know about Barny yet and I thought that it was only right that she should know.'

'I'll come with you, love. You might have a bit of trouble with her, you know, what with you seeing Barny and all that.'

'No, that's OK really, I need to speak to her alone.'

'Well, please yourself. I was only trying to help. Come inside and I will give you directions on how to get there.'

After Doris had given Beth the directions to Wentworth Road, Beth thanked her and went to leave, but Doris shouted out to her. 'Hold on, I don't know what number she lives at, but it's the only house with four or five milk churns in the front garden, you can't miss it.'

She thanked her once again and started on her journey. When she reached Wentworth Road she slowly walked down the road, trying to find the garden with the milk churns in, not knowing what kind of reception she was going to receive from Violet. She finally found the house and knocked on the door. A dirty unshaven man answered. 'Hello,' he said, 'you're a pretty little thing, have you come to see me?'

'No, I haven't, I'm looking for a girl called Violet.'

The man moved closer to her. 'No, I can't say that I know a girl by that name, not living in here anyway, but if you would like to come into my room, I'm sure you can help me nudge my memory.'

'No, thank you,' Beth said. 'The girl Violet, she only moved in yesterday to a friend's room; I think her name's Mary.'

'Ah Mary, yes, I know her and I've seen the new girl a few times, lovely she is, I wouldn't mind tightening her corsets for her. The room's on the top floor.'

Beth walked in and up the stairs and the man followed closely behind her. 'Are you sure you wouldn't like to come and see my room first?' he asked. Just then he put his hand up Beth's dress. She screamed out loud; he then took hold of her arms and tried to kiss her. She tried to get away, but he was too strong. Just then two hands appeared through the railings of the stairs and pulled the man's feet away. He fell back down the stairs, hitting his head on a coal bucket by the door. Beth was crying and shaking. She looked up to thank the person who had saved her from being attacked. It was Violet. She had been in the garden picking flowers when she heard the scream.

'Violet,' Beth said. 'I've been looking for you everywhere.'

'Well, you have found me now, what do you want?'

'I can't tell you here,' she said. 'Can we go to your room?'

'Well, you will have to be quick, I'm meeting Barny soon, I think he is taking me out.'

As they climbed the stairs Beth thanked Violet for getting that man off her. 'Don't thank me,' she said, 'he did the same thing to me when I moved in, so I was just paying him back; I never done it for you.'

'You had better sit down, Violet.'

'Look, what's all this about, you know I don't like you, you know me and Barny's getting back together again. I thought you would have moved back up to turnip land by now. You tell me what you have to say and then go.'

'I've come to talk to you about Barny,' Beth said.

'There is nothing more for you to say about Barny,' Violet replied. 'We are getting back together again and that's all there is to it. I'm afraid you have been pushed out.'

'Why don't you just shut up?' Beth shouted. 'He's dead, Barny is dead.' She then burst into tears.

'You're lying, I know you're lying, you cow, you're just making it up so you can take him away with you; well, it won't work,' she said. Violet fell back on the bed, she could tell by Beth's face that she was telling the truth.

'I'm sorry, Violet, but it is true,' said Beth. She went over and put her arms around her.

'Why,' Violet cried, 'and how, who done it?'

'He fell down some stairs at the police station and he died in the infirmary early this morning.'

'I wasn't with him when he went. Why didn't anyone come and get me?' she asked.

'It all happened so quickly, we didn't know what we were doing.'

Violet turned her head and cried on Beth's shoulder and then lifted her head up. 'You know we are back together,' she said, 'I'm having his baby and we were going to get a flat together. I'm sorry, Beth, you have been so kind coming to tell me, but he has always loved me.'

Beth nodded her head. 'I know,' she said. She couldn't hurt her more by saying that Barny loved her and was going to move away with her and his parents. Anyway, it didn't matter any more, nothing mattered any more. 'Listen, Violet, Mrs Sturt's in a bad way and she knows about the baby and she asked me to come and find you. She wants to see you.'

Violet agreed to go and see Mrs Sturt. Beth got her shawl and they made they way back to Wilford Road. As they passed Violet's parents' house, Beth told her that she had slapped her father round the face that same morning. 'Good,' she said, 'it's about time someone stood up to him.'

Violet went straight into Mrs Sturt's bedroom and Beth went into the kitchen. Fred had come back in and was sitting round the table with Mr Sturt and Billy.

'That door hasn't stayed shut for a second this morning,' said Mr Sturt. 'People have been in and out, paying their respects to Barny.'

'The funeral's tomorrow, Beth, and at three o'clock,' said Fred, 'and the service is at St Saviour's church; that's your uncle's church isn't it? I think that's the only reason we got in there at such short notice.'

'We were going to ask you, Beth,' said Mr Sturt, 'do you think your father would be able to come down and read the service? We know Barny thought a lot of him.'

'Yes, I'm sure he would be proud to,' replied Beth, 'but how could we contact him in time?'

'We have already thought of that,' said Fred. 'If you can write a note then I can give it to the driver of the coal train; he's leaving at four o'clock and will stop and make sure your father gets the message.'

Mrs Sturt then came into the kitchen. 'Are the arrangements going OK?' she asked.

'Yes,' replied her husband. 'We might be able to get Beth's father to take the service.'

'Oh that will be nice,' she replied.

'Well, is it true, is Violet carrying Barny's child?' her husband asked.

'Yes, it's true and a part of Barny is still alive. I will have to look after him again. Like I did when he was a baby before, but the important thing now is that we have got to look after Violet. The poor girl, she has been thrown out of her home and at a time like this. I told her she could stay here, but she said she was quite settled where she was, but she did say we can spend as much time with the baby as we want, when the little mite's born.' She then left the kitchen and returned to her bedroom with Violet.

'You will have to keep an eye on her, the shock hasn't hit her yet,' Billy said.

Beth was looking out of the back window crying; she knew Violet was just putting on an act. She had no doubt that she loved Barny, but only when it suited her. She felt so sick, but at least Mrs Sturt was talking now. It did not matter if Violet was taking her in, as long as she had something to look forward to and she had now, the baby.

Friday afternoon came and Beth's father knocked on the door. He gave Beth a big hug and introduced himself to Barny's parents and then asked if he could talk to them both in private. The three of them went into the bedroom and Mr Sturt shut the door behind them.

The Final Journey

'Now, I don't know if Barny told you or not,' the vicar said, 'but he had been giving me quite a lot of money each week to put by for you. He told me that if anything ever happened to him, then I should come and give you the money.' He then removed a leather pouch from his cloak and gave it to Mrs Sturt. When she opened it she got the shock of her life; there was more money in that small leather pouch than they had ever seen in all of their lives.

'I can't believe this,' said Mrs Sturt with tears in her eyes. 'Even though my Barny is no longer with us, he is still making sure that I am well looked after.'

After they had got over the shock of being given the money, the vicar went through the service with them and told them the words he would like to say about Barny. When they had finished he said a prayer for them and left for the church. He was taken aback by the amount of people already out and lining the roads leading to the church, ready to pay their last respects to Barny

At half past two the funeral carriage pulled up outside the house; it was made from highly polished black yew with glass at both sides and at the back and this was etched with roses all around the edges. It was pulled by two jet-black stallions with black plumes on their heads and highly polished leather straps and brass buckles, and inside was a solid oak coffin with two sprays of the deepest red roses you had ever seen. The largest one at the front of the coffin had the words 'You were more than a son, you were my whole life'. The second one, slightly smaller, read 'My first, my last, my only love'. Fred had the sprays made and he knew the words would be fitting to the two woman whom Barny loved. He was the only one who knew how Barny felt about Beth; even his mother never knew his true feelings. Behind the funeral carriage were a line of carts, stretching half way down Wilford, full of flowers from friends and neighbours.

Barny's family and close friends climbed up into the four carriages that were directly behind Barny's and they slowly moved off at a walking pace, following a man dressed in black with top hat and stick who was leading the first carriage down the middle of the road. As the procession started off, silence came over Wilford Road and, as the men removed their caps and the women, most of them crying, bowed their heads, Barny made his last journey down this infamous road. When they arrived at the church, the police had to move the people away from the gates to make room for the funeral carriage to pull in. The service lasted for over an hour. Beth's father told how Barny had saved his own church from being shut down and how he tried to save a woman from a burning house back in his home village and the stories went on. His parents and friends never knew anything about these good deeds that Barny had done, he never mentioned them, but that was Barny all over.

When the service had finished, the procession moved off, to make the short journey to the cemetery where they held another short service. While this was going on Violet, who had never stopped crying since Barny's coffin arrived outside the house, walked up to the graveside where Barny's coffin was resting delicately across two lengths of timber above the hole; she looked down at the sprays of roses that were going to be lowered down with Barny's coffin. She became more hysterical when she saw the smaller spray and thought that it was from her. But Fred quickly walked over to Beth, who was standing quiet and composed, although her eyes were filled with tears. He told her that Barny had spoken to him a few days before and had told him that she was the only love in his life and the spray was from her, not Violet.

The silence in the cemetery was only broken by the sound of women crying. As they lowered Barny into the ground, the sobbing got louder. Mrs Sturt fainted, but Beth was ready with the smelling salts. She wasn't so quick when Violet fainted, she just thought she was putting it on again and gaining the attention of the crowd as she always did. Beth knew that she and Fred were the only ones there out of all those people who knew that Barny really loved her with all his heart. That's all that mattered to Beth. She never cared that Violet was getting all the limelight because Violet had already told everyone that she and Barny were getting back together again. Beth knew the truth. She knew that she was Barny's one and only true love and that he was moving away with her and not Violet. Beth not only had the pain of losing Barny, she was feeling another pain that made her feel sick – it was the thought of Barny being laid to rest without his best friend being there with him. Bert was still locked up and Beth had tried everything to try and get him out for the funeral just so he could be by his best mate's side for the last few hours, but the courts wouldn't hear of it.

As the funeral came to an end, the people started to leave the cemetery, slowly and silently. Mr Sturt helped his wife away from the graveside and two men helped Violet away. Beth stayed there until everyone had finally left, she then walked up to the open grave and looked in. Her tears were leaving her cheeks and falling on to the top of the coffin. 'Barny,' she said in a whisper. 'I love you so much, I don't care what anyone else says, I know you loved me as much as I love you and I will never ever forget you, as long as I live.' She opened her bag and pulled out a single red rose and then a silk hankie, which smelt of Barny's favourite scent, and threw them both down to where Barny's head was; she then blew him a kiss and slowly walked away.

The next day Beth and her father were getting ready to leave for home and although Mrs Sturt was very grateful to Beth for all that she had done for her, she was still in shock over her son's death and all she seemed to care about was Barny's unborn child, so they just left and, after some time, the people of Wilford Road got back to their normal way of life.

Violet spent a lot of time at the Sturts' house while she was carrying the baby until she gave birth in that small room in Wentworth Road to a baby boy. She named the baby Charles Harold. Mrs Sturt was over the moon. She looked after the baby when Violet went out, which was nearly every night, but she didn't mind. All she used to say was that the baby looked so much like his dad. After two years, Violet met up with the sergeant again, although he wasn't a sergeant any more. His father had died and he was penniless, although he was just starting a new job. They carried on seeing each other for about two years and then he proposed to her again, but with one condition. She couldn't keep baby Charlie. So she asked Mrs Sturt to take him in, which she did. Violet kept in contact with Charlie, but not very often.

Violet married Percy at St Saviour's church, the church where Barny had his last service, and they moved into a flat in Henderson Hill, which was only a five-minute walk from Mrs Sturt's house. Charlie spent his years being taught the trade of carpentry from a very young age by Mr Sturt. He taught him everything he knew, just as he wanted to for his own son. Charlie soon picked up the trade and turned out to be one of the best carpenters around. Mrs Sturt would look at Charlie sometimes, when he was a sleep in the chair or eating his dinner at the table, and all she could see was Barny: he had the same jet black curly hair and the dark skin, but he wasn't built like his father; Barny had been a giant, but Charlie was small and not very broad.

When Charlie was twenty-one, a new family moved into Wilford Road. There were five girls and two boys. The youngest girl was named Daisy. She was dark and very beautiful. Charlie did some work in the new family's house and got very friendly with Daisy. They started going out together and in August 1930, they were married, and moved to a flat in Whitehorse Road.

Daisy gave birth to a baby girl and then a son; they then moved to a three-bedroom terraced house in Boulogne Road, where they had another five girls and another son. It was very hard bringing up eight children, but they were all shown a lot of love and never went without. There were a lot of good times and bad times, a lot of sorrow and a lot of joy, but with six daughters, two sons and twenty-three grandchildren being born, there was always plenty going on, lots of laughs, but also lots of tears. Charlie and Daisy spent thirty-one happy years together until he died at the early age of 51. They went through some really hard times, but always made sure there was food on the table and clothes on the children's backs.

When Charlie died, it left a big gap in Daisy's life; she was absolutely heartbroken when he was taken away from her. She had all of her children around her, but that never made up for losing the only man she had ever loved and had wanted to spend the rest of her life with. It was a big struggle from then on; her children helped her as much as they could, but she was a proud woman and would never accept charity. It was only her strong will and determination that kept the family together and gave them the strong family bond that exists between them to this very day.

One by one they were married and moved out, to bring up their own families, and Daisy was left in the house on her own. The house that held so many sad and happy memories for her and which had always been so full of life and never a dull moment. She spent hour after hour sitting in her chair all alone thinking of the past. Of the only man she had loved and lost but her family were never far away; she would always have her children popping in to make sure she was all right. Then came her grandchildren; there were twenty-six in all and as they grew up, the strong family bond which was shown to her children was now being passed on to her grandchildren.

Daisy spent the next thirty years living in the same house, until suddenly one day she had a stroke. She spent a short time in hospital and then came back home, but needed twenty-four-hour care. Her daughters spent their days looking after her and hired a private nurse to stay with her at night. But Daisy didn't like having strangers in the house and made the nurse's life hell for the first week or so and then her daughters took care of her day and night. They brought her bed down from the bedroom and put it in the living room, but she still had to cope with the outside toilet. She went through some bad times with her illness, it was so sad. In the end they knew she would never be able to cope again with the stairs and the outside toilet. So they applied for a warden flat. It was a big decision to make. Daisy had spent fifty happy years in that house, but they had to think of her well being. They found her a beautiful flat, brand new and not too far from her old house. She spent the next five years in that flat. They didn't know whether she was happy there or not, you could never tell; at least she was safe with a warden on duty twenty-four hours a day.

In the next year or so Daisy's health started to go downhill fast. She spent more time at the doctor's and the hospital until one day the doctor said that they could do no more for her, so they brought her back home and put her in her own bed, surrounded by her own things. They took turns in staying with her, twenty-four hours a day, seven days a week, giving her all the care she needed. She became so bad in the end that they would only allow her own children to sit with her. All of her grandchildren wanted to come and see her, but they said no. They wanted them to remember her how she used to be, happy, loving and caring. Not as she was then: she had lost a lot of weight and looked so sad lying in her bed. When she died, a few weeks later, she had her two sons and two daughters with her, but the rest of her daughters were told quickly and came straight away with their husbands. It was a very sad time for everyone who knew her. I shouldn't think she realised just how much her family really loved her. Everyone, her six daughters, two sons and twenty-six grandchildren, would have given anything just to have spent a little more time with her on their own, just to tell her how much they loved her.

I think the saddest part of this story is how much Daisy has been missed since she's been gone. Nearly all of her grandchildren have families of their own now. She would have had forty-one great-great grandchildren and four great-great-great-grandchildren. Daisy adored children, she was at her happiest when she was sitting in her small living room surrounded by them. Perhaps she can still see her family growing, some people believe that. She might have been there, helping with the birth of all of her grandchildren, no one knows.

The story is full of happy times and sad times, from the time when she first met Barny Sturt's only son and lived in Wilford Road, with her six sisters and three brothers, till the time she left her own family to be reunited with her one and only love, her Charlie. I could go on, but that's another story.

Printed in Great Britain
by Amazon